Soups and Stews the World Over

SOUPS
AND
STEWS
THE WORLD
OVER

by Louise Driggs

Edited by Eleanor Porter

HASTINGS HOUSE, PUBLISHERS

New York

Published simultaneously in Canada by
Saunders, of Toronto, Ltd., Don Mills, Ontario

ISBN: 8038–6698–4
Library of Congress Catalog Card Number: 77–136364

Designed by Al Lichtenberg
Printed in the United States of America

Contents

Part III
STEWS AND BOILED DINNERS

Part IV
FINALE

Introduction

SOUP, *soupe, potage, sopa, suppe, zuppa, soppa, keitto, suimono, caldo*—
the words vary from country to country, according to the language, but
the meaning is the same. Around the world, each country, each region,
each culture has its soups and stews. These may be light, appetite-whet-
ting clear soups, thicker *potages* and purées, or the hearty soups and
stews that are, in reality, a whole meal.

Every type of foodstuff goes into the soup pot—meat, fish, and fowl;
vegetables, fruits, and nuts; oils, butter, and cheese; all kinds of grain;
bread, rice, and pasta; eggs, cream and milk, both sweet and sour; beer
and wine, in fact, all kinds of spirits; vinegar, spices, herbs, and seeds;
tea, coffee, and carbonated beverages.

Soups are served hot, cold, or jellied; dry or liquid; cooked or uncooked. They are drunk from bowls or cups, eaten with spoons, fingers,
or forks, with the occasional help of a knife. Soup may be a part of the
most elegant repast or served as a complete meal. It is savored by the
rich and powerful and by the poor and lowly, and by those in-between.
Eaten by young and old, poets and peasants, the fierce and the meek,
the brave and the cowardly, all people have their soups and stews.

To quote from an old cookbook in my collection: "Soup bears the same
relation to the dinner that a doorway bears to a house. It is safe to say
that no other dish is capable of such variation, and none has received so
much attention from the cooks of all ages and all nationalities."

In the first section of this book are the light soups, those most often
served as an opening course or as an accompaniment to a salad or sandwich. Some are almost hearty enough to be a complete meal. In this section are the consommés and bouillons, usually clear, but sometimes thick-

7

ened a little or enriched with egg or cream. Then there are the cold soups and aspics. Of course, some of the cold soups are delicious, too, when served hot. There are cream soups and *potages*, heavier, but still intended as the first course or to follow an appetizer. And we have a number of sweet soups, often served as dessert or to go along with a salad luncheon, or to be heated and sipped on a cold and stormy night.

In the second section are the recipes for whole-meal soups and chowders. These are the hearty family-style dishes meant to be the main course of the meal. Forks as well as spoons are often needed in their consumption.

Last are the stews and boiled dinners. There is really not much difference between the whole-meal soups and the stews. The stews just tend to be a little more substantial. There are several in which meat, fish, or fowl and vegetables are simmered in liquid. The broth is served as a first course and the rest as the main part of the meal. Sometimes knives are needed in the eating of a stew.

All of my family and many of my friends have made their contributions to this cookbook. My family has traveled extensively and lived all over the world. My mother lived a year in New Zealand and has traveled in Australia, the British Isles, and Germany. My brother has lived in Puerto Rico and Iran, goes to Europe frequently, and has spent considerable time in Germany, France, and Switzerland. All are instructed to bring me recipes and cookbooks.

I spent most of one happy summer in France, Italy, and Switzerland —and a delightful week in Copenhagen. We stayed with an Italian family in Rome and I was by the side of our hostess as she cooked our meals. And I had the opportunity of taking a few days' lessons at the Cordon Bleu in Paris and attending a class in gourmet cooking at the Central Trade School in Copenhagen. This class was part of the training for the young women who were to be stewardesses on Scandinavian Airlines.

My husband grew up in the Philippine Islands and has traveled extensively in the Orient. He spent his "war years" in China and has since had a trip back to Japan. His grandmother and grandfather lived for a number of years in Cuba, and I have one of his grandmother's old Cuban cookbooks.

For a number of years I worked for a spice and herb company and became familiar with all kinds of spices, herbs, and seasonings and with world-wide recipes. I have an extensive collection of cookbooks compiled by women's groups, church, club, lodge, and charity organizations. What interesting recipes you find in these! In regional recipes, I have Creole and Cajun recipes, recipes from the Deep South, and early California recipes.

The area in which I live is a veritable "melting pot" of nationalities. Relatives and friends are often just a generation from a foreign heritage and retain many of the favorite dishes of their parents—Americanized, to be sure.

All of the older and foreign recipes have been modernized and adapted to American measurements and American foods. For most recipes the ingredients are available at the corner grocery or the supermarket, if not every day, then at one time or another. Some, of course, you must purchase at a fancy grocery, specialty shop, or at a delicatessen catering to a particular nationality.

My thanks to all who have helped with this book, not only to those who contributed ideas and recipes but to the many friends and relatives who have helped to eat all of these. They acted as if they enjoyed it; I am sure that I did.

Last of all, I would like to quote from another hundred-year-old cookbook called *Common Sense in the Household:* "It is slovenly to leave rags of meat, husks of vegetables, and bits of bone in the soup tureen. Most soups are better the second day than the first, unless they are warmed over too quickly or left too long upon the fire after they are hot."

I do hope you find here a soup or stew to your special liking: there are many to choose from. Whatever you choose, *eat hearty!*

Part I

SOUPS TO BEGIN OR END A MEAL

The Beginnings: Stocks

A GOOD, well-flavored stock is the beginning of many soups and stews as well as the basis of many sauces. And there is nothing so cheering to mind and body as a cup of hot clear soup. Whether you make the stock from scratch or use one of the very satisfactory short cuts, you will find stock an essential ingredient in many of the recipes in this book.

While it may seem considerable work to make stock, it's well worth the effort. And with a freezer you can keep it for quite some time to use when needed. Several years ago when I attended classes at the Cordon Bleu in Paris, a regular Monday morning procedure was to make the stock pot for all the soups and sauces to be made in class that week. Many European families and most of the restaurants do this, too. Since home freezers aren't as prevalent there, many families keep the stock on the stove simmering all the time, adding bones, bits of meat, cooking liquids, and odds and ends of vegetables, straining and clarifying as needed.

While these recipes for making stock are simpler than many, we would like to suggest that you, too, add any leftover bones, meat, or vegetables that you have on hand. If you haven't the cheesecloth called for in many recipes, use a piece of thin old muslin or cotton or an old linen napkin for straining your stock.

You'll find even more elaborate stocks toward the end of the book, in the recipes for *Pot-au-Feu, Poule-au-Pot, Bollito Misto,* and other boiled dinners from around the world.

TO MAKE BEEF STOCK AND CLEAR SOUP

Beef stock can be dark or light, depending on your preference and its intended use. For darker stock, brown the beef or veal bones—the flavor will be slightly different, too. The amount of salt will vary with the stock's ultimate use. For stock for an elaborate sauce or complicated soup, you may want to use even less salt than we've called for here.

1 *pound or more beef or veal bones*	1 *large stalk celery with leaves*
1½ *to 2 pounds beef ribs, shank, or*	1 *large carrot*
other beef soup meat	1 *medium-size parsnip, if desired*
3 *quarts water*	1 *large onion*
2 *teaspoons salt*	1 *or 2 whole cloves*
4 *or 5 whole black peppercorns*	1-inch *piece bay leaf*
2 *or 3 sprigs parsley*	½ *teaspoon thyme or mixed beef herbs*
1 *leek*	

Use any bones you may have from rib or chuck roasts, steaks, etc., in addition to shank, rib, or other bones purchased at the market. For light stock, do not brown bones. For a darker brown stock, brown bones in a heavy frying pan in a moderately hot oven (400°F.) for 1½ to 2 hours. Combine browned or unbrowned bones with beef soup meat in a large kettle. Add water, salt, peppercorns, and parsley. Heat the liquid to boiling and skim it two or three times. Turn heat down and simmer.

Meanwhile, clean the leek and slice, using part of the green top, and add to soup along with celery stalk and leaves. Scrub carrot and parsnip. Cut into chunks and add to soup. Peel onion, stick it with cloves, and add to soup along with bay leaf and thyme or mixed beef herbs. Simmer soup for 4 to 5 hours. If necessary, skim it from time to time.

Wet a thin piece of muslin or cheesecloth and place in a wire sieve. Strain the finished stock through cloth and sieve. Chill it for several hours or overnight, until the fat hardens on top. Remove hardened fat. The stock is ready to use for soups and sauces. Makes about 2 quarts. Store stock in refrigerator or freeze it for later use.

TO CLARIFY STOCK:

If a clear stock is desired, heat it to boiling. Beat in 2 egg whites with a wire whip, turn heat down, and simmer it for about 30 minutes. Strain it again through a wet cloth and wire sieve.

TO MAKE CONSOMMÉ

If you use a veal knuckle, your consommé will jell beautifully. If not, you may need to add a little gelatin. Soften 1 to 2 tablespoons unflavored gelatin in a cup or so of cold consommé. Add 3 or 4 more cups of consommé and heat until the gelatin is dissolved. Chill until gelatin sets.

1 to 1½ pounds beef stew meat and bones	*½ cup tomato purée*
	1 medium-size onion
1 veal knuckle or 1 pound veal bones	*1 leek*
1 to 1½ pounds chicken backs and necks	*1 medium-size carrot*
	1 medium-size turnip
3 quarts water	*1 clove garlic*
1 tablespoon salt	*1-inch piece bay leaf*
4 or 5 black peppercorns	*2 egg whites*
2 sprigs parsley	

In a large kettle combine stew meat, bones, and chicken and add water. Bring the liquid to a boil, turn heat down to medium and boil for about 1 hour, skimming several times. After 1 hour turn heat down very low, so stock will barely simmer. Add salt, peppercorns, parsley, and tomato purée. Peel onion and cut into 3 or 4 pieces; clean leek and cut into pieces, using part of the green top. Add to simmering stock. Scrape carrot and turnip and cut into 2 or 3 pieces; peel and slice clove of garlic. Add all, with the bay leaf, to stock. Simmer the stock over very low heat for 3 hours.

Wet a thin piece of muslin or cheesecloth and place it in a wire sieve. Strain stock through cloth and sieve. Discard the meat and bones for they will be practically flavorless. Chill stock for several hours or overnight, until the fat hardens. Remove hardened fat. Return the stock to kettle and heat to simmering. Beat in the egg whites with a wire whip. Turn heat down and simmer for about 30 minutes. Strain consommé again through wet cloth and wire sieve. Makes about 2 quarts.

TO SERVE:

Heat consommé to simmering and serve in small soup cups. Or chill it until firm, spoon into soup cups and garnish with chopped parsley, chopped chives, or a spoonful of dairy sour cream.

HURRY-UP BEEF STOCK

In many recipes we call for concentrated beef stock base, bouillon cubes, canned bouillon, and so on. There is no reason why you cannot exchange one for the other. If you make your own beef stock, use it to replace any of these. Or, if beef stock directions are given and you are in a hurry, reverse the procedure. Each brand may vary a little, so be sure to check the directions. Here's how to have beef stock in a hurry:

FROM CONCENTRATED BEEF STOCK BASE
Most label directions for these products suggest that 1 teaspoon makes 1 cup bouillon or stock. These proportions are for a teacup, about 5 or 6 ounces. Since the measurements in recipes are based on a measuring cup, or 8 ounces, you would add 1½ to 2 teaspoons stock base to a measuring cup of hot water for a well-flavored stock.

Most of these stock bases are quite salty, so use further amounts of salt sparingly. Some of these granular products are moist and should be refrigerated as soon as the seal of the jar is broken. Other granular beef stock bases are dry and do not need refrigeration.

FROM BOUILLON CUBES
A bouillon cube usually makes 5 or 6 ounces of stock, so to make 2 cups stock dissolve 3 cubes in 2 cups hot water.

FROM INSTANT BEEF BROTH
Similar to the concentrated beef stock bases in jars, this stock base comes in individual foil or plasticized packages. Each package or envelope makes 5 or 6 ounces stock.

FROM CANNED CONDENSED BEEF BOUILLON OR
CONSOMMÉ
Condensed beef bouillon and consommé comes in 10½-ounce cans. To make a well-flavored stock, dilute with an equal amount of water. However, where a recipe calls for undiluted condensed bouillon, other liquids in the recipe dilute the stock.

FROM CANNED BEEF BROTH
Quite a number of different brands of beef broth are on the market. Can sizes vary slightly, but most are about 14 ounces. Use undiluted.

FROM BEEF BROTH AND SEASONING BASE
Thick and syrupy, this concentrated beef broth base is somewhat similar to the granular stock bases in flavor. Use about 1 teaspoon for each measuring cup of hot water.

TO MAKE CHICKEN STOCK AND CLEAR SOUP

The addition of a veal knuckle or piece of veal shank will give your stock additional flavor. And if you chill it, the stock will jell. If you want a clearer stock, then beat in egg whites and simmer as you would beef stock. A turnip is optional, or you can use other vegetables such as leeks, parsnips, or even a few lettuce leaves. Color of the stock will be better if the vegetables are light colored.

4 to 5 pounds chicken necks, backs, or other bony pieces, or 3- to 3½-pound stewing chicken, cut up
Veal knuckle or piece of veal shank, if desired
2 quarts water
4 teaspoons salt

4 or 5 whole black peppercorns
1 large stalk celery with leaves
1 medium-size onion
2 or 3 sprigs parsley
2 or 3 lemon slices
1 large carrot
1 or 2 turnips or other vegetables

Combine chicken, veal, and water in a large kettle. Bring the liquid to a boil and skim two or three times. Turn heat down and simmer; add salt, peppercorns, and celery, cut up. Peel onion, cut into quarters and add along with parsley and lemon slices. Scrape carrot and turnips, cut into chunks and add to simmering stock. Simmer 2 or 3 hours, skimming from time to time.

Wet a thin piece of muslin or cheesecloth and place in a wire sieve. Strain the stock through the cloth-lined sieve. Chill stock for several hours or overnight, until the fat is firm. Chicken fat will never be very hard. Spoon off fat. Makes 6 or 7 cups. Clarify as you would beef stock.

TO SERVE:

Serve chilled, if desired; or reheat and serve in bouillon cups garnished with chopped chives or parsley or crisp croutons.

HURRY-UP CHICKEN STOCK

As with beef stock, there are a number of different chicken stock products. So inexpensive and easy to use are most of these that you can keep one or two available to use except for the special times when you make your own. As with the beef products you can exchange one for the other. There may be some variation in flavor, but for most recipes, not enough to worry about. For a quickly made chicken stock here's how to proceed:

FROM CONCENTRATED CHICKEN STOCK BASE
All of these products are moist and, like the moist beef bases, should be refrigerated as soon as the seal of the jar is broken. For a good, rich chicken stock dissolve 1 tablespoon in a measuring cup of boiling water. And, if you are using this stock to replace your own homemade stock in a recipe, be sure to taste for the amount of salt.

FROM BOUILLON CUBES
One bouillon cube dissolved in 5 to 6 ounces of boiling water makes a flavorful stock: for 2 cups stock, dissolve 3 bouillon cubes in 2 cups boiling water. There is also a very good imported product available. Each "cube" of this product is ⅝ ounce and makes about 2 cups of rich stock.

FROM INSTANT CHICKEN BROTH
This is similar to the concentrated chicken stock and beef stock bases, except that it is individually wrapped in foil or plasticized packages. Each package or envelope makes 5 or 6 ounces stock.

FROM CANNED CONDENSED CHICKEN BROTH
Most condensed chicken broth is available in 10½-ounce cans. Occasionally, you will find other sizes—even a large size that is 1 quart and 14 or 15 ounces. Dilute with an equal amount of water for a well-flavored stock. Some recipes call for undiluted condensed chicken broth; other liquids in the recipe will dilute the broth.

FROM CANNED CHICKEN BROTH
You will find quite a number of different brands of canned clear chicken broth, varying from about 12 to 14 ounces. There are also larger size cans in several different brands. Use these undiluted.

TO MAKE VEAL STOCK

Veal stock usually should be clear, for its most frequent use is in delicate soups and sauces. You may want to strain it more than once.

3 or 4 pounds veal shank, bones, and/or knuckle	*1 medium-size carrot*
	1 leek
2 or 3 chicken backs or other bony parts, if desired	*1 large stalk celery with leaves*
	2 or 3 sprigs parsley
3 quarts water	*2-inch piece bay leaf*
1 tablespoon salt	*2 or 3 whole cloves*
1 medium-size onion	*2 egg whites*

Combine veal bones, chicken parts, and water in large kettle. Bring the liquid to a boil and skim two or three times. Add salt. Turn heat down and simmer. Peel onion and cut into pieces; scrape carrot and slice; clean leek and slice. Add these to simmering stock along with the stalk of celery and leaves, cut up, parsley, bay leaf, and cloves. Simmer the stock 3 or 4 hours.

Strain the stock through a wire sieve. Chill it several hours or over night, until fat hardens. Scrape off fat. Reheat to simmering. Beat in the egg whites with wire whip and simmer for about 30 minutes. Strain through wet cheesecloth or an old linen napkin. Reheat and strain the stock again, if desired. Makes about 2½ quarts.

TO MAKE LAMB STOCK

Lamb stock is seldom served as a clear soup so the extra step of clarifying the stock can be skipped. Use the bones from a boned roast—leg of lamb, shoulder, or rolled breast of lamb. Or use the bones from a leftover roast along with a lamb shank, or buy a lamb shank or two. Add a beef bone if you don't have enough lamb bones, or even some chicken parts.

Lamb bones from a boned leg of lamb or shoulder roast, or a lamb shank or two	*½ cup chopped celery leaves*
	2 or 3 sprigs parsley
	½ teaspoon mixed herbs for lamb or ¼ teaspoon each rosemary and thyme
2 quarts water	*½ teaspoon dried mint*
1 tablespoon salt	*2 or 3 slices lemon*
1 medium-size onion	*1 clove garlic*
1 medium-size carrot	
1 leek	

Combine lamb bones and water in a large kettle. Bring the liquid to a boil and skim it two or three times. Turn heat down, add salt, and simmer. Peel onion and scrape carrot; cut into pieces and add to simmering stock. Wash leek and cut into pieces and add with chopped celery and parsley. Crush herbs and add, along with mint, to simmering stock. Add the slices of lemon; crush the garlic and drop into stock. Simmer for about 3 hours; skim two or three times. Strain the stock through a wire sieve. Chill stock for several hours or overnight, until fat hardens. Remove fat. Use stock for soups and stews. Makes about 6 cups.

TO MAKE FISH STOCK

Well-seasoned fish stock makes a wonderful base for all kinds of fish soups, chowders, and stews. Use bony pieces or select a less expensive bony fish. Some fish markets sell "chowder fish"—wonderful for making fish stock.

2 to 2½ pounds fish bones and pieces,   *½ cup chopped celery and celery*
  or whole fish cut into pieces   *leaves*
2 quarts water   *2 or 3 sprigs parsley*
1 tablespoon salt   *2 or 3 slices lemon*
1 cup white table wine   *2-inch piece bay leaf*
1 large onion, chopped   *¼ teaspoon ground mace*

Combine fish and water in large kettle. Bring the liquid to a boil, skimming two or three times. Add salt, turn heat down, and simmer. Add white wine, chopped onion, celery, parsley, lemon slices, bay leaf, and mace. Simmer for about 1 hour. Cool stock slightly and strain it through a wire sieve. Chill stock. If you've used a fat fish, you may need to skim off fat. Use stock for soups and stews or as a *court bouillon* (cooking liquid) in which to simmer other fish. Makes about 2 quarts.

HURRY-UP FISH STOCK

If you haven't the time to make fish stock, or haven't the fish available, you can use water instead. Or use a combination of water and white table wine. A half cup of wine and 1½ cups water is a good proportion. Or save any *court bouillon* (cooking liquid) in which you have poached or simmered fish, fresh crab or shrimp. Strain this cooking liquid and keep it on hand in your freezer.

FROM CANNED OR BOTTLED CLAM JUICE

Most clam juice is in 8-ounce bottles or cans. Use as part or all of the stock. There is also a combination of clam and tomato juice, available in a 16-ounce can, which makes an excellent substitute for fish stock in several different soups and chowders.

FROM INSTANT CLAM BROTH AND SEASONING

In individual foil or plastic packages, each package or envelope makes 5 or 6 ounces of stock. Three packages dissolved in 2 cups hot water makes a flavorful stock.

FROM DRIED FISH OR SHRIMP

If you live in an area where you can purchase Japanese or other Oriental foods, then you can buy dried shrimp or fish, or a dried bonito and seaweed combination. These keep indefinitely and make a good fish stock. Check package directions, but generally you would use ¼ cup dried shrimp or ½ cup dried fish to make 2 cups stock. Pour boiling water over dried shrimp or fish. Let stand about 10 minutes, drain, and use liquid for stock.

Some Special Consommés and Bouillons

~~~~~~~

Cranberry Bouillon

Cranberry juice cocktail combined with bouillon makes a piquant and light beginning for a heavy holiday meal, particularly good before a wild game repast or one featuring roast duck or goose.

1 pint bottle cranberry juice cocktail
2 cups beef stock or 1 10½-ounce can condensed beef bouillon and enough water to make 2 cups
½ teaspoon Worcestershire sauce
1 teaspoon onion juice
1 teaspoon seasoned salt, or to taste
⅛ teaspoon Spice Parisienne, quatre épices, or ground nutmeg
½ cup rosé wine
Sliced almonds, stuffed olives, or chives

Combine cranberry juice cocktail and beef stock in a saucepan. Add Worcestershire sauce, onion juice, seasoned salt, and Spice Parisienne. Bring to a boil and simmer 5 to 7 minutes. Just before serving add the rosé wine. Pour into bouillon or soup cups and garnish with roasted sliced almonds, sliced stuffed olives, or chopped chives. Makes 6 servings.

Madrilène aux Pommes
Apple Madrilène

Elegant enough for your nicest dinner party. The apple adds a special touch to madrilène. You can use beef and chicken stock, if you have it, but making madrilène from the stock bases is very easy and the flavor is good.

1 quart water	½ cup sliced celery
1 tablespoon concentrated beef-stock base	3 whole peppercorns
	1 teaspoon seasoned salt
1 tablespoon concentrated chicken-stock base	2 large tart apples
	½ cup water
2 cups tomato juice	¼ cup sherry
1 tablespoon chopped onion	½ cup whipping cream
2 whole cloves	¼ teaspoon salt
½ cup sliced carrots	½ teaspoon curry powder

Combine water, beef- and chicken-stock base, tomato juice, onion, cloves, carrots, celery, peppercorns, and seasoned salt. Simmer 1 hour and strain. Peel and core apples, cut into quarters and slice thinly. Simmer apple slices 5 to 10 minutes in ½ cup water, or until tender but crisp.

When time to serve soup, add apple slices to the clear madrilène. Season with additional seasoned salt, if needed. Add sherry. Whip cream and mix in salt and curry powder. Serve in soup cups, topped with the curried whipped cream.

Consommé Mousseline
Consommé with Cream

Combine the eggs with the broth before heating and be sure not to boil the mixture or there will be some separation. This is an elegant opening-course soup.

2 egg yolks	2 cans (about 14 ounces each) chicken broth, or about 1 quart
¼ cup half and half	
¼ cup sherry	Chopped chives
1 teaspoon arrowroot or cornstarch	

Beat egg yolks, half and half, sherry, and arrowroot or cornstarch until smooth. Beat into chicken broth. Heat over low heat, stirring almost constantly, until soup is hot and has thickened very slightly. Do *not* allow it to boil. Pour into hot soup cups. Sprinkle each serving with ½ teaspoon chopped chives and serve at once. Makes 6 to 8 servings.

Curried Tomato Bouillon

A gourmet soup which is no trouble to make—usually you will have the ingredients right on your shelf. This is especially good to extend a meal for an unexpected guest, or to serve in mugs with a cold supper or outdoor meal.

4 teaspoons concentrated beef-stock base or 4 beef bouillon cubes
3 cups hot water
1 envelope (about 2 ounces) tomato soup mix or 1 8-ounce can tomato sauce
½ teaspoon curry powder
¼ cup cold water
½ teaspoon MSG (monosodium glutamate)
2 tablespoons sherry

Dissolve the beef-stock base or bouillon cubes in the hot water. Mix in tomato soup mix or tomato sauce. Stir over low heat until bouillon and soup mix or sauce are smooth. Heat to simmering and simmer 3 or 4 minutes. Mix together the curry powder, cold water, and MSG. Stir mixture into soup. Just before serving, add sherry. Makes 4 to 6 servings.

Mushroom-Barley Soup

Good for an opening course for luncheon or dinner: the dried mushrooms give a rather exotic flavor. Wait to add the vegetables until just before serving so they will retain their crisp texture.

4 or 5 whole dried mushrooms or 2 or 3 tablespoons dried mushroom pieces
½ cup cold water
1½ quarts beef bouillon or 3 cans (about 14 ounces each) beef broth
¼ cup quick-cooking barley
1 teaspoon seasoned salt
2 tablespoons shredded carrots
2 tablespoons chopped chives or green onions
1 teaspoon chervil or chopped parsley

Soak mushrooms in cold water for 30 minutes or longer. If whole, cut into slices. Combine mushrooms, the water in which they were soaked, bouillon, barley, and seasoned salt in large kettle. Simmer for about 1 to 1½ hours, or until barley is tender. Just before serving, stir in shredded carrots and chopped chives or green onions. Ladle into soup cups or bowls and sprinkle with chervil or chopped parsley. Makes 6 to 8 servings.

Tomato-Orange Bouillon

An unusually flavored opening-course soup. Serve it chilled, also, or add gelatin to all or part and have an aspic.

1 large can (1 quart 14 ounces) or   *1 clove garlic, thinly sliced*
   about 6 cups tomato juice   *1-inch piece bay leaf*
1 medium-size onion, thinly sliced   *1 10½-ounce can condensed beef*
¼ cup sliced celery and celery leaves   *bouillon, undiluted*
1 teaspoon seasoned salt   *½ cup orange juice*
4 or 5 peppercorns   *Orange slices or orange peel*

Combine about half the tomato juice with sliced onion, celery, seasoned salt, peppercorns, garlic, and bay leaf. Simmer until the onion and celery are tender, about 30 minutes. Remove the bay leaf and rub tomato juice and vegetables through a wire sieve. Combine this with the remaining tomato juice, beef bouillon, and orange juice. Simmer 20 minutes longer. Serve hot, garnished with thin slices of orange. If frozen orange juice is used, sprinkle soup with a dash of bottled orange peel. Makes 8 servings.

Green Pepper Consommé

Though this unusually flavored consommé is made from green peppers, because of the tomatoes, it has a delicate pinkish color. Try making it with sweet red peppers at the time of the year they are in the market and it will be even pinker.

3 large green peppers   *1½ to 2 quarts clear beef stock or 3*
2 large tomatoes   *10½-ounce cans beef consommé*
1 large onion   *diluted with 3 cans water*
2 whole cloves   *¼ cup sherry*

Wash green peppers and cut into 6 or 8 pieces. Remove seeds. Peel and cut up tomatoes and slice onion. Combine with cloves and beef stock or consommé and simmer 1½ to 2 hours. Strain the consommé. Reheat the clear soup to simmering and add sherry. Serve in heated soup cups garnished with slivers of green pepper or sliced mushrooms. Accompany with small cheese crackers. Makes 8 to 10 servings.

Madrilène St. Helena
Tomato Madrilène

Preferably, use one of the wonderful red wines from California's Napa Valley—Gamay, Zinfandel, or Cabernet. But any good red table wine will do. Serve *Madrilène St. Helena* as an opening course along with crisp Melba toast. Excellent chilled and served very cold, too.

1 to 1½ pounds ripe red tomatoes	*1 teaspoon onion salt*
1 10½-ounce can condensed beef consommé, undiluted	*¼ teaspoon coarsely ground black pepper*
1 cup red table wine, such as Zinfandel, Gamay, or Cabernet	*½ teaspoon chervil*
	Chopped chives

Scald and peel tomatoes, and cut into chunks. Blend them in electric blender until smooth. Strain them through a wire sieve to remove all seeds. Combine the puréed tomatoes with the consommé, red wine, onion salt, pepper, and chervil, and heat to simmering. Pour into soup cups and top with chopped chives. Serve very hot, or chill and serve cold. Makes 6 servings.

Zwiebelsuppe mit Bier
Onion Soup with Beer

This German *Onion Soup with Beer* is a specialty of my friend Barney Vogel, for many years a commercial photographer in San Francisco, and a host who likes to cook for his guests. He makes it to serve aboard his power cruiser on the Sacramento River.

4 tablespoons butter	*1 11- or 12-ounce can beer*
3 large onions, thinly sliced	*¼ teaspoon marjoram*
2 10½-ounce cans condensed beef bouillon, undiluted	*¼ teaspoon thyme*
	Salt and pepper to taste
1½ cups water	*Grated Gruyère or Parmesan cheese*

Melt butter in saucepan; add sliced onions and cook until yellow but not brown. Add canned bouillon, water, and beer. Crush marjoram and thyme and stir into soup. Simmer 30 to 35 minutes. Add salt and pepper to taste. Ladle soup into mugs or bowls and sprinkle with grated cheese. Serve with bread sticks, rye Melba toast, or toasted French bread. Makes 4 to 6 servings.

Moravian Beef and Mushroom Broth

If you can get wild mushrooms, you will have the more distinctive flavor of the original middle-European soup. Or, for a real quickie, use a 4-ounce can of sliced mushrooms.

2 10½-ounce cans condensed beef bouillon, undiluted
1 cup red table wine
1 cup water

½ teaspoon caraway seeds
1½ cups sliced fresh mushrooms
1 teaspoon arrowroot or cornstarch
1 tablespoon cold water

Combine the beef bouillon with the wine and water. Crush caraway seeds slightly and add to broth. Simmer about 20 minutes. Strain out caraway seeds. Add sliced mushrooms and simmer 15 to 20 minutes, or until mushrooms are tender. Combine arrowroot or cornstarch with cold water and stir into the soup. Simmer until broth thickens slightly, stirring constantly. Serve at once in soup cups or small bowls. Good with crisp seasoned rye wafers. Makes 6 servings.

Kraut 'n' Beer Soup

A refreshingly piquant soup to start a meal. Serve it hot with caraway seasoning, or, for a good cold soup on a hot day, combine chilled ingredients and skip the simmering. Top with a blob of dill-flavored sour cream —½ cup dairy sour cream and ½ teaspoon each seasoned salt and dill weed.

1 cup rich chicken stock or 2 chicken bouillon cubes dissolved in 1 cup hot water

1 cup sauerkraut juice
½ cup light beer
⅛ teaspoon caraway seeds

Combine chicken stock, sauerkraut juice, and beer. Crush caraway seeds and add to soup. Simmer over very low heat for 15 to 20 minutes. Serve hot, accompanied by rye crackers. To serve chilled, combine chilled stock, sauerkraut juice, and beer. (Be sure first to skim off *all* fat from the stock.) Serve in chilled cups with a sprinkling of dill weed or a spoonful of dill-flavored sour cream. Makes 4 to 6 servings.

Irish Clear Soup

If you're careful you will end up with about 3 quarts of the most beauti-fully clear, flavorful bouillon you have ever tasted. Actually, you are making stock and then clarifying it. Irish whiskey gives it a special flavor. Traditionally in Ireland, *Clear Soup* is served before Christmas dinner. Christmas is a good time to serve it here in this country, too, and it is excellent before any large festive dinner.

3 to 4 pounds beef shank	*6 whole black peppercorns*
Veal bones	*1 whole bay leaf*
4 quarts water	*1 sprig parsley*
2 large onions	*1 tablespoon salt*
2 whole carrots	*¼ teaspoon thyme*
2 outside celery stalks	*2 egg whites*
1 whole leek	*¼ cup Irish whiskey*
6 whole cloves	

TO MAKE THE BEEF STOCK:

Combine beef shank, veal bones, and water in a large kettle. Bring to a boil and skim off any scum that forms. Turn heat down to simmer. Meanwhile, peel onions and cut in half crosswise. Scrub carrots, but do not scrape. Scrub celery stalks; be sure there are some green leaves, too. Clean leek, using part of green tops. Add vegetables to simmering soup along with cloves, peppercorns, bay leaf, parsley, and salt. Crush thyme and add to stock. Simmer slowly 5 to 6 hours, skimming occasionally if needed. Cool slightly. Wet a piece of muslin or cheesecloth and place it in a wire sieve. Strain the stock through the cloth and sieve. Chill it until the fat hardens on top and remove the fat.

TO CLARIFY THE STOCK:

Bring stock to a boil and beat in the egg whites with a wire whip. Turn the heat down and simmer the bouillon for about 30 minutes. Strain it again through wet cloth and wire sieve.

TO SERVE:

Heat 4 to 6 cups of *Clear Soup* to simmering; add Irish whiskey and when soup is again simmering, pour into bouillon cups and serve at once. Crisp crackers, Melba toast or toasted slivers of Irish bread go well with *Clear Soup*. Four to 6 cups of soup will serve 6 to 8.

Yoghurt Corbasi
Turkish Yoghurt Soup

At first glance this might seem like a cream soup, but it is really very light and if all the fat is skimmed from the lamb stock, it is so low in calories that it can fit into a dieter's menu.

1 quart lamb stock (see recipe in section on stock)	1 tablespoon flour
	1 cup yoghurt
2 tablespoons butter	1 teaspoon dried mint

Skim off any remaining fat from lamb stock and heat it. In a saucepan melt butter and stir in flour, until it is well blended. Add lamb stock slowly; bring to simmering, stirring constantly. Simmer for 4 or 5 minutes, or until soup is smooth and slightly thickened. Mix in the yoghurt; reheat just to simmering but do *not* boil. Sprinkle with dried mint and pour into soup cups. Serve with crisp sesame crackers. Makes 6 servings.

Oyster Soup Louisiane

A very old and very elegant soup recipe from New Orleans. Serve this as an opening course for one of your most special dinners.

¼ cup butter	1½ to 2 cups champagne or 1 half-bottle
3 dozen fresh oysters, or 1 quart, or 3 10-ounce jars, preferably Gulf or Louisiana oysters	2 beef bouillon cubes or 2 teaspoons concentrated beef-stock base
Dash Tabasco sauce	Salt to taste
1 teaspoon celery salt	2 tablespoons chopped parsley
¼ cup very fine, dry crumbs of French bread, toasted	

Melt butter in heavy saucepan, or use an electric frying pan or chafing dish if you wish to make this on or near your dining table. Add oysters and liquor, Tabasco, and celery salt. Cook over high heat until edges of the oysters curl. Sprinkle them with toasted French-bread crumbs. Pour in the champagne and add bouillon cubes or beef-stock base. Simmer, stirring, until bouillon cubes are dissolved and soup thoroughly heated, but do not overcook oysters. Add additional salt to taste, if desired. Ladle into hot soup cups and sprinkle each serving with chopped parsley. Serve with thin fingers of Melba toast. Makes 6 servings.

Irish Turtle Soup

The British usually add Madeira to their *Turtle Soup,* but the Irish prefer a good slug of rum or their own Irish whiskey. I think the rum, particularly a light rum, gives the best flavor.

3 or 4 cups Irish Clear Soup *or 2*   *1 10-ounce can turtle meat or 1 cup*
10½-ounce cans condensed beef con-   *cooked turtle meat and stock*
sommé diluted with 2 cans water   Salt to taste
                                        ¼ *cup rum or Irish whiskey*

Pour the *Clear Soup* into saucepan or kettle. Cut canned turtle meat
into bite-size pieces and add to soup along with the turtle stock from the
can. If using fresh or frozen turtle meat, cook it first until tender, then
cut it into bite-size pieces. Measure about ½ to ¾ cup of turtle meat and
fill cup with turtle stock from the cooking. Combine with Clear Soup or
bouillon. Heat to simmering; add additional salt, if needed. Just before
serving stir in rum or whiskey. When soup simmers again, pour into
bouillon cups and serve at once. Makes 6 servings.

Dashi
Japanese Clear Soup

My good friend Pearl Kimura makes her clear soup a number of different
ways and I have tried them all. Of course, the various Japanese ingredients, such as *Dashi no Moto,* are available in California cities and other
localities where there are communities of Japanese Americans. But if you
can't get these special foods, then there are very plausible substitutes.

The true clear soup is very delicate in flavor—and very clear. In Japan
it is more often served between courses or at the end of a meal than at
the beginning. My friend Pearl, who says she cooks either American
Japanese-style or Japanese American-style—she's not sure which—starts
her meal with this clear soup. And she is very careful about the garnishes:
the colors should be delicate, yet still offer a contrast. Arrangements
should be in threes, as in Japanese flower arrangements.

Here are several different ways to make this delicate clear soup.

4 cups boiling water
½ teaspoon MSG (monosodium glutamate)
One of the following:
1 envelope or bag (¾ ounce) Dashi no Moto (a specially packaged mixture of powdered bonito and kelp or seaweed)
or

1 cup dried bonito and 1 piece seaweed or kelp
or
½ cup dried shrimp
or
1 pound fresh fish pieces, head, bones, pieces for chowder, and ½ teaspoon salt

THE SOUP

Combine water and MSG and bring to a boil. Add any of the suggested fish ingredients. Simmer for 8 to 10 minutes. Strain through a wire sieve lined with a wet muslin cloth or cheesecloth. Or just pour off the top, very clear portion of the *Dashi*. Use any remaining *Dashi* for *Miso Shiru* (bean curd soup) since the *Dashi* need not be so clear. (See recipe for *Miso Shiru*.)

THE GARNISH

Reheat the clear soup. Taste and add MSG, salt, or soy sauce, if needed. Be careful in adding soy sauce, for it may not be so attractive in color, depending upon your garnish. While soup simmers, add thin slices of mushroom, 3 slices for each serving. Ladle soup and mushrooms into fragile low soup cups and garnish each cup with a tiny twist of lemon peel. The delicate colors will show better if cups are light-colored inside.

Or use tiny cooked shrimp, 3 to a serving, with a sprinkling of thinly sliced green onion tops or a small sprig of water cress; or 3 small pieces of snow peas or green beans with a tiny pink shrimp, or slices of water chestnut with water cress or green onion tops. Or, if available, use tiny cubes of *tofu* (soy bean curd) with a touch of green. Be sure garnish is gracefully small. Do not crowd cups. Makes about 4 servings of ¾ cup each.

Bouillon de Radis
Radish Bouillon

Radish Bouillon makes a nice light opening course for a special dinner. With gelatin added, it's good as an aspic.

2 *bunches radishes*	*1-inch piece bay leaf*
2 *pounds beef bones*	1 *clove*
1 *cup sliced carrots*	3 *quarts water*
1 *cup sliced onion*	¼ *teaspoon thyme*
1 *leek, sliced*	2 *tablespoons salt*
2 *or 3 sprigs parsley*	

Wash radishes well. Slice one bunch. Combine slices and well-washed tops in large kettle with beef bones, sliced carrots, onions, leek, parsley, bay leaf, clove, and water. Bring mixture to a boil and turn down to simmer. Simmer a few minutes, skimming several times. Then crush thyme and add to soup with salt. Simmer the soup 2½ to 3 hours.

Meanwhile, slice remaining radishes in thin slices. When ready to serve, strain the soup through a sieve. Pour the clear bouillon into soup cups and garnish with sliced radishes.

Makes 2 to 2½ quarts bouillon, enough to serve 6 or 8 hot, and plenty left to make *Radish Aspic* for another 6 or 8 servings.

For *Radish Aspic*, see Cold Soups and Aspics.

SECTION 3

Aspics and Cold Soups

ASPICS

*

Radish Aspic

Soften 1 envelope plain gelatin in ¼ cup cold water. Combine with 2 to 3 cups *Radish Bouillon* (see recipe). Heat, stirring occasionally, until gelatin is dissolved. Chill until aspic begins to set, then mix in ½ cup or more of thinly sliced radishes. Chill until aspic is set. To serve, spoon into chilled soup cups. Top with a spoonful of sour cream and sprinkle with dill weed or chopped chives.

Jellied Cucumber Soup with Shrimp

Summer or winter try this sophisticated soup for an opening course for dinner or for luncheon. A drop or two of green food coloring will deepen the delicate green color.

2 *large cucumbers*	2 *tablespoons lemon or lime juice*
¼ *cup chopped onion*	1 *cup dairy sour cream*
2 *cups chicken stock*	2 *teaspoons finely chopped crystal-*
½ *teaspoon seasoned salt*	*lized ginger*
2 *envelopes unflavored gelatin*	1 *cup cleaned cooked shrimp*
½ *cup cold water*	*Chopped chives, chervil, or dill weed*

33

Pare cucumbers, cut into chunks and combine with chopped onion and chicken stock. Add seasoned salt. Simmer for about 30 minutes, or until the cucumbers are very tender. Force them through a wire sieve or food mill or purée in a blender. Soak the gelatin in the cold water and add to hot cucumber purée. Stir until gelatin is dissolved. Let the soup chill until it begins to set. Blend in lemon or lime juice and dairy sour cream. Add crystallized ginger. Chill soup in bowl for several hours, or until it is firm. Spoon into soup cups or bowls, garnish with chilled shrimps and sprinkle with chopped chives, chervil, or dill weed. Serve with crisp onion-flavored crackers. Makes 6 to 8 servings.

Artichokes with Clam Madrilène Aspic

Here's an unusual opening course with a touch of elegance. The *Clam Madrilène* (without the gelatin) can be served hot. Or the aspic can be spooned into avocado halves or chilled soup cups with a sprinkling of chopped chives or chervil. The *Remoulade Sauce* is good, too, with fried fish.

8 *medium-size fresh artichokes*	*¼ teaspoon lemon peel*
3 *cups tomato juice*	2 *envelopes unflavored gelatin*
1 *teaspoon Worcestershire sauce*	1 *8-ounce bottle clam juice*
1 *teaspoon seasoned salt*	*⅓ cup yoghurt*
1 *teaspoon onion juice*	Remoulade Sauce

Trim artichokes and cook in boiling salted water until tender. Let them cool. Spread the leaves apart and remove the chokes and some of the center leaves. Chill several hours or overnight.

Meanwhile, make *Clam Madrilène:* Combine tomato juice, Worcestershire sauce, seasoned salt, onion juice, and lemon peel and simmer 10 minutes. Soften gelatin in clam juice. Pour hot tomato juice over the softened gelatin and clam juice and stir until the gelatin is dissolved. Cool the soup and blend in yoghurt. Pour into a pan or bowl and chill several hours or overnight until firm.

When ready to serve, spread the chilled artichokes apart and spoon the madrilène into the center. Serve with *Remoulade Sauce* as a dip for the artichokes. Makes 8 servings.

REMOULADE SAUCE

Combine 1 cup mayonnaise, 1 teaspoon dry mustard, 2 teaspoons each capers, chopped parsley, and anchovy paste, and 2 tablespoons chopped gherkins. Mix well and chill.

Mushroom Aspic Tarragon

This is the kind of opening course to serve preceding a rather heavy, formal dinner or luncheon.

1 envelope unflavored gelatin	2 tablespoons lime juice
⅓ cup white table wine	¼ teaspoon tarragon
2 4-ounce cans sliced mushrooms	Dairy sour cream
1 cup well-seasoned, clear chicken stock	Chopped chives

Soften gelatin in wine. Drain mushrooms. Combine the mushroom liquid with chicken stock and heat to boiling. Pour liquid over softened gelatin and stir until gelatin is dissolved. Add lime juice; crush tarragon and stir into gelatin mixture. Chill it until syrupy. Mix in the mushrooms and chill until firm. Spoon the aspic into chilled soup cups. Top with a spoonful of dairy sour cream and sprinkle with chopped chives. Serve with crisp Melba toast. Makes 6 to 8 servings.

Another way to serve *Mushroom Aspic Tarragon* is to mold it in 6 or 8 individual molds. Unmold on small plates and garnish with watercress.

Avocado Aspic with Red Caviar

Of course you can use black caviar here, but the red is much less expensive and makes an interesting contrast with the green of the avocado —nice at holiday time. Or serve this as an opening course for a late spring or midsummer luncheon or supper.

1 envelope unflavored gelatin	1 teaspoon seasoned salt
½ cup cold water	½ teaspoon chili powder
3 ripe avocados	Dash Tabasco sauce
2 tablespoons finely chopped onion	½ cup dairy sour cream
2 tablespoons chopped canned green chilis	1 tablespoon lime juice
	Red caviar

Soften gelatin in cold water. Meanwhile, cut avocados in half, remove the seeds and peel. Mash the avocados or sieve or blend in electric blender until smooth. Mix in finely chopped onion, green chilis, seasoned salt, chili powder, Tabasco, sour cream, and lime juice. Dissolve gelatin over hot water or very low heat. Mix it into avocado mixture. Chill the aspic until firm. Spoon it into stemmed glasses or chilled soup cups and garnish each serving with a spoonful of red caviar. If preferred, spoon into individual molds and chill until firm. Turn out onto small plates and top with caviar. Makes 6 to 8 servings.

Green Pepper Aspic in Cantaloupe

A delicious and unusual opening course for a summer luncheon. The aspic will keep several days in the refrigerator. You can make the hot consommé for a small dinner party and make the rest into aspic and serve a few days later.

2 *cups cold* Green Pepper Consommé	2 *or 3 cantaloupes*
(*see Consommés and Bouillons*)	*Dairy sour cream*
1 *envelope unflavored gelatin*	*Paprika or chopped parsley*

Soften gelatin in ½ cup of the cold *Green Pepper Consommé.* Heat remaining 1½ cups of consommé to simmering; pour it over gelatin and stir until dissolved. Chill the aspic until firm. Cut cantaloupes into thirds or halves and remove all seeds. Spoon the aspic into cantaloupes and top each serving with a spoonful of dairy sour cream. Sprinkle with paprika or chopped parsley. Makes 6 servings.

COLD SOUPS

Iced Tomato Soup

When the weather's sizzling this makes a refreshing opening course. Or start out a heavy, rich meal with this chilled soup. On a chilly day, serve it piping hot.

3 cups tomato juice
1 tablespoon chopped chives
2 tablespoons soy sauce
1 teaspoon MSG

1 tablespoon lemon juice
Dash cayenne pepper
½ teaspoon chervil or 1 teaspoon
    chopped parsley

Combine tomato juice, chopped chives, soy sauce, MSG, lemon juice, cayenne pepper, chervil or parsley and mix thoroughly. Chill until very cold and serve in soup cups accompanied by crisp crackers. Or heat to simmering and serve hot. Makes 6 servings.

Roquefort Tomato Glacé

Particularly good as an opening course for a wild duck dinner or to go along with venison, pheasant or other game. A good sprinkling of shrimp or crab makes it a refreshing and filling soup for a hot summer day.

2 tablespoons crumbled Roquefort
    cheese
1 3-ounce package cream cheese
1 teaspoon onion juice
1 teaspoon Worcestershire sauce
1 teaspoon seasoned salt

⅛ teaspoon white pepper
2 tablespoons lemon juice
2 cups tomato or vegetable juice cock-
    tail
2 egg whites
Chopped chives

Blend together thoroughly Roquefort cheese, cream cheese, onion juice, Worcestershire sauce, salt, pepper, and lemon juice. Add tomato juice, mix thoroughly, and freeze until mushy. Beat the egg whites until stiff but not dry. Break up the frozen mixture and carefully beat it into the beaten egg whites. Return the glacé to the freezer until ready to serve. Glacé is best, however, if not completely frozen. Spoon it into chilled soup cups or sherbet glasses and sprinkle with chopped chives. Makes 6 servings.

Cream Cheese Chicken Soup

So easy to make and so good on a hot day! Try serving it before a crab or shrimp Louis salad along with rye wafers or Melba toast.

1 8-ounce package cream cheese
1 can (about 14½ ounces) chicken
    broth or 2 cups well-seasoned
    chicken stock

½ teaspoon seasoned salt
1 teaspoon onion juice
½ cup white table wine
Chopped chives

Let cream cheese soften a little and combine with chicken stock, seasoned salt, onion juice, and wine in a blender. Blend until smooth. Chill thoroughly and pour into chilled soup cups. Sprinkle with chopped chives. Makes 4 to 6 servings.

Clam Madrilène Frappé

Calorie counters will like this cold, refreshing frozen soup—a good opening course for a hot weather meal or for an elaborate dinner.

3 cups vegetable juice cocktail	*½ teaspoon dill weed*
1 teaspoon celery salt	*1 8-ounce bottle clam juice*
1 teaspoon onion juice	*½ cup yoghurt*
1 teaspoon lemon juice	*Chopped chives*

Combine vegetable juice cocktail, celery salt, onion juice, lemon juice, and dill weed and simmer the soup for about 10 minutes. Cool and stir in clam juice, then beat in yoghurt. Freeze until mushy. Spoon into chilled soup cups or sherbet glasses and sprinkle with chopped chives. If the frappé has frozen hard shave it off with a heavy spoon or ice cream scoop. Accompany with crisp whole-wheat or rye crackers or Melba toast. Makes 6 servings.

Bouillon de Betterave
Beet Bouillon

Serve this cold soup at your most special ladies' luncheon. Rosé wine is good, but the sparkling wine gives a more luxurious touch.

4 chicken bouillon cubes	*3 tablespoons red wine vinegar*
2 cups hot water	*1 cup pink champagne, sparkling burgundy, or rosé wine*
1 1-pound can julienne-cut beets	
1 6-ounce can frozen concentrated pink lemonade	*1 cup dairy sour cream*
	2 tablespoons chopped chives
½ teaspoon garlic salt or to taste	*¼ teaspoon salt*

Dissolve bouillon cubes in hot water in mixing bowl. Add the undrained beets and frozen pink lemonade. When lemonade is melted, stir in garlic salt and vinegar and mix thoroughly. Let chill until time to serve. Mix together sour cream, chives, and salt.

At serving time, add champagne to soup. Serve soup, very cold, in bouillon cups or glass bowls. Top each serving with sour cream and chives. Accompany with crisp sesame-seed or matzoth crackers. Makes 6 to 8 servings.

Soup Sengali

Exotic yet easily made, *Soup Sengali* precedes a summer luncheon or dinner with style. You can serve it hot, but probably like it better cold.

1 cup shredded or flaked coconut	1 teaspoon curry powder
3 cups chicken stock	½ to 1 teaspoon seasoned salt
1 medium-size onion	Dash white pepper
1 medium-size apple	Chopped salted peanuts
1 cup half and half	

Combine shredded or flaked coconut and chicken stock. Peel onion and apple and chop coarsely. Add to coconut and chicken stock mixture. Simmer 30 to 40 minutes, or until onion and apple are very tender. Let cool slightly, then blend in electric blender, and press through a wire sieve. Discard any coconut that will not go through sieve. Blend in half and half. Add curry powder and seasoned salt to taste (amount depends on saltiness of chicken stock) and white pepper. Chill for several hours. Serve in chilled soup cups, garnished with chopped salted peanuts. Makes 6 servings.

Pink Velvet

Easy to whip up in no time on a hot day for lunch or dinner, yet special enough for the nicest party! Make the stock from chicken seasoned stock base or bouillon cubes, or use canned chicken bouillon.

2 4½-ounce jars baby food strained beets	½ cup dairy sour cream
2 cups chicken stock	½ teaspoon salt, or to taste
	Chopped chives or chervil

Combine strained beets, chicken stock, and dairy sour cream. Blend well with a wire whip, rotary beater, or electric mixer. Season to taste with salt (amount depends on saltiness of chicken stock). Chill the soup. Pour into soup cups and sprinkle with chopped chives or chervil. Any crisp cracker, especially onion- or other flavored crackers, goes well with this. Makes 6 servings.

Iced Green Pea Soup

Adapted from an old, old recipe supposed to have been a favorite of
Queen Victoria. Her version was much, much richer than this one, for it
used a very large amount of sweet butter. We presume she had it served
hot. It's very good hot as well as icy cold.

1 10-ounce package frozen green
   peas, or about 3 cups shelled fresh
   peas
6 green onions, sliced, tops and all
1 teaspoon dry mint
¼ cup chopped parsley
4 cups chicken or veal stock

½ teaspoon salt or to taste
½ teaspoon sugar
½ cup dairy sour cream
½ cup sherry
Chopped chives
1 cup shredded lettuce, outside green
   leaves

Combine green peas, sliced onions, mint, chopped parsley, shredded
lettuce, and stock in a soup kettle. Bring to a boil and add salt (amount
depends on saltiness of stock) and sugar. Turn heat down and simmer
the soup for about an hour or until vegetables are very tender. Let mixture cool and blend until smooth in an electric blender or force it through
a fine wire sieve. With a wire whip beat in sour cream until well blended
with soup. Stir in wine. Chill soup until very cold. Serve in soup cups
and garnish with chopped chives. Tiny cheese crackers go well with this.
Makes 6 to 8 servings.

Okrosha
Cold Russian Soup

In Russia *Okrosha* is made with kvass, a beer-like drink made by fer-
menting rye bread. Since it is not readily available in this country (though
you can make it), and since many Americans don't especially like it, use
wine with the addition of sparkling water.

1 cup diced fresh cucumber
¼ cup diced dill pickle
¼ cup thinly sliced green onion
¼ cup chopped parsley
1 cup yoghurt
1 cup white table wine
1 cup diced cooked chicken
1 cup small cooked or canned shrimp

2 or 3 teaspoons seasoned salt
¼ teaspoon cracked black pepper
1 teaspoon prepared mustard
¼ teaspoon tarragon
⅛ teaspoon fennel seeds
1 cup chilled sparkling water
3 or 4 ice cubes
2 hard-cooked eggs

Combine diced cucumber, dill pickle, sliced onion and parsley in large bowl. Stir in yoghurt and wine and add chicken and shrimp. Add 2 teaspoons of the seasoned salt, cracked black pepper, and mustard. Crush the tarragon and fennel seeds and mix into soup. Chill several hours or overnight.

Just before serving, mix in sparkling water and ice cubes. Peel and chop hard-cooked eggs. Mix chopped eggs into soup. Add remaining teaspoon seasoned salt, if needed. Ladle into soup plates. Serve with dark rye bread. Makes 6 to 8 servings.

Okrosha
American-Style

Bottled cola drink and frankfurters give the American touch to this cold Russian soup. Almost any kind of cold leftover cooked meat or poultry can be used. Keep a bowl of this refreshing soup on hand for hot weather luncheons. It will keep for several days and the flavor actually improves.

1 quart buttermilk	*1 teaspoon dry mustard*
1 6-ounce bottle cola drink	*1 teaspoon dill weed*
½ cup dairy sour cream	*1 teaspoon seasoned salt*
1 1-pound can diced beets	*1 cup diced frankfurters or ham*
¼ cup thinly sliced green onion	*1 cup diced cooked chicken, veal or*
½ cup diced cucumber	*beef*
2 tablespoons chopped parsley	*1 hard-cooked egg*

Combine buttermilk, cola drink, and dairy sour cream in a large bowl. Stir in diced beets and beet liquid. Add green onion, cucumber, and parsley. Mix in mustard, dill weed, and seasoned salt. Add diced cold meats. Chill several hours or overnight. Just before serving, peel and chop hard-cooked egg and mix into soup. Ladle into soup plates. Pretzels or pretzel sticks or nuggets make a good accompaniment.

Soupe Maste va Khiar
Persian Cold Yoghurt Soup

A soup acquired in Iran. Though the raisins seem an odd ingredient, don't let it frighten you—they are delicious. Or you can use diced cooked beets instead. The soup is unbelievably refreshing on a hot day.

½ cup seedless raisins
Boiling water
1 cup cold water
3 cups yoghurt or buttermilk
½ cup half and half
1 cup pared, chopped cucumber
   (about 1 medium-size cucumber)

¼ cup chopped green onion
2 teaspoons salt
½ teaspoon ground white pepper
1 teaspoon dill weed
1 hard-cooked egg
1 tablespoon chopped parsley

Pour boiling water over the raisins and drain. Add raisins to cold water and chill for about an hour. Meanwhile, combine yoghurt or buttermilk, half and half, chopped cucumber, chopped green onion, salt, and pepper. Crush dill and stir into yoghurt mixture. Chill for about an hour, then combine with raisins and water. Just before serving, peel and chop hard-cooked egg and add to soup. Be sure soup is very cold. Sprinkle with chopped parsley. Makes about 6 servings.

Yoghurt Soup from the Caspian Sea

The Caspian Sea is a favorite vacation area for Russians and Iranians—the two countries on its shores. Which country this came from, I don't know; a friend who made a trip through the Near East gave it to me. It's almost as much a salad as a soup—especially refreshing in hot weather.

1 quart yoghurt
1 jar or can (about 4 ounces) cocktail
   sausages or 5 or 6 ounces smoked
   cocktail sausages

3 cups shredded red cabbage
1 medium-size red onion
Salt to taste
¼ cup chopped parsley

Spoon yoghurt into a deep mixing bowl and chill. If sausages are in brine, heat to simmering. Let cool in liquid, then drain. Or fry smoked cocktail sausages until done and let them cool. Simmer shredded cabbage in a small amount of water until tender but still crisp. Drain and chill. Peel red onion and cut into thin slices; cut slices in half and separate the pieces. Mix together yoghurt, sausages (cut in half, if desired), cooked cabbage, and onion pieces. Add salt to taste and sprinkle with parsley. Chill thoroughly. Spoon into chilled soup cups or glass bowls. Serve as a first course or as an accompaniment to a hot or cold sandwich. Makes about 6 servings.

Fruit and Sweet Soups

~~~~~

Holiday Fruit Soup

From a collection of pioneer recipes, this soup was probably Scandinavian. More unusual than a fruit cocktail, it makes a good opening course for holiday meals. It is good, too, as a dessert, or serve it cold as an opening course for a summer luncheon or supper.

2 quarts water	½ orange
1 cup sugar	½ lemon
½ teaspoon salt	3 apples
¼ cup quick-cooking tapioca	3 fresh peaches or 1 10-ounce package
1 cup cut-up pitted prunes	frozen peach slices
½ cup raisins	1 stick cinnamon

Bring water to a boil in a large kettle and add sugar, salt, and tapioca. Add prunes and raisins. Slice the orange and lemon into thin slices and then into quarters. Remove any seeds. Add slices to soup. Pare apples and slice thinly. Peel peaches, if using fresh peaches, and slice. Add sliced apples and peaches to soup along with stick of cinnamon. Simmer for 1 hour. Serve hot or cold, accompanied by thin sesame crackers. Makes 8 to 10 servings.

Fruktsoppa
Swedish Fruit Soup

My British friend Eleanor met her Swedish husband at the University of Wisconsin. This soup was often on the table at smorgasbord gatherings of her husband's family. It is good to serve at a Sunday brunch.

2 cups mixed dried fruit (about 12
ounces)—apricots, peaches, pears
and prunes
½ cup seedless raisins
2 quarts water
½ cup sugar
1 teaspoon lemon peel
2-inch piece of stick cinnamon

⅛ teaspoon salt
½ teaspoon aromatic bitters
3 tablespoons quick-cooking tapioca
½ cup raspberry syrup, or other red
fruit syrup
Dairy sour cream
Toasted finely sliced almonds

Combine the dried fruit with cold water in a large kettle and let soak 1 hour. Add sugar, lemon peel, cinnamon, and salt and simmer for 1 hour. Stir in bitters and tapioca and cook about 10 minutes longer, or until tapioca is clear. Remove from heat and stir in fruit syrup. Cool, then chill for several hours in refrigerator. When ready to serve, spoon into soup bowls or glass fruit bowls. Top with sour cream and sprinkle with sliced almonds. Makes about 8 servings.

Danish Apple Soup

Friends who go skiing like to serve cups of this hot soup when they come in from the slopes. Chilled, it makes a good opening course for a summer salad luncheon.

1½ pounds tart cooking apples
2 quarts water
½ teaspoon lemon peel
½ teaspoon ground cinnamon
¼ teaspoon salt

2 tablespoons cornstarch
⅔ cup sugar
1 tablespoon lemon juice
½ cup sweet white wine

Core apples and cut them into quarters but do not peel. Combine with 1 quart water in a kettle and add lemon peel, cinnamon, and salt. Simmer until tender. Cool slightly and force through food mill or wire sieve. Blend the cornstarch with a little water and stir into remaining quart of water. Stir into apples. Simmer 10 to 15 minutes. Add sugar, lemon juice, and wine. Reheat to simmering and serve hot in cups, sprinkled with crumbled crisp zwieback. Makes 6 to 8 servings.

Sparkling Cherry Soup

Equally good as an opening course for a midsummer Sunday brunch or as a light dessert, you can top this cold fruit soup with sweetened whipped cream or dairy sour cream sweetened with a little brown sugar.

1 1-pound can pitted sour cherries	1 tablespoon cold water
½ cup water	1 bottle or can (7 or 8 ounces) lemon-lime carbonated beverage, such as 7-Up, or gingerale
½ cup red wine, sweet or table wine	
½ cup sugar or to taste	
1-inch piece of stick cinnamon	Whipped cream or dairy sour cream
1 teaspoon cornstarch	

Reserve several cherries for garnish. Pour rest of cherries and juice in an electric blender and blend until almost smooth. Empty into saucepan and add water, red wine, sugar, and cinnamon. Simmer for about 10 minutes. Blend cornstarch into cold water and stir into cherry mixture. Cook, stirring constantly, until soup thickens slightly. Chill until very cold. A short time before serving, remove stick of cinnamon. Blend in lemon-lime beverage or gingerale. Serve in glass bowls or sherbet glasses, topped with whipped cream or sour cream and a half cherry. Makes 6 servings.

Strawberry Soup

A version of an elegant dessert served at a famous supper club, this sweet soup is particularly good to follow a gala dinner.

Most gourmet food stores carry pink sugar—other colors, too. If you can't find it, make your own by sprinkling 2 or 3 drops of red food coloring onto a tablespoon or two of granulated sugar. Rub with a spoon until sugar is evenly colored.

2 boxes fresh strawberries	Dash of salt
1 cup water	1 tablespoon arrowroot or cornstarch
1 fifth of port	Whipped cream or dairy sour cream
2 tablespoons sugar	Whole strawberries
2 tablespoons lemon juice	Pink sugar

Wash and hull strawberries, reserving a few whole ones for garnish. Cut the rest in two if very large. Combine with water and about ¾ of the wine. Bring to simmering and add sugar, lemon juice, and salt. Mix together the arrowroot or cornstarch and the remaining port and stir into soup. When soup simmers again and has thickened slightly, remove from heat. When slightly cool, pour into a large glass bowl. Chill for 5 or 6 hours.

To serve, garnish with whipped cream or sour cream, top with whole strawberries, and sprinkle with pink sugar. Spoon into glass bowls or sherbet glasses and serve with crisp sugar cookies. Makes 6 servings.

Danish Buttermilk Soup

Wonderfully refreshing when the weather is warm, serve this cold sweet soup as a light dessert. Or for a summer luncheon, serve it with an assortment of finger sandwiches—chicken, cucumber, crab, or cream cheese and nut.

2 egg yolks	Dash of salt
4 to 6 tablespoons sugar	Fresh strawberries cut in half, fresh
1 quart buttermilk	peach slices, blueberries, or other
1½ teaspoons lemon juice	fresh fruit
¼ to ½ teaspoon lemon peel	Toasted slivered almonds

Beat egg yolks and sugar in mixing bowl until lemon-colored. (Amount of sugar depends on your taste.) Beat in buttermilk. When well blended add lemon juice, lemon peel, and a dash of salt. Chill until very cold. Serve in glass bowls topped with fresh strawberries or other fresh fruit and a sprinkling of toasted slivered almonds. A spoonful of strawberry jam with a blob of whipped cream is good, too. Makes 6 servings.

Prussian Beer Soup

A spirit-warming soup based on beer to serve on a chilly afternoon. It has just a touch of sweetness. Popular at ski resorts, served like a hot toddy. You can make the soup ahead, then warm slightly and add the sweet wine and rum. Don't simmer the soup after the egg is added—just heat a little, or the smoothness will vanish. Too much heat after the wine and rum is added will eliminate the light lift of the alcohol. Hot toast fingers or crisp crackers topped with melted cheese go well with this.

¼ cup butter	2 slices lemon
1 tablespoon flour	3 or 4 tablespoons sugar
1 quart light German beer	1 egg yolk
1-inch piece of stick cinnamon	¼ cup sweet white wine
Small piece ginger root, dry or fresh	2 or 3 tablespoons light rum

Melt the butter and mix in the flour. Add beer and bring to a boil. Add cinnamon stick, ginger root, lemon slices, and sugar. Taste before adding the last tablespoon; you may like it without the extra sugar. Simmer 15 to 20 minutes. Beat egg yolk in a bowl. Strain the soup into the egg yolk, beating constantly with a wire whip. Return soup to saucepan. Just before serving heat soup just to simmering. Add wine and rum and pour into cups or mugs. Sprinkle with nutmeg and serve at once. Makes about 6 servings.

Claret Wine Soup

The friend in Tennessee who makes this soup says her friends like it best in the summertime served very, very cold. But it can be served hot also. She has sage in her garden, so uses fresh sage.

1 fifth claret wine	1 teaspoon dry sage
½ lemon, thinly sliced	or 1 tablespoon chopped fresh
1-inch piece of stick cinnamon	sage leaves
2 tablespoons sugar, or to taste	1½ cups water
	2 egg yolks

Combine wine, lemon slices, cinnamon, and sugar and simmer 15 minutes. Meanwhile, simmer sage in water for 15 minutes. Strain the water into the wine mixture. Lift out the lemon slices and cinnamon stick. Beat egg yolks well, add a little of the hot soup and mix well. Then stir into soup. Heat just to simmering, but do not boil. Serve hot, or chill until very cold and serve well chilled with thin, crisp toast or sweet crackers. Makes 6 to 8 servings.

Valley of the Moon Wine Soup

This hot sweet soup is definitely one to be served on a chilly evening after a day out of doors—or for lunch on a winter's day. The wine I like best for it is the delightful Château La Salle, a light sweet muscat wine from The Christian Brothers winery in Napa, California.

3 eggs
1 tablespoon flour
3 tablespoons sugar
Dash of salt
¼ teaspoon ground nutmeg

2 cups water
6 to 8 thin slices lemon
2 cups sweet white wine
½ cup brandy

Separate eggs. In the top of a double boiler beat egg yolks with flour, 2 tablespoons of the sugar, salt, and nutmeg. Add water and lemon slices and cook over very low heat, stirring constantly, until just barely simmering. Place top of double boiler over bottom, with water just barely simmering. Beat egg whites with remaining tablespoon of sugar. Fold them into the hot liquid, blending carefully until whites are slightly set. Just before serving, blend in sweet wine and brandy. Ladle from a hot tureen or casserole into heated mugs or cups. Hot fingers of toast or melted cheese on crackers go well with this. Makes about 6 servings.

Cream Soups and Potages

~~~

MOSTLY VEGETABLE SOUPS
*

THIS FIRST GROUP of soups is made from various vegetables, stocks, and cream or milk. The entire section comprises soups that are tasty and somewhat substantial.

More satisfying than a bouillon or a consommé, a *potage* is considered an opening course in most parts of the world. But, when accompanied by a salad or a sandwich, most Americans regard a hearty serving of this kind of soup as the main course of a luncheon or supper. *Potages* are usually thicker than clear soups, almost always made thicker from the addition of vegetables, meat, fish or seafood, poultry, game, grain, or nuts. Sometimes the soup is puréed, sometimes not; sometimes cream or milk is added, sometimes the thickening is egg or starch.

Black Forest Soup

From the Black Forest of Germany comes this onion soup made with beer. The beer gives it a slight yeasty flavor.

2 tablespoons butter	½ cup dairy sour cream
2 cups thinly sliced onions	1 egg yolk
2 cups beef stock	Dash cayenne pepper
2 12-ounce cans or bottles beer	Salt to taste
1-inch piece bay leaf	Grated Gruyère cheese

49

Melt butter in heavy kettle and add sliced onions. Cook onions over low heat until tender and yellow but not brown. Add beef stock, beer, and bay leaf. Simmer for about 30 minutes. Beat together sour cream and egg yolk. Stir into soup. Heat soup just to simmering, but do not boil. Add cayenne pepper and salt, if needed. Ladle into soup bowls and sprinkle with grated Gruyère cheese. Serve with rye Melba toast. Makes about 6 servings.

Potage Choux de Bruxelles
Brussels Sprouts Soup

A friend who lives down on the Monterey Peninsula, where lots of Brussels sprouts grow, told me how to make this soup. The wife of one of the growers did the original version.

1 *pound fresh Brussels sprouts*	2 *cups half and half*
1 *cup water*	⅛ *teaspoon white pepper*
1 *teaspoon salt*	½ *cup dairy sour cream*
4 *tablespoons butter*	½ *teaspoon seasoned salt*
4 *tablespoons flour*	2 *teaspoons chervil*
4 *cups well-seasoned chicken stock*	

Trim and wash Brussels sprouts. Add water and salt and cook 10 to 15 minutes, or until barely tender. Lift out 12 of the sprouts—fewer if sprouts are large. Cool these and cut in half. Meanwhile, cook the remaining sprouts another 5 minutes. Blend them in electric blender, along with any cooking liquid, until smooth. Melt butter in a large saucepan over low heat and stir in the flour. When well mixed stir in the chicken stock and cook, stirring constantly, until mixture comes to a boil and is thickened and smooth. Stir in puréed sprouts, half and half, pepper, and sprout halves. Heat just to simmering. Combine sour cream, seasoned salt, and chervil. Ladle soup into bowls or cups and top with a spoonful of the seasoned sour cream. Makes 6 to 8 servings.

Potage Crème de Topinambour
Cream of Jerusalem Artichoke Soup

Jerusalem artichokes don't come from Jerusalem nor are they like the globe or French artichoke. They are similar to potatoes and you'll most often find them these days where organic foods are sold. You'll find recipes for cream soups like this one in French cookbooks—hence, its glamorous name. But the Irish make a similar *potage*—and a friend of mine told me she first became acquainted with the Jerusalem artichoke in a seventh-grade foods class.

1 *pound Jerusalem artichokes*	1 *teaspoon salt or to taste*
3 *tablespoons butter*	⅛ *teaspoon white pepper*
2 *medium-size onions, chopped (about*	1 *cup rich milk or half and half*
2 *cups)*	*Ground mace or nutmeg*
4 *cups chicken or veal stock*	*Chopped toasted hazelnuts or slivered*
1 *clove garlic*	*almonds, or croutons*
½ *bay leaf*	

Scrub the artichokes and scrape off the outside skin. Cut into ½-inch slices.

Melt butter in a kettle or saucepan, add sliced artichokes and chopped onions and cook until light yellow but not brown. Add the stock. Crush garlic and add to soup along with bay leaf, salt (exact amount will depend on saltiness of stock) and pepper. Simmer until artichokes are very tender, about 1 hour. Let cool slightly and purée in electric blender or force through a food mill or fine wire sieve. Add milk and heat the soup just to simmering. Sprinkle each serving with a dash of ground mace or nutmeg and garnish with toasted nuts or croutons. Makes 8 servings.

Asparagus-Leek Cream Soup

Springlike in flavor and color, *Asparagus-Leek Cream Soup* makes a good opening course for a simple luncheon or supper.

2 *leeks*	¼ *teaspoon white pepper*
½ *pound fresh asparagus*	*Salt to taste*
2 *cups chicken stock*	1 *teaspoon cornstarch*
2 *cups half and half or undiluted*	½ *teaspoon chervil or* 1 *teaspoon*
evaporated milk	*chopped parsley*

Wash leeks thoroughly and slice very thin, using just a little of the green tops. Wash asparagus and cut off ends and scales. Cut into ½-inch pieces. Reserve the tips.

In a kettle combine sliced leeks, asparagus and chicken stock. Simmer until tender. Add asparagus tips and half and half or evaporated milk.

Season with white pepper and salt to taste. Heat to simmering. Blend the cornstarch with a little cold water and stir into soup. Cook until soup thickens slightly. Sprinkle with chervil or chopped parsley. Accompany with crisp crackers. Makes 6 servings.

Mushroom-Avocado Soup

This recipe for a present-day soup from the Philippine Islands was brought back by a friend who made a recent Pacific voyage on a freighter. My family, who spent many years in the Philippines a long time ago, all think it excellent and wish they could have had some recipe like this years ago.

2 *tablespoons butter*	1 *tall can (1⅔ cups) evaporated milk*
2 *tablespoons finely chopped onion*	1 *ripe avocado*
1 *tablespoon finely chopped celery*	*Salt to taste*
½ *cup sliced fresh mushrooms*	⅛ *teaspoon black pepper*
2 *tablespoons flour*	2 *or 3 slices of bacon or 2 table-*
2 *cups chicken stock*	*spoons chopped cashew nuts*

In the top of a double boiler over direct heat, melt butter and add chopped onion and celery. Cook over low heat until onion and celery are tender but still crisp. Add the mushrooms and cook 2 or 3 minutes longer. Blend in the flour, stir in the chicken stock and evaporated milk and cook, stirring constantly, until soup begins to simmer. Set top of double boiler over simmering water.

Peel the avocado and mash or force through a coarse sieve. (Avocado should not be too smooth.) Blend it into soup. Add salt to taste and pepper. Meanwhile fry bacon until crisp, drain and crumble. Serve soup in cups or bowls, sprinkled with crisp bacon or chopped nuts. Makes 6 to 8 servings.

Potage d'Automne
Autumn Soup

The friend who gave me this recipe gave it this fancy name to disguise the fact that it's made from staples from her pantry shelf. She tells me it dates from her younger days, when her mother made it in the late fall when there were few, if any, fresh vegetables available in the stores.

2 10½-ounce cans undiluted beef bouillon
1 can (1 pound, 14 ounces) whole tomatoes
1½ cups chopped onions
2 medium-size potatoes, pared and cut into cubes
1 teaspoon seasoned salt
¼ teaspoon sweet basil
¼ teaspoon marjoram or ½ teaspoon soup herbs
1 can (about 1 pound) cream-style corn
2 cups half and half
Additional salt and pepper to taste

Combine the beef bouillon, tomatoes, chopped onions, and potatoes in a kettle. Add seasoned salt. Crush sweet basil and marjoram or soup herbs and add to soup. Simmer soup until onions and potatoes are tender. Add the cream-style corn and half and half. Heat to simmering. Season with additional salt, if needed, and pepper to taste. Serve with crisp crackers. Makes about 8 servings.

Fresh Corn Bisque

This is especially good as an opening course for a midsummer meal of cold meats or seafood salad. You can substitute a can of whole-kernel corn for the fresh corn—but it won't be quite the same.

2 cups fresh corn, cut from cob
2 tablespoons butter
¼ cup chopped onion
¼ cup chopped green pepper
2 cups chicken stock
1½ teaspoons seasoned salt
⅛ teaspoon white pepper
1 cup half and half
½ teaspoon sweet basil

Cut the kernels from about 4 medium-size ears of fresh corn to make 2 cups. Melt butter in saucepan. Add onion and green pepper and cook over low heat until soft. Add chicken stock, corn, seasoned salt, and white pepper. Cover and simmer about 30 minutes. Let cool slightly and blend in electric blender until smooth. Press through wire sieve into saucepan. Add half and half. Crush the sweet basil and stir into soup. Heat just to boiling. Serve very hot, with cheese crackers. Makes 6 servings.

Sopa de Calabacitas
Zucchini Soup

So simple and still so good, this cream soup has an early California-Mexican origin. It's a wonderful opening course for luncheon or dinner and is good, too, served icy cold.

1 pound zucchini	1 tablespoon butter
1 large onion, chopped (about 1 cup)	2 cups light cream
2 cups water or chicken stock	or half and half
1 teaspoon seasoned salt	Additional salt to taste
⅛ teaspoon white pepper	Chopped parsley

Wash and trim zucchini. Cut it into slices and combine with chopped onion, water or chicken stock, seasoned salt, and pepper. Simmer until zucchini is tender. Cool slightly and blend in electric blender until smooth, or force through a food mill. Add butter, cream, and additional salt to taste. (Amount of salt will depend on saltiness of chicken stock.) Heat just to simmering. Pour into soup cups and sprinkle with chopped parsley. Makes 6 to 8 servings.

Celery and Olive Soup

Serve this *Celery and Olive Soup* with a sandwich for lunch, or as an opening course for an otherwise skimpy supper.

1 cup thinly sliced celery	4 cups milk
¼ cup chopped onions	2 teaspoons salt or to taste
1 cup water	⅛ teaspoon cracked black or seasoned
3 tablespoons butter or margarine	pepper
2 tablespoons flour	2 tablespoons sherry
½ cup sliced stuffed green olives	

Simmer the sliced celery and onions in water until crisp but tender, about 7 or 8 minutes. Meanwhile, melt butter in a saucepan. Stir in the flour and add sliced green olives. When flour is well blended, add the milk. Cook over low heat, stirring constantly, until soup is simmering and slightly thickened. Add celery and onions along with the water in which they were simmered. Mix well and season with salt and pepper. Add sherry. Serve with crisp crackers. Makes 6 to 8 servings.

Potage Marseillaise
Marseille Vegetable Soup

During World War II, a Frenchwoman who had escaped from Occupied France gave lessons in French cooking in San Francisco. She taught her students to make this *potage*. In those days when meat, butter, and eggs were all scarce, a hearty *potage* such as this was often the main course at lunch or supper.

3 *tablespoons olive oil or butter*	*Pinch of saffron*
2 *cups sliced onions*	3 *or 4 large fresh tomatoes*
2 *cups chopped celery and celery*	2 *slices French bread cut in cubes*
leaves	(*about 1 cup*)
¼ *cup chopped green pepper*	4 *cups hot water*
2 *cloves garlic, thinly sliced or*	2 *egg yolks*
crushed	3 *tablespoons sherry*
¼ *teaspoon thyme*	*Grated Swiss cheese*
1-*inch piece bay leaf*	*Fried croutons*
1 *teaspoon salt*	

Heat oil or butter in a kettle. Add onions, celery, green pepper, and garlic, and cook, stirring occasionally, until vegetables are limp but not brown. Crush thyme and add to vegetables along with bay leaf, salt, and saffron. Peel the tomatoes and cut into chunks. Add tomatoes and French bread cubes. Cover and simmer over very low heat about 1 hour. Force soup and vegetables through food mill or wire sieve. Add hot water and simmer 30 minutes. Beat egg yolks slightly. Stir 1 cup of the hot soup into egg yolks, then add to soup gradually, stirring. Cook until thickened slightly and heated through, about 5 minutes. Stir in sherry. Serve in soup plates and sprinkle with grated cheese and fried croutons. Makes 6 servings.

TO MAKE CROUTONS:

Fry French bread cubes in olive oil or butter until crisp and brown. Drain on paper towels.

Soupe Printemps
Spring Soup

During the days of Victory Gardens, a friend used to make this soup with her first green onions (or scallions) and parsley. Many years have gone by and she lives in smaller quarters. Now she uses chives and parsley from her windowbox. You can use frozen or dried chives and the very convenient dried parsley. (Use only about 2 to 3 tablespoons of dried parsley instead of a half-cup fresh.) In those days she simmered chicken feet, necks, and so on to make the stock. Today she uses chicken stock base or bouillon cubes. (Incidentally, what a lovely springlike green color and flavor this soup has!)

2 tablespoons butter
½ cup chopped parsley
¼ cup thinly sliced green onions with tops or chopped chives
2 to 3 tablespoons flour

½ teaspoon salt
⅛ teaspoon white pepper
2 cups chicken or veal stock
2 cups milk
1 hard-cooked egg, chopped or sliced

Melt butter in a saucepan and stir in chopped parsley and onions or chives. Cook gently 2 or 3 minutes and stir in flour. Blend well. Add salt and pepper to stock and stir into parsley and onions. Then add milk and cook, stirring constantly, until soup has come to a boil and is slightly thickened. Pour into soup bowls and sprinkle with chopped egg. Or arrange egg slices on soup. Makes 6 servings.

Zuppa di Verdura
Green Soup

During the 1960 Olympic Games in Rome, Signora Rovelli took "paying guests" into her home. Many Roman housewives helped to house and feed travelers from all over the world. Signora's dinner at night often began with her very excellent "green soup." She made it with chicken stock and spinach. However, a dear friend whose parents came from Italy says her mother made it with beef stock and chard. Either way, it's good.

3 tablespoons olive oil
½ cup chopped onion
1 clove garlic, crushed or finely
    chopped
¼ cup finely chopped parsley
6 cups rich beef or chicken stock
2 cups shredded chard or spinach

1½ to 2 cups diced zucchini or Italian
    squash
½ teaspoon sweet basil or Italian herbs
Salt and pepper to taste
Fried Italian or French bread
Grated Parmesan cheese

In a large kettle pour olive oil; add onions, garlic, and parsley and cook over low heat until onions are tender but not brown. Add stock, chard or spinach, and squash. Crush the herbs and add to soup. Simmer gently until vegetables are tender. Add salt and pepper to taste. Ladle into soup plates or bowls. Top with slices of French or Italian bread lightly fried in olive oil. Sprinkle with grated Parmesan. Makes 6 servings.

Creole Soup

The piquant flavor from the cayenne and horseradish along with the dark brown *roux* is typical of Creole cookery.

¼ cup butter
¼ cup chopped onion
¼ cup chopped green pepper
3 tablespoons flour
1 1-pound can tomatoes
1 quart beef stock
¼ teaspoon thyme

½ teaspoon salt or to taste
⅛ teaspoon black pepper
Dash cayenne pepper
¼ cup salad or soup macaroni
1 to 2 tablespoons bottled horse-
    radish in vinegar

Melt butter in kettle; add onion and green pepper and cook until vegetables are soft. Lift out and reserve. Stir in the flour. Turn up heat and cook, stirring constantly, until flour has turned a deep brown. Be careful not to burn the flour, however. Return the vegetables to this brown *roux*. Add tomatoes and beef stock. Simmer about 1 hour, or until vegetables are tender.

Cool slightly and force the soup through wire sieve or food mill. Return it to kettle. Add seasonings (amount of salt will depend on saltiness of beef stock). Meanwhile, cook the macaroni in lightly salted water until barely tender. (Use large-size macaroni, if desired, and cut cooked macaroni into rings.) Just before serving, add the macaroni and horseradish to soup. (The amount of horseradish depends on the "heat" of the horseradish and your taste. Two tablespoons of a hot horseradish sauce makes quite a zesty soup.) This is especially good for lunch along with toasted cheese sandwiches. Makes 6 servings.

Fresh Tomato Soup

Especially good at the peak of the tomato season when tomatoes are truly vine-ripened. And this soup is good, too, chilled. If fresh tomatoes are not really ripe, then good canned whole peeled tomatoes are an excellent substitute.

3 or 4 large ripe tomatoes or 1 1-pound can whole peeled tomatoes

1 pint half and half

1½ teaspoons seasoned salt, or to taste
Dash of white pepper
¼ teaspoon sweet basil
Chopped parsley or chervil

Scald the tomatoes and peel them. Scoop pulp out of the inside. Chop outside portion coarsely. Press the pulp through a wire sieve. (Don't be disturbed if a few seeds escape you.) Discard seeds in sieve and add sieved pulp to chopped tomato. Add half and half; both the tomatoes and cream should be cold.

If using canned tomatoes, chop outside section of tomatoes coarsely. Press pulp and juice through a wire sieve, discard seeds, and add sieved juice and pulp and chopped tomato to half and half. If tomatoes are canned with salt, then a lesser amount of seasoned salt may be desired.

Crush sweet basil and stir into soup. Heat over very low heat, stirring frequently, just to simmering. Do not boil or let simmer very long or soup will curdle. Season to taste with seasoned salt and white pepper. Ladle into soup cups or bowls and sprinkle with parsley or chervil. Makes 4 servings.

COLD TOMATO SOUP:

Chill soup and serve very cold. To retain the completely fresh, uncooked flavor of the tomato, do not heat the soup at all. Mix the ingredients and chill several hours or overnight.

Potage Santé
Sorrel Soup I

In Paris where this was made at a cooking class, the chef used sorrel. Since sorrel is not available everywhere in this country, make it with water cress. It is then *Potage Cressonière*.

2 leeks	3 teaspoons salt
3 tablespoons butter	1 bunch sorrel or water cress
4 medium-size potatoes	2 tablespoons butter
1½ quarts water	½ cup dairy sour cream

Wash well, clean and slice leeks into thin rings, using a little of the green tops. Sauté them in 3 tablespoons butter until soft. Pare and cube potatoes and add to leeks. Add water and salt. Simmer 1 hour, or until vegetables are very tender. Press through a wire sieve or food mill.

Wash the sorrel or water cress, cut off stems, and chop coarsely. Cook in 2 tablespoons butter until barely wilted, 2 or 3 minutes. Add to soup. Blend in sour cream. If serving from a soup tureen, as it was served in France, spoon sour cream into tureen and pour hot soup over it. Ladle into soup bowls or plates. Serve with bread sticks or toasted French bread. Makes 6 servings.

Potage Oseille
Sorrel Soup II

Like *Potage Santé* this soup can be made with water cress, since sorrel is almost impossible to buy in most markets. However, my dear friend and French teacher, Madame Woodmansee, who gave me this recipe, also brought me sorrel. A friend of hers grows it and brings her some often to make this, her favorite soup.

1 bunch sorrel, about ½ pound (or as the French say, a good handful)	2 or 3 tablespoons heavy cream
	1 teaspoon salt
4 tablespoons butter	¼ teaspoon pepper
1 quart water	⅛ teaspoon sugar, if desired
1 egg yolk	

Wash sorrel and chop coarsely. Place in a heavy top-of-the-stove casserole. Over low heat wilt the sorrel. Add butter and water and mix with a wooden spoon. Simmer for 10 to 15 minutes, or until sorrel is tender. Just before serving, beat egg yolk with the cream. Stir in a little of the hot soup, then add egg yolk to soup in casserole. Heat just to simmering. Season with salt, pepper, and sugar, if desired. Serve at once with crisp crackers or croutons, as an opening course. Makes about 4 to 6 servings.

NOTE: If soup seems a bit tart to you, add the sugar. Sugar, we feel, also brings out the delicate flavor of the sorrel.

Anchovy Bisque

From a collection of very old recipes: Anchovy Bisque was supposed to have been served at Delmonico's Restaurant during the Gay '90's.

½-*pound piece or slice of white fish,*   1 *whole clove*
   such as halibut, sole, or cod   3 *or 4 black peppercorns*
1½ *quarts water*   ¼ *teaspoon paprika*
2 *teaspoons salt*   ¼ *teaspoon thyme*
½ *cup sliced carrots*   4 *tablespoons butter*
½ *cup chopped onion*   4 *tablespoons flour*
1 *leek, thinly sliced*   2 *tablespoons anchovy paste*
½ *cup sliced celery*   1 *cup light cream or half and half*
2 *or 3 sprigs parsley*   6 *anchovy filets*
1-*inch piece bay leaf*

Combine fish and water in a large kettle. Bring to a boil and turn heat down to simmering. Skim the liquid and add salt, carrots, onion, leek (including a part of the green tops), celery, parsley, bay leaf, clove, peppercorns, and paprika. Crush the thyme and add to soup. Simmer for 1 hour. Strain this stock.

Melt butter and blend in flour until smooth, but do not brown. When well blended, stir in fish stock. Add anchovy paste. Stir with a wire wisk, until soup comes to a boil and is slightly thickened. Just before serving add the cream or half and half. Cut each anchovy filet into 2 or 3 pieces and add to the bisque. Serve as an opening course accompanied by crisp crackers or Melba toast. Makes 6 or 8 servings.

Greek Lemon Egg Soup

A young friend who has lived since a small girl with older Greek friends gave me this recipe. Its tart lemon flavor makes it a good opening course for a substantial dinner or lunch. A heartier version is *Avgolemono*.

4 *cups chicken stock*
⅓ *cup small rice-shaped pasta or rice*
1 *egg*
1½ *tablespoons lemon juice*
Salt to taste

Heat chicken stock to boiling. Slowly add pasta or rice and simmer until done, about 15 minutes. Meanwhile, beat egg white until stiff but not dry. Beat egg yolk slightly, then blend into beaten egg white. Stir in the lemon juice. Slowly pour some hot stock into the egg and lemon mixture, stirring vigorously. Return to saucepan and heat soup just to simmering, but do not boil or egg will curdle. Add salt to taste. Serve at once in heated soup cups, accompanied by crisp crackers. Makes 6 servings.

Potage Alsacienne
Pork and Cabbage Soup

The wonderful pork and cabbage of the Alsatian area of France is the inspiration for this soup. It's an attempt to duplicate the tasty soup served in a small inn near Strasbourg.

4 *ounces salt pork*
3 *cups shredded cabbage*
1 *teaspoon salt*
¼ *teaspoon pepper*
⅛ *teaspoon ground allspice*
2 *cups diced potatoes*
2 *quarts chicken or veal stock*

Cut salt pork into cubes and fry them in a heavy kettle until crisp and brown. Drain off excess fat, if desired. Add the cabbage, cover and steam about 10 minutes. Add salt, pepper, allspice, potatoes, and stock and simmer about 1 hour. Sprinkle with chopped chives or parsley. Serve with rye wafers or rye bread. Makes 6 servings.

Potage Cousinette
Vegetable and Sausage Soup

Reminiscent of the soups of the Alsatian countryside, this soup makes a hearty lunch along with dark bread. Use any of the dried sausages, with or without garlic, but if you use one with a heavy garlic flavor you may want to omit the garlic in the soup.

2½ *quarts water*	¼ *teaspoon ground white pepper*
1 *cup chopped fresh spinach*	¼ *teaspoon thyme*
½ *cup chopped onion*	¼ *teaspoon marjoram*
½ *cup thinly sliced carrots*	1-*inch piece bay leaf*
2 *leeks, thinly sliced*	1 *cervelat sausage, about 8 ounces, or*
2 *tablespoons chopped parsley*	*salami or pepperoni sausage*
1 *clove garlic, chopped*	2 *cups finely chopped cabbage*
1 *teaspoon salt*	1 *cup diced potato*

In a large kettle combine water, chopped spinach and onion, sliced carrots and leeks, chopped parsley, garlic (if desired), salt and pepper. Bring to a boil. Crush thyme and marjoram and add to soup along with bay leaf. Turn heat down and simmer for about 30 minutes. Peel the casing from sausage, add it and simmer another 30 minutes. Add chopped cabbage and diced potato and simmer 30 to 40 minutes, or until vegetables are tender. Remove the sausage from soup and slice it. Place two or three slices in each soup bowl and ladle hot soup over sausage. Serve with black peasant bread or dark rye bread. Makes 6 to 8 servings.

Poor Man's Soup

From a collection of old church cookbooks, there is also a similar version of this recipe in a *Godey's Lady's Book* of the 1860's. Not too different is a peasant soup from Portugal called "green soup." In spite of its name, *Poor Man's Soup* is very tasty and is excellent for lunch with a sandwich.

6 *cups hot water*	¼ *teaspoon black pepper*
4 *cups pared diced potatoes*	½ *pound fresh spinach*
1 *cup chopped onion*	2 *tablespoons bacon or ham drippings*
2 *teaspoons salt*	1 *tablespoon flour*

Combine hot water, potatoes, chopped onion, salt, and pepper. Simmer until potatoes are tender; then mash without draining. Wash spinach well, chop coarsely and add to soup. Simmer 10 to 15 minutes, or until spinach is tender. Melt bacon or ham drippings and blend in the flour. Stir into soup. Simmer soup for about 5 more minutes, or until slightly thickened. Serve with grilled cheese or tuna sandwiches. Makes 6 servings.

Turkish Wedding Soup

This delicious soup is served at Turkish wedding parties. Small cups make a good opening course, but a generous plateful makes a good luncheon or supper—and it's tasty chilled, too.

2 to 2½ pounds lamb stew meat: *3 egg yolks*
    neck slices, ribs, or shoulder   *2 tablespoons lemon juice*
3 quarts water
1 large onion   GARNISH
1 medium-size carrot   *¼ cup butter*
1 tablespoon salt   *2 teaspoons paprika*
4 tablespoons butter   *Dash cayenne*
⅓ cup flour

Combine lamb and water in a large kettle. Peel and cut onion into quarters; scrape carrot and cut into several pieces. Add to kettle along with salt. Simmer over very low heat for 3 to 4 hours, or until meat falls from the bones. Skim soup frequently. Let cool until fat hardens and skim off all fat. Strain the broth.

Cut the meat from bones and trim off all fat. Cut meat into ½-inch cubes. Discard bones and onion and carrot. Melt butter in a large kettle; stir in flour and brown lightly. Stir in the broth and cook, stirring constantly, until soup thickens slightly.

Beat egg yolks and lemon juice together. Spoon in a half cup or so of hot soup, mix well and then stir into soup. Add meat cubes and heat just until soup is ready to simmer; do not allow to boil.

Meanwhile, for garnish, cream together butter and paprika; add a dash of cayenne. Spoon soup into cups or soup plates. Top with creamed butter and paprika. Serve at once. Or chill until very cold and serve cold. Makes 8 to 10 servings for opening course, about 6 whole-meal servings. Serve with crisp bread sticks or flat Armenian or Turkish bread, if available.

SOUPS MADE WITH
PEAS AND BEANS

*

Lentil and Mushroom Soup

If you like a *potage* very thick and hearty, then use the smaller amount of chicken stock. Either way it's filling enough for a luncheon main course.

1 cup lentils	1 egg yolk
4 to 6 cups chicken stock	½ teaspoon arrowroot or cornstarch
¼ pound fresh mushrooms	2 cups rich milk or half and half
¼ teaspoon summer savory	Salt to taste
1 tablespoon butter	2 tablespoons sherry

Wash and drain lentils. Combine in a large kettle with chicken stock. Wash mushrooms; reserve 5 or 6. Chop rest of mushrooms and add to lentils and stock. Crush summer savory and add to soup. Cover and simmer about 1½ hours, or until lentils are very soft. Cool slightly. Press through a wire sieve or blend in electric blender until smooth. Pour back into kettle.

Slice reserved mushrooms and sauté them gently in butter. At serving time, heat soup to simmering. Beat together egg yolk and arrowroot or cornstarch along with about a half cup of the milk. Stir in a little of the hot soup and then stir egg mixture into soup. Add mushrooms and remaining milk or half and half. Add salt to taste: the amount will depend on saltiness of chicken stock. Heat just to simmering and add sherry. Ladle into soup cups or bowls and sprinkle with crisp croutons. Or accompany soup with crisp crackers. Makes 8 servings.

Double Green Pea Soup

A hearty *potage* especially good for lunch or supper on a cold wintry day. If you can't find the whole dry green peas then use dry green split peas.

1 cup dry whole green peas (about ½ pound)
Water
5 cups chicken stock
1 cup white table wine
½ cup chopped onion
½ cup chopped celery and celery leaves

2 tablespoons chopped parsley
1 10-ounce package frozen green peas
½ cup undiluted evaporated milk or half and half
Chopped chives
Crisp bacon, crumbled, or frizzled Canadian bacon

Wash dry peas and cover with water; soak overnight. Next morning drain peas and add chicken stock and wine. Bring to a boil, turn down to simmer, and add chopped onion, celery, and parsley. Simmer for about 3 hours, or until dry peas are soft. (Dry whole peas do not disintegrate as split peas do.) Let peas cool sightly and purée about half of soup in a blender.

Return to soup kettle. Add the frozen peas and continue to cook until they are tender. Stir in evaporated milk or half and half. Season with salt, if needed. Sprinkle with chopped chives and crumbled bacon. Serve in soup bowls accompanied by crisp onion-flavored crackers. Makes 6 to 8 servings.

Potage Émeraude au Fromage
Emerald Soup with Cheese

A thick hearty *potage* with a piquant flavor that invites speculation as to just what makes it different from most split pea soups. It's the cheese and the horseradish! A soup plate or bowl of it will make a main course for lunch or supper. A small cup goes well with a sandwich or salad.

1 cup green split peas
1½ quarts water
2 tablespoons chopped parsley
½ cup chopped onion
½ cup chopped celery and celery leaves
1 teaspoon seasoned salt

1 teaspoon salt
¼ teaspoon black pepper
8 ounces process sharp Cheddar cheese spread
2 tablespoons prepared horseradish
4 to 6 slices bacon

Wash split peas and combine with water in a large kettle. Add chopped parsley, onion, celery, seasoned salt, salt and pepper. Simmer until peas are tender, about 1½ hours. Cool slightly and press through wire sieve or blend until smooth in an electric blender. Return to kettle.

Add cheese spread and horseradish. Heat slowly and blend in cheese with a wire whip. Add additional salt to taste. Cut bacon into ½-inch pieces. Fry until crisp. Drain on paper towels. Ladle soup into bowls or cups. Garnish with crisp bacon. Makes 6 to 8 servings.

Cajun Black-Eyed Pea Soup

The Cajuns or Acadians were refugees from Nova Scotia. Of French heritage, they came to Louisiana in the 18th century and settled in the bayous instead of the cities. Their cookery is slightly different from that of the city Creoles but it, too, is influenced by French, Spanish, German, Negro, and Choctaw and Chickasaw Indian food habits and customs.

1½ cups dry black-eyed peas	½ teaspoon thyme
2 pounds ham hocks or ham bone	1 tablespoon flour
8 cups water	1 tablespoon bacon or ham drippings
1 cup chopped celery	Salt and pepper to taste
½ cup chopped onion	Slices of lemon and hard-cooked egg
1-inch piece bay leaf	

Combine black-eyed peas, ham hocks or bone, and water in large kettle. Add chopped celery, chopped onion, and bay leaf. Crush thyme and add to soup. Simmer until peas · are done, about 1 hour. Remove ham hocks and bay leaf; press soup through sieve or purée in food mill or in a blender. Return to kettle. Blend flour and drippings and cook until browned. Stir into soup slowly and simmer until soup is thickened. Season to taste with salt and pepper. Cut meat from bone into ½-inch cubes and add to soup. Serve hot, with slices of lemon and hard-cooked egg.

Beans 'n' Beer 'n' Bacon Soup

Except for the bacon garnish there's not a bit of meat in this soup, but the beer gives it a meaty flavor. Serve it as a hearty luncheon soup or as the opening course for a light supper.

1 cup dry navy or Great Northern beans	1 1-pound can tomatoes
	2 teaspoons salt
1½ quarts water	⅛ teaspoon black pepper
½ cup chopped onion	½ teaspoon crumbled sage
¼ cup chopped carrot	1 cup beer, light or dark
¼ cup chopped celery	3 or 4 slices bacon

Wash beans and cover with water. Bring to a boil and boil rapidly for 5 minutes. Turn off heat and let soak 1 hour. Drain off liquid and cover with 1½ quarts warm water. Add chopped onion, carrot, and celery, tomatoes, salt, and pepper. Bring to a boil, then turn down to simmer. Add crumbled sage. Simmer for 1½ to 2 hours, or until beans and vegetables are tender. Let cool slightly. Lift out about 1 cup of beans and vegetables. Blend remaining soup in an electric blender until smooth. Return soup to kettle and add the whole cooked beans and the beer. Simmer about 10 to 15 minutes. Meanwhile, cut bacon in ½-inch pieces. Fry until crisp and drain. Ladle soup into bowls and garnish with crisp bacon bits. Makes 6 generous servings.

Piedmont Black Bean Soup

This soup comes from the Piedmont section of the Carolinas (not Italy) and is typical of the black bean soups of this part of the South.

1 pound dry black beans	¼ teaspoon dry mustard
3 quarts cold water	2 leeks, thinly sliced
Ham bone and rind	1-inch piece bay leaf
2 tablespoons fat trimmed from ham	2 teaspoons salt or to taste
or 2 tablespoons butter	¼ teaspoon black pepper
1 cup chopped onion	1 cup Madeira or dry sherry
1 cup chopped celery	2 hard-cooked eggs
¼ cup chopped parsley	Thin slices lemon
1 tablespoon flour	

Pick over and wash beans. Cover with cold water and soak overnight. Next morning drain beans and in a large kettle combine beans with cold water. Add ham bone and rind and bring to a boil. Turn down to simmer. Meanwhile, in a skillet fry out fat cut from ham, or melt butter. Add onion, celery, and parsley and cook until limp. Stir in flour and mustard and cook, stirring constantly, until flour is lightly browned. Stir mixture into simmering beans. Add thinly sliced leeks and bay leaf, salt and pepper. Simmer 3 to 4 hours, or until beans are very tender. Lift out ham bone and rind and bay leaf. Let soup cool slightly, then force soup through a wire sieve or blend until smooth in a blender. Just before serving, reheat soup to simmering. Add Madeira or sherry. Chop the hard-cooked eggs and mix into soup. Ladle soup into soup cups. Top each with a thin slice of lemon. Serve as an opening course or a more generous serving as a main course soup for luncheon or supper. Makes 10 to 12 servings for an opening course, or 5 to 6 servings for luncheon or supper.

Potage Viennoise
Green Bean Soup

This thick peasant-style soup, with fresh-baked or French bread, a salad, and fruit and cheese, makes a complete meal. Use a can of green beans instead of the fresh, if you prefer.

½ pound green beans	*1 stalk celery*
1 quart chicken stock	*2 tablespoons chopped parsley*
¼ cup barley	*1-inch piece bay leaf*
½ cup green split peas	*1 cup rich milk or half and half*
2 tablespoons chopped onion	*1 egg yolk*
1 medium-size carrot	*Salt and pepper to taste*

Cut ends off green beans and cut into ½-inch lengths. Simmer in boiling salted water to cover until barely tender. Drain liquid from beans and reserve beans. Combine the liquid with chicken stock, barley, split peas, and chopped onion in a large kettle. Bring to a boil, then turn heat down to simmer. Scrape carrot and slice; slice celery stalk. Add vegetables to soup with chopped parsley and bay leaf. Simmer for 1½ to 2 hours or until barley and vegetables are tender. Let cool slightly. Press soup through a wire sieve, or blend until smooth in an electric blender. Beat egg yolk and half and half together. Add a little hot soup to mixture, then blend into soup. Add drained beans. Heat soup just to simmering. Do not boil or egg will curdle. Season to taste with salt and pepper. Serve at once. Makes 6 servings.

Miso Shiru
Japanese Bean Curd Soup

Miso soup is a staple in the life of Japanese people—and it is one of the most nutritious soups in their cuisine. In Japan it is most often eaten for breakfast. We like it for lunch or supper. I have made it with Japanese ingredients and also with my Americanized *Miso*, or bean paste, and instead of *Tofu*, or bean curd, have used ricotta or smooth cottage cheese. However, there are innumerable ingredients that can be used instead of *Tofu*—spinach, bean sprouts, shredded turnips or carrots, shrimp or fish, or mushrooms. The *Dashi* for *Miso Shiru* needn't be clear. And, of course, you can use other fish stock or even other soup stock, if you like.

4 cups Dashi (*see recipe*)
½ cup Miso *or bean paste*
2 ounces Tofu *or bean curd, cut into
small cubes or long slender pieces*

¼ cup finely sliced green onion
MSG, salt, or soy sauce to taste

Heat the *Dashi* to simmering; add bean paste and stir to blend into soup. Add bean curd and when soup is simmering again, season to taste with MSG, salt, or soy sauce. Some *Miso* is quite salty, so taste first. Ladle into soup bowls and sprinkle with sliced green onion. Makes 6 servings.

Miso American-Style
Bean Paste

½ cup soy beans *or Mung beans*
Water
2 tablespoons sake (*Japanese wine*)
2 tablespoons vinegar

1 tablespoon soy sauce
2 teaspoons MSG
1 teaspoon salt

If using soy beans, soak overnight in water to cover. Next morning drain and cover with warm water. Simmer slowly until tender, 4 to 5 hours. (Soy beans take considerable time to cook.) Use just enough water to cover beans; when beans are cooked, there should be almost no water left. Mung beans do not need to be soaked and will cook much quicker. Mung beans will be done in about 1 to 1½ hours. Pour cooked beans into an electric blender. Add sake, vinegar, soy sauce, MSG, and salt. Blend until smooth. Makes about 1½ cups *Miso*.

A FEW CHEESE SOUPS
*

Italian Cream of Cheese Soup

If you live where you can get it, a freshly grated Italian Romano cheese is best in this soup. However, the packaged Parmesan or ready-grated Italian cheese from the supermarket is good, too.

2 *cups veal stock*
2 *cups milk, or 1 quart milk if you have no veal stock*
3 *or 4 carrot slices*
2 *thick onion slices*
⅛ *teaspoon mace*
1 *clove garlic, sliced in half*

½ *cup freshly grated Romano or Parmesan cheese, or other firm Italian cheese*
2 *egg yolks*
Salt and pepper to taste
Chopped parsley

Combine veal stock and milk in top of a double boiler. Add carrot and onion slices, mace, and garlic. Place over very gently simmering water and simmer for 1 hour. Lift out carrot and onion slices and garlic. (Strain these out if easier and return liquid to top of double boiler.) Stir in cheese. Beat egg yolks, add a little of the hot soup, and then stir eggs into soup. Heat throughly, but do not boil. Add salt and pepper to taste, the amount depending on seasoning of veal stock. Pour into hot soup cups and sprinkle with parsley. Serve as first course accompanied by small bread sticks or crisp pizza-flavored crackers. Makes 6 to 8 servings.

Australian Pumpkin-Cheese Soup

A favorite recipe from Down Under. Make it with fresh pumpkin or use the rest of a can of pumpkin after making a pie. Good with that turkey sandwich a day or so after Thanksgiving.

1 *quart chicken stock*
2 *cups pared, diced pumpkin or 1 to 1½ cups cooked or canned pumpkin*
½ *cup lentils*

¾ *cup shredded Cheddar cheese*
Salt and pepper to taste
Croutons tossed in hot bacon drippings

Combine chicken stock, pumpkin, and lentils. Simmer about 1 hour, or until pumpkin and lentils are tender. Press through a sieve or food mill. Return to kettle and add shredded cheese. Heat, stirring constantly, until cheese is melted. Season to taste with salt and pepper. Serve at once,' sprinkled with croutons. Do not overheat or cheese will become stringy. Makes 6 servings.

Cottage Cheese Soup

Good to go along with a sandwich for a Saturday lunch or a light supper. This high-protein soup can be completely meatless if you use vegetable stock (made with bouillon cubes, if you like) instead of chicken stock. Cut down or omit the cayenne, if you like a little less "heat."

2 tablespoons butter	⅛ teaspoon each cayenne pepper and nutmeg
2 tablespoons chopped onion	
1 cup thinly sliced celery	1 cup cottage cheese with chives (or
1 tablespoon flour	1 cup plain cottage cheese and 1
1½ to 2 cups chicken stock	tablespoon chopped chives)
1½ cups milk	½ teaspoon salt or to taste
½ teaspoon paprika	1 tablespoon toasted slivered almonds

Melt butter in saucepan; add chopped onion and sliced celery and cook over low heat until vegetables are limp but not brown. Stir in flour. Add chicken stock and milk and cook, stirring constantly, until soup begins to simmer. Add paprika, cayenne pepper, and nutmeg. Mix in cottage cheese and chives. Add salt to taste. Reheat just to simmering. Serve in soup cups, sprinkled with toasted slivered almonds and accompanied by onion-flavored crackers. Makes 6 servings.

SOUPS MADE WITH NUTS

*

Potage de Canard aux Marrons
Duck Soup with Chestnuts

This makes a delicious finish to the carcass of a roast duck. It's rich and filling enough to make a complete meal when served with a salad and hot rolls.

Roast duck carcass	1 1-pound can tomatoes
2 quarts water	½ cup red table wine
1 pound chestnuts	2 teaspoons salt
1 medium-size onion	⅛ teaspoon black pepper
2 medium-size carrots	½ teaspoon thyme
1 cup sliced celery	1-inch piece bay leaf
1 leek	

Combine duck carcass and water in a large kettle. Bring to a boil. Turn down heat to simmer.

Meanwhile, spread chestnuts out on flat pan. Place in moderate oven, 350°F. When chestnuts are hot, take out a few at a time. Peel them and remove inside skin. Add peeled chestnuts to simmering duck carcass. Peel and slice onion; scrape and slice carrots. Add to soup along with sliced celery. Clean leek and slice; add to soup, including some of green top. Add tomatoes, red wine, salt and pepper. Crush thyme and add along with bay leaf. Continue to simmer another hour, or until duck meat begins to fall from bones. Lift carcass out along with 6 to 8 whole chestnuts. Let soup and vegetables cool slightly and blend until smooth in an electric blender. Return to soup kettle. Take duck meat off of bones and cut into strips or pieces. Cut whole chestnuts in half. Return duck meat and chestnuts to soup. Heat thoroughly. Ladle into soup plates and serve at once. Makes 6 to 8 servings.

Black Walnut Soup

During drouth years the pioneers on the western plains could often count on black walnuts. The roots of black walnut trees grow deep and can get moisture other plants cannot. So to them Black Walnut Soup was an emergency food—to us somewhat exotic.

2 tablespoons butter or lard
3 tablespoons flour
1 quart beef stock
1-inch piece bay leaf
1 cup light cream or half and half
⅛ teaspoon black pepper
Dash cayenne pepper
Salt to taste

BLACK WALNUT BALLS
¾ cup finely chopped black walnuts
¼ cup dairy sour cream
¼ teaspoon marjoram
2 tablespoons flour

Melt butter or lard in a heavy kettle and stir in flour. When blended, add beef stock. Cook, stirring constantly, until soup comes to a boil. Add bay leaf and turn heat down so soup will barely simmer.

Meanwhile, combine chopped black walnuts and sour cream. Crush marjoram and mix into walnut mixture along with flour. With a half-teaspoon measuring spoon, form small balls and drop them into simmering soup. Simmer for 15 to 20 minutes. Add cream, pepper, cayenne, and salt to taste. Continue heating until soup simmers again. Serve at once for lunch or supper, accompanied by fresh bread or rolls and butter, and pickled peaches. Makes 6 servings.

Nigerian Groundnut Soup

A first-course soup made with peanuts and fish stock. Throughout Central Africa the groundnut or peanut is a "staff of life." In reality a legume rather than a nut, the groundnut or peanut is highly nutritious. Use either a freshly roasted unsalted peanut or canned dry roasted peanuts.

1 cup roasted peanuts
3 cups fish stock or bottled clam juice
2 or 3 small hot dry red peppers
½ cup chopped fresh green pepper or
  chopped canned green chilis

½ cup chopped onion
Salt to taste
Croutons

Crush peanuts with rolling pin, or grind or crush by blending in an electric blender. (Do not grind too fine or blend too long, or nuts will become peanut butter.) Heat fish stock. (You make stock from fish bones and odds and ends of fish and fish skin and strain it. Or use liquid from cooking crab or other seafood, or bottled clam broth.) Crush red peppers and add to stock along with chopped green pepper or chilis and chopped onion. Simmer until vegetables are tender. Stir in crushed peanuts. Simmer about 10 minutes, stirring frequently. Add salt to taste, depending on the saltiness of the roasted nuts. Pour into soup cups and top with crisp croutons made from French bread. Makes 6 servings.

Nut Soup

From a cookbook given to a bride married in the fall of 1906 comes this recipe. There's the suggestion that 2 cups of cooked lima beans can be added to the soup to make it more nourishing, but it seems plenty nourishing as it is. If you, like many others, have a big bowl of mixed nuts around at holiday time, then use enough to make this soup. Make the stock from turkey bones. It's a good soup to fill out a rather skimpy meal.

½ cup shelled filberts or hazelnuts
½ cup shelled almonds
1 quart chicken or turkey stock or 1
  quart water
1 slice onion

2 stalks celery, chopped (about 1 cup)
½ teaspoon salt, or to taste
⅛ teaspoon white pepper
1 cup rich milk or cream, or 1 cup
  undiluted evaporated milk

Blanch nuts, if needed; or if using salted nuts, rub off excess salt. Chop coarsely and combine with stock or water in a kettle along with onion slice and chopped celery. Simmer 35 to 40 minutes, or until nuts and vegetables are tender. Rub through a wire sieve or food mill or blend in an electric blender. When ready to serve, add salt and pepper to taste, and milk or cream. Heat to simmering and pour into soup cups or small bowls. Since this soup is quite rich, it will make from 6 to 8 servings. Accompany with Melba toast, crisp crackers, or rye wafers.

Part II

SOUP
MAKES THE MEAL
Whole-Meal Soups
and Chowders

You CAN CALL OUR SOUPS and chowders peasant fare, soul food, or just plain home cooking, whatever you like. Each calls for ingredients that are liked and are easy to obtain in the part of the world where the recipe originates. Hard-working people have lived by them and enjoyed them. In this country, you may have to search a little for some of the ingredients or make some substitutions. Many of these will make intriguing meals for family or guests. For what may be "poor man's soup" in one part of the world may be an exotic repast in another.

SECTION 1

Mainly Poultry

Avgolemono

Almost every Greek family has its own version of *Avgolemono*, the traditional soup with egg and lemon. Here is one that is more of a whole-meal soup than many (see *Greek Lemon-Egg Soup*). It comes from a college friend of my sister-in-law whose grandparents came to this country from Greece.

3½-pound stewing chicken	*1 cup rice or rice-shaped pasta*
2 quarts water	*3 eggs*
1 tablespoon salt	*¼ cup lemon juice*
Celery leaves	

Cut up stewing chicken. Place in a large kettle and add water, salt, and celery leaves. Simmer very slowly about 2 hours, or until chicken is tender. Let stock cool.

Lift chicken from stock and remove from bones in bite-size pieces. Measure 1½ cups chicken pieces.

Skim fat from stock. Measure 6 cups of stock into a large kettle. Bring to a boil and add rice or pasta.

Meanwhile, separate eggs. Beat the whites until stiff. Beat egg yolks lightly and stir gently into egg whites along with lemon juice. When rice or pasta is tender, pour egg mixture slowly into soup, mixing carefully. Add pieces of chicken. When thoroughly heated, serve at once. Makes 6 servings.

NOTE: If any soup is left over, reheat in a casserole in a slow oven, adding additional chicken stock, if needed.

Chinese Noodle Soup with Braised Chicken

Copied from a soup served at a popular Chinese restaurant in San Francisco, this is a Cantonese soup. It can be a whole meal or a part of a Chinese feast.

4 to 8 chicken thighs, drumsticks, or wings
1 teaspoon sugar
1 teaspoon chopped fresh ginger or chopped candied ginger
2 tablespoons soy sauce
2 tablespoons sherry
1 tablespoon salad oil
4 cups chicken stock
1½ cups coarsely chopped Chinese greens or Chinese cabbage
4 ounces Chinese noodles or spaghetti
1 teaspoon MSG

Cut tips off chicken wings. Arrange chicken pieces in glass plate or bowl. Combine sugar, chopped ginger, soy sauce, and sherry. Pour this over chicken and let marinate several hours. Lift marinated chicken out. Brown it lightly in salad oil. Cover and cook until done. (Do this ahead of time, if you like.)

Add any of the leftover marinade to the chicken stock and heat to simmering. Add greens and cook until they are barely tender. Meanwhile, cook the noodles in boiling salted water until tender. Drain noodles and add to soup. Add chicken and any of its pan drippings. Heat to boiling. Add MSG. Pour out into tureen or ladle into soup bowls, arranging chicken and greens on top. (Chopsticks or tongs are good for this job.) Serve at once. Makes 4 to 6 servings.

Chicken Chow Mein Chowder

Since it is as American as chop suey or chow mein, certainly no true Chinese restaurant would call any soup a chowder. But most people who like Chinese-American food will like this. It's a wonderful late supper dish, particularly after an evening of bridge or poker. For the stock and cooked chicken you can simmer a stewing chicken in 2 or 3 quarts of water. You'll have enough cooked chicken for something else—salad, sandwiches, or a casserole.

¼ cup peanut oil
¼ pound fresh mushrooms, thinly sliced
½ cup green pepper strips
⅓ cup thinly sliced green onions
½ cup thinly sliced celery
2 quarts strong, clear chicken stock
1½ to 2 cups cooked chicken, cut in strips

2 tablespoons soy sauce
1 teaspoon MSG
1 1-pound can mixed Chinese vegetables
Steamed rice
Chow mein noodles

Heat peanut oil in a large kettle. Add sliced mushrooms and cook for 5 to 10 minutes, or until mushrooms are tender. Add green pepper strips, sliced green onions, and sliced celery. Cook these vegetables 2 or 3 minutes in the oil, then add the chicken stock. Simmer about 15 minutes, or until vegetables are barely tender. Add the cooked chicken, soy sauce, and MSG. Drain the canned Chinese vegetables and add to soup. Heat soup to boiling. Ladle into soup plates or bowls over balls of steamed rice. Sprinkle with crisp chow mein noodles. Makes 6 to 8 servings.

Mizutaki

An Americanized version of a favorite Japanese cold-weather dish. If you can't find some of the Japanese ingredients, leave them out or make substitutions. Use fresh or canned mushrooms or Italian or South American dried mushrooms. Instead of seaweed use additional water cress or spinach, and for the Chinese cabbage use Swiss chard or other greens. The bean curd, of course, can be omitted and additional chicken, clams, or oysters added.

6 or 8 dried mushrooms, about ¼ cup
1 piece seaweed (kombu)
8 cups water
2 whole chicken breasts, 1 to 1½ pounds, or 1½ pounds beef sirloin, very thinly sliced
1 10-ounce can small whole clams

7 or 8 ounces bean curd, fresh or canned (tofu)
1 pound Chinese cabbage, cut into strips
1 cup water cress or spinach, firmly packed

In a large kettle soak dried mushrooms and seaweed in the 8 cups water for about 30 to 40 minutes. Bring to a boil, skim off foam, and turn down to simmer. Cut chicken from bones and into bite-size pieces. Or cut beef into strips. Add to soup and simmer for about 30 to 40 minutes, or until chicken or beef is tender. When time to serve, add clams and their broth. Cut bean curd into ½-inch cubes and add along with cabbage and water cress or spinach. Ideally, this last should be done on a table stove, or *hibachi*, for the vegetables should be hot but still crisp. Ladle broth into cups or bowls. Then serve the meat and vegetables accompanied by steamed rice and *Momijii-Oroshi* and *Pon-Zu Sauce*. Makes 6 servings.

TO MAKE MOMIJII-OROSHI:

Grate *daikon* (large white radish) or white turnip to make ½ cup. Stir in 1 tablespoon soy sauce and 2 crushed hot dry red peppers.

TO MAKE PON-ZU SAUCE:

Combine 2 tablespoons each lemon juice, soy sauce, and stock from soup. Sprinkle with chopped green onions.

South American Turkey and Bean Soup

Make this with a stewing chicken or with a turkey carcass and use up pumpkin or squash left from autumn decorations or from making pies.

Turkey carcass or 2½- to 3-pound stewing chicken
8 cups water
1 tablespoon seasoned salt
1 tablespoon salt
½ cup chopped onion
½ cup chopped celery
¼ teaspoon crushed hot dry red chili pepper
2 tablespoons chopped green pepper

½ pound fresh green beans, or 1 cup canned or frozen
¼ cup rice
2 cups pared, diced potatoes
1 cup pared, diced pumpkin or yellow squash, summer or winter
1 cup green peas, fresh or frozen
2 hard-cooked eggs, chopped
2 tablespoons chopped parsley

Break up turkey carcass and place in large kettle, or cut up stewing chicken. Add water, seasoned salt, and salt. Simmer 2 or 3 hours or until all pieces of turkey or chicken fall from bones and stock is flavorful. Strain the stock. Cool and remove turkey or chicken meat from bones and reserve.

To make soup, skim off any excess fat from stock. Add chopped onion, celery, crushed chili pepper and green pepper. Simmer gently. Cut green beans in 1-inch pieces and add to soup along with rice, potatoes, and pumpkin or squash. Simmer until vegetables are done. Add green peas and reserved pieces of turkey or chicken. Cook until peas are done. Ladle into soup plates or deep bowls. Combine chopped eggs and parsley and sprinkle over soup. Serve with toasted rolls, crisp toast, or hot corn sticks. Makes 6 generous servings.

Mainly Fish

⁓ ⁓

Green Pea and Lobster Chowder

Here is an adaptation of a chowder served by a small inn on the West Coast, which specializes in all kinds of fish and seafood. If you cook fresh or frozen lobster or lobster tails, then use the stock instead of water.

2 tablespoons butter
¼ cup chopped onion
½ cup thinly sliced celery
3 cups water or stock
2 vegetable bouillon cubes
1 cup pared, diced potato
6 to 8 ounces cooked fresh or frozen lobster or lobster tails

1 10-ounce package frozen peas
¼ teaspoon thyme
1 cup half and half
Salt to taste
⅛ teaspoon black pepper
2 tablespoons chopped parsley

Melt butter in a kettle. Add onion and sliced celery and cook until vegetables are soft but not brown. Add water or stock, bouillon cubes, and diced potato. Simmer until potatoes are tender. Slice the lobster and add to soup with frozen peas. Crush thyme and stir into soup. Simmer until peas are done. Add half and half; season to taste with salt. Stir in pepper. Ladle into soup bowls and sprinkle with parsley. Serve with toasted pilot crackers. Makes 4 or 5 servings.

Pacific Northwest Chowder

Similar to the *soupes* of the Mediterranean, like *Bouillabaisse*, is this prize-winning recipe from the Pacific Northwest, but the fish and seafood called for are those most readily available in the region.

2 to 2½ pounds firm white fish, such as sea bass, black cod, or halibut
1 quart water
2 teaspoons salt
3 medium-size onions
⅓ cup olive oil
1 clove garlic
1 medium-size carrot
2 large tomatoes
1-inch piece bay leaf
1 cup chopped or ground fresh clams, or 1 can (6½ to 7 ounces) minced clams
1 cup fresh or frozen cleaned shrimp
1 cup white table wine
2 tablespoons lemon juice
2 green onions
¼ teaspoon coarsely ground black pepper

Cut fish into chunks. Combine water and salt. Slice one onion and add to salted water along with fish. Simmer about 10 minutes or until fish is barely tender. Lift fish from stock and reserve. Strain stock and reserve.

Heat olive oil in a large kettle. Slice the remaining two onions and add to oil. Crush garlic or chop finely and add to onions. Slice the carrot into thin crosswise slices. Peel tomatoes, remove seeds, and cut into chunks. Add vegetables to kettle along with the bay leaf. Sauté for a few minutes, then add undrained clams and shrimp. Add the reserved fish stock and simmer about 30 minutes. Stir in white wine and lemon juice and add the cooked fish. Simmer about 5 minutes. Cut the green onions, tops and all, into thin slices. Sprinkle green onions and black pepper over chowder just before serving. Serve with bread sticks. Makes about 6 servings.

Creole Oyster Soup

A trip to Louisiana some years ago brought me this recipe. Of course, in Creole country the oysters are from the Gulf. But Pacific oysters are especially good in this soup. They need to be cooked a little longer than the Gulf oysters.

1½ to 2 pounds soup bones or boiling beef
2 quarts hot water
4 teaspoons salt
¼ teaspoon thyme
1-inch piece bay leaf
2 tablespoons butter
⅓ cup sliced green onions
3 tablespoons chopped parsley
1 teaspoon chervil
2 dozen medium-size oysters or 2 10-ounce jars medium-size Pacific oysters
2 teaspoons arrowroot or cornstarch

Combine soup bones or boiling beef and hot water in a large kettle. Add salt, thyme, and bay leaf and simmer 3 or 4 hours. Strain stock from the meat and bones. Chill it and remove the fat. Cook green onions, parsley, and chervil in butter about 10 minutes, stirring. Add beef stock and bring to a boil. Add oysters and simmer them until edges curl. Moisten arrowroot or cornstarch in a little cold water and stir into soup. Heat soup to simmering and ladle into soup plates or bowls. Serve with crisp toast or toasted French bread. Makes 4 to 6 servings.

Gulf of Alaska Crab Soup

A friend brought back this recipe from an Alaskan vacation some years ago—before Alaska was a state. There it is made with king crab. Recently, king crab has been plentiful and inexpensive—at least in the western United States—but any other crabmeat, fresh, frozen, or canned, may be used. The original called for even more cayenne pepper, but the soup is quite hot this way. You may like to cut down on the cayenne; taste to be sure.

3 cups clear chicken stock
3 cups crabmeat—freshly cooked, frozen, or canned
1 teaspoon onion juice
1 teaspoon chopped parsley
⅛ teaspoon cayenne pepper
2 cups milk
2 egg yolks
½ cup heavy cream or evaporated milk
Paprika

Heat chicken stock to simmering. Add crabmeat, onion juice, parsley, and cayenne. Simmer until crabmeat is thoroughly heated. Beat egg yolks and milk together with an electric or rotary beater or in an electric blender. Stir into soup. Heat just to simmering. Whip cream and salt it lightly. Garnish soup with cream and a dash of paprika. Or stir cream or evaporated milk into soup and sprinkle with paprika. Serve with fresh homemade bread, sourdough bread, toast, or crackers. This is a very rich soup, and bread and salad are enough to make a meal.

Crab Bisque

Scotch whisky gives this hearty soup an unusual flavor. It makes a good supper for a cold winter night.

4 tablespoons butter
2 tablespoons finely chopped onion
1 pound crabmeat or about 2 cups
½ to 1 teaspoon salt

½ cup leftover mashed potatoes or 3 tablespoons instant mashed potato flakes
3 cups milk

Freshly ground black pepper
½ cup heavy cream
2 tablespoons Scotch whisky
Chopped parsley

Melt butter in top of a double boiler and stir in finely chopped onion. Over direct heat cook until onion is limp but not brown. Add potato slowly and mix well. Add milk, stirring constantly. Add crabmeat, salt, and pepper. Cook over boiling water 15 minutes, stirring occasionally. When thoroughly heated, add cream. Just before serving stir in whisky. Ladle into soup plates or bowls; sprinkle with parsley. Serve with hot rolls or crisp toast. Makes 4 to 6 servings.

Cullen Skink
Finnan Haddie Soup

In the land of my forebears—Scotland—the Findon haddock, or here in the United States finnan haddie, is one of the choicest of the smoked fish. Recipes for *Cullen Skink* vary according to locality and family. Our version we like for a late Sunday breakfast or brunch along with oatmeal scones—really just biscuits with quick-cooking oats substituted for part of the flour.

1½ to 2 pounds finnan haddie
6 cups water
1 medium-size onion, chopped (about 1 cup)
2 cups rich milk or half and half

1 cup instant mashed potato flakes
1 tablespoon butter
Salt to taste
⅛ teaspoon coarsely ground black pepper

Wash fish and cut it into 3- or 4-inch squares. Combine in a large kettle with water and chopped onion. Simmer until fish is done, about 30 to 40 minutes. (If fish is cooked from frozen stage, it may take a few minutes longer.) Lift fish out of kettle and let cool slightly. Remove any skin and bones. Reserve the fish and return all skin and bones to kettle. Simmer for 1 hour and strain. Just before serving add rich milk and reserved fish to stock. Heat to simmering. Add potato flakes gradually, stirring as soup thickens slightly. When simmering again, add butter, additional salt to taste, and pepper. Serve from soup plates or bowls accompanied by hot oatmeal scones or hot biscuits and lime marmalade. Makes 4 servings.

Seljankakeitto
Finnish Fish Soup

Finnish people, wherever they may live, like to have lots of fresh fish. A favorite way to cook it is in a whole-meal soup. If you can get your hands on a whole fresh fish, then try *Seljankakeitto*. Striped bass is particularly good made into this *keitto,* or soup, with its tart seasonings of capers and dill pickle.

4- or 5-pound whole fish, or 2 or 3 pounds fish fillets, white fish such as white or ling cod, striped bass, or white sea bass	1 8-ounce can tomato sauce
	4 or 5 whole allspice
	2 teaspoons capers
	2 teaspoons anchovy paste
3 tablespoons butter	½ teaspoon dill weed
2 cups chopped onions	¼ cup chopped dill pickle
½ cup sliced fresh mushrooms	3 or 4 lemon slices
1 tablespoon flour	2 or 3 tablespoons chopped parsley
6 cups stock (2 to 4 cups of fish stock and the rest chicken or veal stock)	

Skin fish and cut from the bones into chunks. From the bones, skin, and head make fish stock. (Use about 1 quart of water and season as suggested in recipe *How to Make Fish Stock.*) Refrigerate pieces of fish until ready to make soup.

Melt butter in a large top-of-the-stove casserole. Add chopped onions and sliced mushrooms and cook until tender, but not brown. Stir in flour. Strain the fish stock and add enough chicken or veal stock to make 6 cups. Add to onions and mushrooms and cook, stirring constantly, until soup simmers. Add tomato sauce and allspice and simmer about 15 minutes. Add fish chunks, capers, anchovy paste, and dill weed. Simmer until fish is done but still firm. Stir in chopped dill pickle. Float lemon slices on top of soup and sprinkle with parsley. Serve with hardtack, rye Melba toast, or Finnish rye loaf. Makes 6 to 8 servings.

Laksloda
Finnish Salmon Chowder

Years ago when going to school in New York City I shared an apartment with a friend from Astoria, Oregon, whose mother and father were born in Finland. Later when I visited her in Astoria I became acquainted with a number of Finnish favorites made by those who had migrated to that delightful spot on the Columbia River. If you live where smoked salmon is plentiful and relatively inexpensive, then use the larger amount. It's delicious, however much you use. And you can use kippered salmon instead, if it's easier to get.

½ to 1 pound thinly sliced smoked salmon or ½- to 1-pound piece
3 or 4 medium-size potatoes
1 medium-size onion
1 tablespoon flour
3 cups rich milk or half and half
10 to 12 whole allspice
½ teaspoon coarsely ground black pepper

Separate thin slices of salmon or break piece into chunks. Pare and slice potatoes; peel and cut onion into thin slices. Butter a 2-quart casserole; arrange a layer of potato slices using about ⅓, and top with a layer of onion, using about half of the onion. Sprinkle with half of the flour and top with half of salmon. Add a second layer of all and top with remaining potato slices. Pour milk over potatoes; add whole allspice and sprinkle with pepper. Bake in a moderately slow oven, 300°F., for about 1 hour or until vegetables are tender. Serve in soup plates accompanied with hardtack or crisp rye wafers or with rye bread. Makes about 6 servings.

Kaen Ron
Thailand Soup

In Thailand there are many *kaens,* or soups, and most, like this one, have both meat and fish. The seasoning most often used is a fish sauce called *Nam Pla.* It is unavailable in this country; anchovy paste and soy sauce make a good substitute. The soy bean threads are available in cities that have Oriental groceries; otherwise, use regular Chinese noodles or thin vermicelli or spaghetti.

4 ounces pork tenderloin or lean boneless shoulder
½ breast of chicken, about 4 ounces
1 quart well-seasoned chicken stock
6 or 8 dry mushrooms, about ¼ cup
½ cup water
1 large onion, thinly sliced
1 clove garlic
1 teaspoon anchovy paste
2 teaspoons soy sauce
2 or 3 ounces soy bean threads or 1 cup Chinese noodles
4 ounces cleaned raw shrimp or prawns
1½ cups pared, cubed cucumber
1 or 2 eggs
2 or 3 tablespoons chopped fresh coriander (Chinese parsley) or chopped fresh parsley

Cut pork and chicken into ½-inch cubes. Add to chicken stock in a kettle. Heat to simmering. Soak mushrooms in water for about 20 minutes. Slice thinly, if whole; add mushrooms and water to soup along with thinly sliced onion. Crush garlic and stir into soup along with anchovy paste and soy sauce. Simmer until pork and chicken are tender, about 20 minutes more. Add soy bean threads or noodles, raw shrimp, and cucumber. Simmer another 10 minutes, or until shrimp are cooked. Stir in unbeaten eggs, one at a time. Pour into soup tureen and sprinkle with chopped parsley. Ladle into soup plates or bowls and serve steamed rice separately. Makes about 6 servings.

Korean Fish Soup

Different from the soups, stews, and chowders of the Western world is this *soupe* from Korea. Still basically the same—for meat, fish, and vegetables are all included—this is the hearty stew of the peasant-fisherman of the Orient. To serve, dip the broth out into soup cups or small bowls, then eat the meat, fish, and vegetables separately with rice.

1 tablespoon sesame seeds	1 medium-size turnip
4 to 6 ounces beef sirloin, very thinly sliced	1 pound fresh or frozen cod, haddock, halibut, or other firm white fish
3 tablespoons soy sauce	½ teaspoon finely chopped crystallized ginger
2 green onions, thinly sliced	
1 clove garlic, chopped	¼ cup rice wine or sake, or dry vermouth
6 cups hot water	
¼ teaspoon black pepper	Salt, if needed
1 1-pound can bean sprouts or 1 pound fresh bean sprouts	

Toast sesame seeds until brown in heavy pan, stirring constantly so seeds will not burn. Crush seeds. (The easiest way is to whiz seeds a few seconds in a blender, but you can do it in a mortar with a pestle, or with a wooden spoon.) Cut beef into pieces about 1-inch square. Sear in a Dutch oven or heavy kettle. Stir in 1 tablespoon soy sauce, sliced green onions, garlic, and sesame seeds. Add hot water, pepper, and remaining 2 tablespoons soy sauce. Drain canned bean sprouts, or wash fresh sprouts, and add to soup. Wash, pare, and cut the turnip into ½-inch cubes and add to soup. Simmer the soup until meat and vegetables are almost done. Cut the fish into pieces about 2 inches square. Add to soup along with crystallized ginger. Continue simmering 15 to 20 minutes, or until fish is done. Add wine or vermouth. Add salt, if needed, but the soy sauce probably will make the soup salty enough. Serve with bowls of steamed rice. Makes 4 servings.

Abalone Chowder

A true California recipe, for California abalone cannot be "exported" from the state. You can make *Abalone Chowder* with the canned abalone from Mexico or the Orient. If you do, use the liquid and add water to make 2 cups.

4 slices bacon	2 cups hot water
3 or 4 slices fresh abalone, about ½ pound	1 teaspoon Worcestershire sauce
1 cup chopped onion	2 cups half and half
1½ cups pared, diced potato	Salt to taste
1 clove garlic	⅛ teaspoon pepper
	Paprika

Cut each piece of bacon into 5 or 6 pieces. Fry until lightly browned but not crisp. Pour off most of the fat. Pound the abalone slices on both sides and cut into 1-inch squares. Add abalone to bacon along with chopped onion and diced potato and cook until lightly browned. Crush garlic and add to abalone and vegetables. Add hot water and Worcestershire sauce. Simmer until the abalone and vegetables are tender. Stir in half and half, salt to taste and pepper. Ladle chowder into soup plates or bowls and sprinkle with paprika. Serve with thin slices of toasted French bread. Makes six servings.

Chinese Abalone Soup

Entirely different from *Abalone Chowder* is *Chinese Abalone Soup*. Made from canned abalone from Mexico, Australia, or the Orient, the soup will need either Chinese greens or Chinese cabbage, if available to you. If not, Swiss chard, spinach, or other greens will do. Another interesting touch is the seaweed—obtainable only in cities where considerable Oriental food is sold.

1 1-pound can abalone	1 to 1½ cups coarsely chopped or sliced Chinese greens or cabbage
6 or 8 dried mushrooms, about ¼ cup	2 tablespoons soy sauce
½ cup water	¼ to ½ cup crumbled seaweed (if available)
6 cups chicken stock	
1 5-ounce can bamboo shoots	

Drain liquid from abalone and reserve. Cut abalone into ½-inch cubes. Soak dried mushrooms in water for about 20 minutes. In a kettle combine the chicken stock, cubed abalone and liquid, and the mushrooms and water in which they were soaked. Simmer for 30 to 40 minutes. About 20 minutes before serving, add bamboo shoots and Chinese greens. Toast seaweed in moderately slow oven, 300°F., while soup is simmering. At serving time stir soy sauce and crumbled seaweed into soup. Spoon into bowls and serve at once. Makes 6 to 8 servings.

Psarosoupa
Greek Fish Soup

The ancient name was *Kakavia* and it's said to be the *bouillabaisse* of the Greek fishermen. It is served in an earthen pot, often placed in the middle of the fishing boat. The fishermen sit around and help themselves.

2 *pounds firm white fish such as cod,*	1 *clove garlic, finely chopped*
haddock, halibut, perch, or pike	1 *quart water*
¼ *cup olive oil*	¼ *bay leaf*
2 *medium-size onions, sliced*	2 *teaspoons salt*
2 *medium-size potatoes, sliced*	6 *whole black peppercorns*
2 *medium-size carrots, thinly sliced*	¼ *teaspoon oregano*
1 *small celeriac or celery root, pared,*	2 *tablespoons lemon juice*
cut into quarters, and thinly sliced	3 *tablespoons chopped parsley*

Trim fish and cut into serving-size pieces. Heat olive oil in a large soup pot. Add onions, potatoes, carrots, celery root, and garlic. Cook the vegetables gently in oil for 5 to 10 minutes. Add water, bay leaf, salt, and peppercorns and simmer about 30 minutes, or until vegetables are tender. Crush the oregano and add to the soup with lemon juice and fish and continue to simmer until the fish is done, about 20 minutes. Meanwhile, fry slices of French bread in hot oil until crisp and brown. Arrange fried bread in soup plates. Lift fish and vegetables out of the hot soup and arrange on hot platter. Ladle the hot broth over the fried bread. Sprinkle soup and fish with chopped parsley. After the hot broth is eaten, the fish and vegetables are served in the soup plates. Makes 6 servings.

Bouillabaisse

There are as many different versions of *bouillabaisse* as there are French fishermen. The seasonings vary little, but the kinds of fish and seafood do. Naturally, a *bouillabaisse* made in the south of France will have different varieties of fish and seafood from a *bouillabaisse* made in San Francisco or New Orleans or North Africa. The secret is in using the largest variety of fish and seafood possible. Use any or all of those suggested, or other kinds, if desired.

1 to 2 pounds fish, almost any fish you like or that is available can be used—striped or sea bass, haddock, cod, red snapper, redfish, mackerel
1 to 1½ pounds lobster, fresh or frozen
1 pound raw or green shrimp
1 dozen oysters or clams
½ pound crabmeat
2 large onions, sliced
2 leeks, thinly sliced
1 carrot, thinly sliced
3 medium-size tomatoes, peeled and cut into chunks
1 quart water
1 cup white table wine

Any stock or liquid from steaming clams, or 1 8-ounce bottle clam juice
1 clove garlic, crushed
½ bay leaf
2 thin slices lemon with peel
4 thin slices orange with peel
3 whole allspice
⅛ teaspoon fennel seeds, crushed
¼ teaspoon thyme
1 tablespoon salt
1 small whole hot red pepper
2 pinches saffron
¼ cup olive oil
3 tablespoons chopped parsley

Remove any bones from fish and cut into chunks. Cut lobster meat into cubes. Shell the shrimp and remove black vein. Open clams or oysters by steaming in small amount of water, and remove from shells. Reserve any liquid. (Or make some stock by simmering bones from fish, lobster and shrimp shells, in 1 to 1½ cups of water. Strain and reserve.)

In a large soup pot arrange the sliced onions, leeks, carrot, and tomatoes. Add the water, wine, and reserved stock or clam juice. Add crushed garlic, bay leaf, lemon and orange slices, allspice, fennel seeds, thyme, salt, red pepper, saffron, and olive oil. Simmer for about 30 minutes. Arrange fish and seafood carefully in the soup pot and simmer about 20 minutes, or until fish and seafood are done. Carefully remove bay leaf, orange and lemon slices, allspice, and red pepper. Sprinkle the soup with chopped parsley. Ladle soup and an assortment of fish and seafood into each soup plate over slices of toasted French bread or crisp toast. Makes 8 servings.

Mainly Meat

～⁓⁓

*

Borsch

Russian Soup

You'll need a very large pot for this version of the classic Russian soup. I make the whole amount and then freeze a part of it. When I reheat a portion I usually add an 8-ounce can of julienne-cut beets to each quart or so, for beets tend to lose their color. If you have any extra beef bones, be sure and add these when you make the stock.

3 to 3½ pounds beef shanks, soup meat, or boiling beef
2 quarts water
½ cup vodka
2 tablespoons salt
½ bay leaf
6 to 8 whole black peppercorns
2 carrots, thinly sliced (about 1½ cups)
2 stalks celery and leaves, thinly sliced (about 1½ cups)

2 medium-size onions, thinly sliced, (1½ to 2 cups)
2 cups peeled fresh tomatoes, cut up, or 1 1-pound can whole tomatoes
1 1-pound can julienne-cut beets
2 cups sliced cabbage
1 tablespoon vinegar
Dairy sour cream
Dill weed or parsley

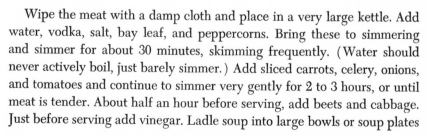

Wipe the meat with a damp cloth and place in a very large kettle. Add water, vodka, salt, bay leaf, and peppercorns. Bring these to simmering and simmer for about 30 minutes, skimming frequently. (Water should never actively boil, just barely simmer.) Add sliced carrots, celery, onions, and tomatoes and continue to simmer very gently for 2 to 3 hours, or until meat is tender. About half an hour before serving, add beets and cabbage. Just before serving add vinegar. Ladle soup into large bowls or soup plates and top with a spoonful of sour cream. Sprinkle with dill weed or parsley. Rye or black bread or crisp rye wafers or Melba toast or a plain boiled potato make a good accompaniment. Makes 10 to 12 servings.

Rassolnik
Russian Dill and Kidney Soup

I tasted this hearty soup the first time many years ago at a Russian restaurant in New York City, where I was a student. Then during World War II I came across a version of it in a group of recipes prepared for Russian war relief.

2 quarts chicken stock or stock from roast fowl such as duck, goose, or turkey
2 tablespoons barley
1 large onion, chopped (about 1½ cups)
1 cup each diced turnip and carrot
½ cup thinly sliced celery
1 small beef or veal kidney (about 1 pound)
1 tablespoon butter
1 tablespoon flour
½ cup diced dill pickle
½ cup liquid from dill pickles
Salt to taste
1 cup dairy sour cream

Bring chicken stock to a boil in a large kettle. Add barley and cook until it is tender, about 1 hour. Add chopped onion, diced turnip and carrot, and sliced celery. Wash the kidney. Cut it in thin slices and cut out fat and tubes. Add to soup and simmer until vegetables are tender. Melt butter in a small pan and stir in flour. Add about 1 cup of liquid from soup, stirring, then stir mixture into soup. Bring to a boil, stirring constantly. Just before serving, add diced dill pickle, liquid from pickles, and salt to taste. (The amount will depend on saltiness of stock and dill pickles.) Bring to a boil, stir in sour cream, and serve at once with rye or black bread. Serve as a main dish for luncheon or supper. Makes about 6 servings.

Sopa de Albóndigas
Meatball Soup

From a collection of early California recipes, this soup is just mildly hot. Made from very lean beef and beef stock with all the fat skimmed off, it makes a very tasty low-calorie meal.

2 medium-size fresh tomatoes	¼ teaspoon black pepper
1 4-ounce can green chilis	⅓ cup fine dry bread crumbs
½ cup chopped onions	1 egg
2 teaspoons ground coriander	1 tablespoon salad oil
¼ teaspoon oregano	2 quarts beef stock
¾ pound lean ground beef	Additional salt, to taste, if needed
1 teaspoon salt	

Peel and dice tomatoes; chop green chilis. Combine tomatoes, chilis, onions, and coriander. Crush oregano and add to mixture. Measure 1 cup of mixture and combine with ground beef, salt, pepper, and bread crumbs. Add egg and mix until thoroughly combined. Shape into ½-inch meatballs. Cook remaining vegetable mixture in salad oil in a large kettle until onions are soft, about 5 minutes. Add beef stock and simmer 45 minutes. Drop meatballs into soup and simmer 20 to 25 minutes. Add additional salt, if needed. Serve in bowls along with crisp fried tortillas, corn chips, or hot corn sticks. Makes 6 servings.

Ben Verdusco's Tortilla Soup

Mr. Ben is a very talented hair stylist whose parents were born in Mexico. He says that his blonde Scotch-Irish wife just *can't* seem to make *Tortilla Soup* like his mother used to. This one, he says, tastes more like he remembers it. If you haven't time to fry the tortillas (or haven't them available), corn chips make a good substitute.

2 to 3 pounds beef shanks or boiling beef	4 or 5 peppercorns
Beef bones, if available	2 tablespoons chopped parsley
2 quarts water	½ teaspoon ground coriander
4 teaspoons salt	1 large carrot, sliced
1 1-pound can tomatoes	2 or 3 zucchini, sliced (about 1½ cups)
1 large onion, chopped (about 1½ cups)	2 small ears corn, cut into 1-inch pieces
2 cloves garlic, finely chopped or crushed	3 or 4 tortillas
	Salad or cooking oil

In a large kettle combine beef shanks, bones, and water. Bring to simmering and skim. Add salt, tomatoes, onion, garlic, peppercorns, chopped parsley, and ground coriander. Simmer soup over very low heat about 2 hours, or until meat is tender. Remove meat and bones from soup and when cool, cut meat from bones into cubes. Chill the soup and remove the hard fat. Return meat to soup and add sliced carrot. Simmer for about 30 minutes. Add zucchini and corn, and cook an additional 20 minutes.

Meanwhile, cut the tortillas into thin strips. Fry until crisp in hot oil and drain on paper towels. Just before serving add tortillas to soup. Bring soup to simmering and serve while tortillas are still crisp. Make sure that each serving has a few pieces of corn and some of each vegetable. Makes 6 servings. (Corn is lifted out with a soup spoon and eaten with fingers, as corn on the cob is.)

Locro de Patata
Potato Soup

This is really an early California soup rather than a typically Mexican one.

3 tablespoons butter or margarine
2 medium-size onions, chopped
2 medium-size potatoes, pared and cut into cubes
4 cups water
2 teaspoons seasoned salt
1 canned green chili, chopped
6 to 8 ounces Monterey Jack cheese

½ cup dairy sour cream
1 avocado
1 tablespoon lemon juice
10 to 12 ounces small smoked pork sausages
⅛ teaspoon crushed dry hot red pepper (or ¼ teaspoon chili powder and a dash of cayenne pepper)

Melt butter in a heavy kettle; add chopped onions and cook over low heat until onions are soft and yellow but not brown. Add cubed potatoes and water. When water is simmering stir in seasoned salt and chopped green chili. Simmer until potatoes and onions are tender. When ready to serve, cut cheese into cubes and stir into soup along with sour cream. Peel avocado and cut into cubes; sprinkle with lemon juice. Divide avocado cubes into 4 soup bowls or plates. Fry pork sausages until done; cut in two. Ladle hot soup over avocado and add pieces of sausage. Sprinkle with dry red pepper or chili powder. Serve with crisp tortillas or corn chips. Makes 4 generous servings.

Ashe Reshte
Persian Noodle Soup with Meatballs

Ashe is the Persian word for soup and a cook is an *Ash-Paz* or "maker of the soup." Soups are as important today in the cuisine of modern Iran as they were in ancient Persia.

SOUP

¼ cup lentils
¼ cup dry black-eyed peas
4 to 5 cups water
1½ teaspoons salt
1 cup fine egg noodles
½ cup chopped parsley

MEATBALLS

½ pound ground beef
⅓ cup finely chopped or grated onion
¼ teaspoon cinnamon
¼ teaspoon fine-grind black pepper
½ teaspoon salt

SPICE GARNISH

2 teaspoons dried mint
½ teaspoon black pepper
¼ teaspoon cinnamon

Wash lentils and black-eyed peas; combine in a large kettle with water and salt. Simmer until almost tender, about 30 to 40 minutes. Add noodles and parsley.

Make meatballs by mixing beef, onion, cinnamon, pepper, and salt. Blend well. Shape into 1-inch meatballs. Drop into simmering soup and cook for about 30 more minutes, or until meatballs are done and noodles tender. Crush the dried mint and combine with pepper and cinnamon. Ladle soup into soup plates or large bowls and sprinkle with the mixed spices. Makes 6 servings.

Margaritsa
Greek Easter Soup

Lamb is the traditional Easter meat in Greece—and a hearty soup using the bony parts along with the liver and heart is traditionally eaten at Easter time. (The Greek Church uses a slightly different calendar.)

1½ pounds lamb liver and heart
2 or 3 pounds lamb neck bones, ribs,
  or other stew meat with bones
3 quarts water
1 tablespoon salt
2 tablespoons butter

1 cup sliced green onions
¼ cup rice
¼ teaspoon white pepper
4 eggs
⅓ cup lemon juice
Dill weed or chopped fresh dill

Wash liver and heart and combine in a large kettle with lamb stew meat, water and salt. Simmer until meat is tender, skimming frequently. Strain the stock and chill stock and meat separately. Skim off hardened fat from the stock. Cut meat from bones and cut off all the fat. Cut meat into ½-inch cubes. Melt butter in a frying pan. Add meat, onions, and rice and cook until lightly browned. Measure stock and add enough water to make 3 quarts. Combine meat mixture and diluted stock in a large kettle. Add pepper and additional salt to taste. Simmer until the rice is done, about 25 to 30 minutes. When time to serve, beat eggs with lemon juice. Stir in 2 or 3 tablespoons of hot soup and then stir egg mixture back into soup. Heat just to simmering, but do not boil. Ladle into soup bowls or plates and sprinkle with dill. Makes about 8 servings. Armenian cracker bread, matzoth, or crisp sesame crackers, buttered and toasted, are good with this soup.

Scotch Broth

My Scottish relatives and ancestors may call this "broth," but my present friends and relatives—even the Scotsmen among them—regard it as a whole meal, especially when served with *Skirlie*, either the old-fashioned version or the modern one similar to fried polenta or cornmeal mush.

¼ *cup pearl barley*	*2 leeks*
½ *cup dry peas, yellow or green*	*1 cup diced carrot*
2 pounds lamb neck slices	*1 cup diced white turnip*
6 cups cold water	*½ cup shredded carrots*
1 tablespoon salt	*½ cup chopped kale*
¼ *teaspoon black pepper*	*1 tablespoon parsley*

Soak the barley and dry peas overnight in water to cover. Next morning, drain them and place in a large kettle. Add lamb neck slices, water, salt and pepper. Clean and slice leeks, using some of green portion. Add to soup and add diced carrot and turnip. Simmer soup slowly for 2 to 2½ hours, or until vegetables and meat are very tender. Remove the meat bones, if desired. Just before serving, add shredded carrots, kale, and parsley. Bring just to simmering and serve accompanied by *Skirlie*, oatmeal scones, steamed rice, or mashed potatoes. Makes 6 to 8 servings.

Mutton Broth, Indienne

Don't let the name fool you; this is a *soupe*—almost a stew, for you can serve it for a hearty lunch or light evening meal. A British civil servant in India brought this home to England many years ago. In most parts of this country, lamb is easier to buy than mutton, but either is good.

1 to 1½ pounds lean lamb or mutton
   stew meat
1 medium-size carrot, chopped (about
   ¾ cup)
1 medium-size turnip, chopped (about
   ¾ cup)
2 stalks celery, chopped (about 1
   cup)
1 small white onion, chopped (about
   3 tablespoons)
3 tablespoons chopped green pepper

1 large or 2 small leeks
1 teaspoon curry powder
2 quarts hot water
½ teaspoon lemon peel
3 to 4 teaspoons salt
2 tablespoons Worcestershire sauce
½ small eggplant
1 8-ounce can tomato sauce
¼ cup rice
¼ cup sherry
Chopped parsley or chervil

Cut lamb, or have cut, into 1-inch cubes. Heat a large heavy kettle and brown the lamb. (Most lamb has enough fat so that there's no need to add extra.) When lamb is well browned, pour off excess fat. Add chopped carrot, turnip, celery, onion, and green pepper. Clean and slice leeks thinly, using some of green part. Add the vegetables to the lamb and stir in curry powder. Cook, stirring occasionally, until vegetables are softened and slightly brown. Add hot water, lemon peel, 3 teaspoons salt, and Worcestershire sauce. Simmer until lamb and vegetables are tender, about 30 minutes. Pare eggplant and cut into cubes; add to soup along with tomato sauce and rice. Simmer the soup 15 to 20 minutes more, or until eggplant and rice are done. Just before serving stir in sherry. Ladle into soup plates and sprinkle with chopped parsley or chervil. For a heartier meal, omit the rice in the soup. Steam rice separately and ladle soup over it in soup bowls or plates. Makes 6 generous servings.

Coddle

My good Irish friend says that this Saturday night supper for the Dublin working man was a traditional dish in his family, transported to the American Middle West. Considered a hangover preventative by any hard-drinking Irishman, it would be waiting for him at home after several hours at the local pub. The amount of bacon and sausage would depend on the financial circumstances at the moment. Original Dublin versions didn't call for browning the meat, but most American versions do.

½ to 1 pound thick-sliced or whole piece of bacon	3 medium-size potatoes
½ to 1 pound pork sausages	1 tablespoon chopped parsley
3 medium-size onions	Salt and pepper to taste
	1 to 1½ cups water

Cut bacon slices into 2-inch lengths, or cut piece of bacon into thick slices and into 2-inch lengths. Brown bacon in a heavy frying pan. Drain on paper towels. Prick sausages and brown in frying pan. Drain along with bacon. Arrange bacon and sausages in a casserole or heavy kettle. Slice onions and arrange on bacon and sausages. Pare and slice potatoes and place on top of onions. Sprinkle with chopped parsley. Sprinkle layers of onions and potatoes with salt and pepper to taste. (The amount will depend on saltiness of bacon and sausage.)

Pour off all but a tablespoon or two of the drippings in the frying pan. Add 1 cup of water to drippings and bring to a boil. Pour over *Coddle*. If needed, add additional water until almost to the top of the potatoes. Cover and bake in a moderate oven, 350°F., until potatoes and onions are very tender, about 1 hour. Uncover for last 10 to 15 minutes of cooking and brown slightly, if desired. (Traditionally, *Coddle* is simmered on top of the stove instead of in the oven.) Serve with Irish Soda Bread or homemade whole-wheat bread. Makes 6 servings.

January Soup

An English friend of my sister's doing graduate work at one of the Eastern universities contributed this hearty soup. If ham was a part of her family's Twelfth Night feast, then *January Soup* was sure to follow.

FOR THE SOUP
1 cup lentils
2 tablespoons butter
1 onion, chopped (about 1 cup)
1 carrot, chopped (about 1 cup)
2 stalks celery, chopped (1 to 1½ cups)
1 quart beef stock
2 cups milk

1 tablespoon flour
Salt and pepper to taste

FOR THE HAM BALLS
1 cup ground or finely chopped cooked ham
1 tablespoon flour
¼ teaspoon dry mustard
Dash pepper
1 egg

Soak the lentils overnight or for several hours in water to cover. Melt butter in a large heavy pot or kettle. Add chopped onion, carrot, and celery and sauté the vegetables about 10 minutes, stirring so they won't burn. Add stock and a teaspoon or so of salt, depending on saltiness of stock. Simmer for about 1½ hours, or until vegetables are very soft. Cool soup slightly and rub through a wire sieve or blend until smooth in an electric blender. About 30 minutes before time to serve, add 1½ cups milk and reheat. Add additional salt and pepper if necessary.

Mix thoroughly the ham, flour, mustard, and pepper. Beat egg and mix well with ham mixture. Shape into small balls with a teaspoon. Drop balls into soup and simmer for 10 minutes.

Combine the remaining ½ cup milk with 1 tablespoon flour. Stir into soup and simmer for 5 minutes. Serve in soup plates or bowls accompanied by oatmeal bread or hot scones. Makes 6 servings.

New Zealand Kidney Soup

In New Zealand, a great deal of mutton is raised and after a butchering the kidneys are apt to find their way into a hearty whole-meal soup. In this hemisphere we would most often use lamb kidneys. If you have only two or three lamb kidneys, then add sliced hard-cooked eggs to the soup just before serving.

6 to 8 lamb kidneys	2 potatoes, diced (about 2 cups)
2 or 3 slices bacon	2 teaspoons salt
1 medium-size onion, diced or chopped	¼ teaspoon black pepper
(about 1 cup)	1 tablespoon flour
1½ quarts water	2 tablespoons cold water
1 carrot, diced (about 1 cup)	1 teaspoon lemon juice
2 stalks celery, sliced (about 1 cup)	1 teaspoon Worcestershire sauce
1 turnip, diced (about 1 cup)	

Wash kidneys, cut them in half and cut out tubes. Cut each half into two or three pieces. Fry bacon in large kettle until crisp, drain on paper towel and reserve. Add kidney pieces and onion to bacon drippings and cook until kidneys are no longer pink and onion is lightly browned. Take out about half of kidney pieces and reserve along with bacon. To kidney and onion in kettle add water, carrot, celery, turnip, potatoes, salt, and pepper. Simmer until very tender, about 2 to 3 hours. Let soup cool slightly and purée in blender or press through a food mill.

When time to serve, mix flour and cold water and stir into soup. Bring soup to a boil, stirring constantly, and simmer until it is thickened. Crumble the bacon and add bacon and reserved pieces of kidney to the soup. Add lemon juice and Worcestershire sauce. Ladle into soup plates, serving some of the bacon bits and pieces of kidney into each plate. Or top each serving with slices of hard-cooked egg. Serve with whole-wheat bread or rolls or crackers. Makes 6 servings.

Maul Dasch
Pork Shanks and Dumplings

Packets of dough filled with chopped green onion are simmered in broth made with fresh pork shanks. *Maul Dasch* is a Midwestern version of an old German recipe.

6 fresh pork shanks	1 tablespoon bacon drippings
2½ quarts water	or lard
1 tablespoon salt	4 tablespoons water
2 large fresh tomatoes	2 teaspoons salt
or 1 cup canned tomatoes	2 cups small white bread cubes
4 or 5 bunches green onions (about	3 eggs
2 dozen)	1½ cups flour (approximately)

In a large kettle arrange pork shanks; cover them with 2½ quarts water and add salt. Peel tomatoes, cut up and add to pork shanks. Simmer about 2 hours, or until shanks are tender.

Meanwhile, clean and slice onions, along with some of the green tops. Melt bacon drippings in a frying pan. Add the onions, 4 tablespoons water and 1½ teaspoons salt. Cook until onions are soft, then mix in bread cubes.

Beat eggs with ½ teaspoon salt. Add about 1½ cups flour to make a stiff dough. Roll dough out on a floured board into a rectangle 12 × 16 inches. Cut it into twelve 4-inch squares. On each square place a spoonful or two of the onion filling. Fold over square to form a triangle. Seal the edges by pressing down with tines of a fork. Let the dumplings dry on the board.

When pork shanks are almost tender add the dumplings to the hot broth and simmer gently about 30 minutes. To serve, spoon a pork shank in each soup plate along with two dumplings; fill with hot broth. Crisp coleslaw seasoned with dill weed and a sweet-sour mustard sauce make good accompaniments. Makes 6 generous servings.

Danish Split Pea Soup

In downtown Copenhagen home economists from the Danish Department of Agriculture give food demonstrations—in three languages, no less. This whole-meal soup is from a recipe passed out to the audience. A good friend likes to take this soup in a large pot on board his boat.

1 pound yellow split peas	*½ cup chopped onions*
3 quarts water	*¼ teaspoon thyme*
1-pound piece of bacon or lean salt	*1 to 1½ pounds Danish Canadian-*
pork	*style bacon*
1 medium-size celery root	*1 can or jar Danish cocktail frankfurt-*
3 leeks	*ers*
1½ cups diced carrots	*Salt to taste (about 2 teaspoons)*
2 cups pared, diced potatoes	*¼ teaspoon black pepper*

Simmer split peas in 1 quart water until tender, about 1 to 1½ hours. Meanwhile, in a large kettle, combine piece of bacon or salt pork with 2 quarts of water and bring to a boil. Pare celery root, cut into quarters and then into thin slices. Cut leeks into thin slices. Add celery root and green portion of leeks to soup. Simmer for about 1½ hours, or until bacon or salt pork is almost done. Add rest of leek slices, carrots, potatoes, and chopped onions. Crush thyme and stir into soup. If Canadian bacon is uncooked, add it whole to the soup now. Continue cooking until vegetables and meat are done. Force the cooked split peas through a wire sieve or purée in blender. Add these to soup and heat to simmering. If Canadian bacon is canned or table-ready, add it now to soup along with cocktail frankfurters. Add additional salt, if needed, and pepper. When thoroughly heated, lift out and slice Canadian bacon and salt pork. Pour soup into bowls or large cups and garnish each serving with 2 or 3 frankfurters. Serve the sliced meat along with soup, accompanied by dark rye or pumpernickel bread. A good mustard sauce goes well with the meat.

Polish Bread Soup

From a friend whose grandmother was a Polish Jewish immigrant to this country many, many years ago comes this *Polish Bread Soup.* My friend no longer observes Jewish dietary laws, so this soup isn't kosher. However, it's easy to see how it once was made to conform to those food customs.

½ pound Jewish rye bread
  or any dark rye bread with caraway
  seeds
½ cup chicken or turkey fat
  or bacon drippings
1 cup chopped onions
2 quarts chicken or turkey stock

2 teaspoons garlic salt
⅛ teaspoon pepper
1 pound Polish sausage
1 8-ounce can or 1 cup sauerkraut,
  drained
½ cup dairy sour cream
1 egg

Cut bread into ½-inch cubes. Melt fat or drippings in a large kettle. Add bread cubes and cook over medium heat until bread is toasted. Add chopped onions and cook about 5 minutes, tossing onions and bread cubes frequently. Add chicken or turkey stock, garlic salt, and pepper. Simmer about 30 to 40 minutes, or until onions are tender and bread dissolved. Let the soup cool slightly and force through a wire sieve or blend until smooth in an electric blender. Return to kettle. Skin and slice the sausage and add to soup along with drained sauerkraut. Simmer about 20 to 25 minutes. Just before serving beat together sour cream and egg; add a little hot soup to mixture and then stir into soup. Heat just to simmering, but do not let boil. Serve at once with split and toasted bagels. Makes 6 servings.

Oxtail Soup

There are many versions of *Oxtail Soup*. This one is especially pleasant, for the vegetables are puréed to a smooth *potage*, the meat cut from the oxtails and then returned to the soup. A generous soup plate makes a wonderful supper or lunch.

2 to 3 pounds oxtail
2 quarts beef stock
¼ teaspoon sweet basil
¼ teaspoon oregano
1-inch piece bay leaf
1 tablespoon chopped parsley
1 tablespoon seasoned salt
4 or 5 peppercorns

¼ cup chopped onion
1 8-ounce can tomato sauce
½ cup red table wine
1 cup chopped carrots
½ cup chopped turnips
1 cup chopped celery
2 teaspoons cornstarch
1 tablespoon cold water

Have oxtails cut into 2-inch lengths and trim off excess fat. Heat a small piece of the fat in a large, heavy kettle. Brown the oxtails in the fat; pour off any excess fat. Add stock; crush basil and oregano and add to oxtails along with bay leaf, chopped parsley, seasoned salt, and peppercorns. Bring to a boil, skim, and add chopped onion, tomato sauce, red wine, carrots, turnips, and celery. Cover and simmer soup 2 or 3 hours, or until oxtails are very tender. Remove oxtails from soup. Cool the soup slightly and purée in an electric blender. Return soup to the kettle. Remove the meat from the bones and cut into ½-inch cubes. Add these to soup. Mix cornstarch with cold water and stir into soup. Heat soup to boiling, stirring constantly. Serve at once with toasted hard rolls spread with soft cheese. Makes 8 servings.

Chinese Oxtail Soup

From Hawaii where many of the Americans are of Chinese descent, *Chinese Oxtail Soup* calls for raw peanuts. When cooked in the soup, they seem more of a vegetable than a nut. If you have trouble finding raw peanuts, use roasted peanuts—slightly different results, of course. This is good, though prunes and peanuts sound unlikely.

1 oxtail, 2 to 2½ pounds	*⅛ teaspoon sugar*
½ pound raw or roasted peanuts	*¼ cup soy sauce*
2 or 3 thin slices ginger root, fresh or	*6 prunes, pitted and cut in half*
dried	*Salt to taste, about 1 tablespoon*
2 quarts water	*2 tablespoons sherry*

Have oxtail cut into pieces. Trim off excess fat. Cover meat with cold water and bring to a boil. Drain off the water and pat pieces of meat dry. Render a small piece of the fat in a large heavy kettle. Add oxtail and brown slowly.

Meanwhile, shell peanuts; cover with hot water and remove red skins. Discard water. Add ginger root to browned oxtails. (Soak dried ginger in water for a few minutes.) Add skinned or roasted peanuts and 2 quarts water. Simmer for about 1 hour, then add sugar, soy sauce, and prunes. Simmer for another half hour and then add salt to taste. Continue to simmer another half hour or so, or until meat is very tender. Just before serving add sherry and remove pieces of ginger root. Makes 6 generous servings.

Turkish Tripe Soup

A Navy wife passed on to me this recipe acquired during a tour of duty in the Near East.

2 pounds beef tripe
Cold water
6 cups hot water
1 tablespoon salt
¼ teaspoon pepper

2 eggs
½ cup lemon juice
1 clove garlic
Paprika

Cut tripe in strips. Add just enough cold water to cover and bring to a boil. Drain the tripe and rinse with cold water. Place it in a kettle with the hot water, salt, and pepper. Simmer until tender, about 3 hours. Lift out tripe; let it cool and chop finely or grind in coarse grinder of food chopper. Beat eggs with lemon juice. Crush the garlic and add to egg and lemon mixture. Stir this into the broth in which the tripe was cooked. Heat just to simmering, but do not boil. Spoon tripe into soup plates and pour hot soup over tripe. Sprinkle with paprika. In Turkey a crisp, lightly leavened bread is served with a soup such as this. One of the crisp Swedish breads or the Jewish matzoth go well, too. Makes 4 to 6 servings.

Czechoslovakian Tripe Soup

Czech families would accompany *Tripe Soup* with potatoes or a hearty, peasant-type bread. My family and friends like it with pizza.

1½ to 2 pounds beef tripe
Cold water
2 quarts well-seasoned beef stock
2 cloves garlic

½ teaspoon marjoram
2 tablespoons butter
2 tablespoons flour
Chopped parsley

Wash tripe and cover it with cold water. Bring to a boil and boil for about 10 minutes. Pour off the water. Let tripe cool until it can be handled easily. Cut it into thin julienne strips. Cover with beef stock. Crush garlic and marjoram and add to tripe. Simmer over low heat for 2½ to 3 hours, or until meat is very tender. Just before serving, melt butter in a frying pan. Stir in flour and cook, stirring constantly, until mixture is well browned. Add a cup or so of the stock and stir until smooth and then stir the mixture into soup. Simmer another 5 or 10 minutes. Ladle into soup bowls or plates and sprinkle with chopped parsley. Makes 6 servings.

Turtle Soup—Flying Sportsman

In Loreto, Baja California, on the Sea of Cortés, is the Flying Sportsman Inn. The fishing is wonderful around this old Mexican village. While we were there on a fishing trip, the local fishermen ran into a school of turtles, so we soon had *Turtle Soup*. Lucilla, the cook at the Flying Sportsman, made it with the turtle flippers; she calls it *Sopa Aletus*. I watched her make it—and though turtle flippers aren't available to me, a delicious substitute is available with canned turtle or fresh frozen turtle meat.

1 10-ounce can turtle meat or 1 to 1½ cups cooked fresh or frozen turtle
¼ cup salad oil or shortening
½ cup chopped onions
3 to 4 cups beef stock
1 8-ounce can Spanish-style tomato sauce

1 clove garlic
¼ to ½ teaspoon oregano
⅛ teaspoon black pepper
1 cup cooked, canned, or frozen mixed vegetables
Salt to taste

Drain canned turtle meat. Reserve liquid and cut turtle into bite-size pieces. If using fresh or frozen turtle, simmer until tender in salted water. Cut into bite-size pieces and reserve broth.

In a soup pot or kettle, heat the oil or shortening. Add onions and cook until soft and yellow, but not brown. Add beef stock, tomato sauce, and liquid from turtle meat. When soup is simmering crush garlic and oregano and stir into it. Add turtle meat, pepper, and mixed vegetables and simmer for about 30 minutes. Add salt to taste, if needed. Makes 6 servings for an opening course or 2 or 3 for a main course.

Pendennis Turtle Soup

A soup that made Kentucky famous—as is said also about *Burgoo*. Made in Kentucky from land rather than sea turtles, this can be made from fresh, frozen or canned turtle meat.

2 tablespoons butter
1½ to 2 pounds veal or beef bones
2 medium-size carrots
2 medium-size onions
3 tablespoons flour
2 quarts water
2 teaspoons salt
1 1-pound can tomato purée
3 or 4 cloves
¼ teaspoon thyme

1½ to 2 cups diced cooked turtle meat and its stock or 1 can (10 ounces or larger) turtle meat
Additional salt to taste
⅛ teaspoon pepper
½ cup dry sherry
1 thin slice lemon
1 thin slice grapefruit
2 hard-cooked eggs, chopped

Melt butter carefully in a heavy kettle. Add veal bones and brown

slowly. Scrape and slice carrots; peel and slice onions. Add vegetables to veal bones and brown. Stir in flour and brown carefully, stirring. Do not let it burn. (This brown *roux* is one of the flavor secrets of this soup.) Add water and salt and simmer slowly for 2½ hours. Cool this stock slightly and strain. To the stock add tomato purée and cloves. Crush thyme and stir into soup. Simmer for about 3 minutes. Add diced cooked turtle meat and its stock, or cut canned turtle meat into cubes and add to soup with juice from can. Simmer until thoroughly heated. Add additional salt to taste and pepper. Just before serving remove the cloves and stir in sherry. Cut slices of lemon and grapefruit into 6 or 8 small pieces. Ladle soup into cups. Garnish each serving with a small piece of lemon and grapefruit and chopped hard-cooked egg. Makes 8 servings.

NOTE: *To cook fresh or frozen turtle meat:* Cover with water and add 1 teaspoon salt for each pound of meat. Simmer about 2 hours or until tender. Remove meat from bones and cut into cubes.

Gibelotte
Mushroom and Rabbit Soup

The original recipe was translated from the French—a choice one from Touraine, where wild rabbit and field mushrooms are used. In the original the rabbit was pounded and sieved into a purée, but we like it better cut into chunks. And it's just as delicious with fresh or frozen rabbit from the market and cultivated mushrooms. I like to make the stock from beef or veal bones, but canned bouillon or bouillon cubes are good, too.

1 rabbit, about 2 to 2½ pounds	½ bay leaf
2 quarts beef or veal stock	¼ teaspoon each rosemary,
1 cup white table wine	basil, and thyme
1 teaspoon salt	¼ teaspoon curry powder
¼ teaspoon pepper	1 pound fresh mushrooms
3 medium-size onions	3 egg yolks
1 sprig parsley	½ cup heavy cream
1 clove garlic	

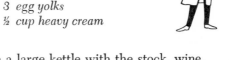

Cut the rabbit into pieces. Place in a large kettle with the stock, wine, salt, and pepper. Peel and slice onions and add to soup along with parsley.

Crush or chop garlic and add garlic and bay leaf. Crush herbs and stir into soup along with curry powder. Simmer over very low heat until rabbit is tender, about 1 to 1½ hours. Lift out rabbit pieces and cool. Remove the meat from bones and cut into bite-size pieces. Strain the stock.

Wash mushrooms and slice. Take about half the mushrooms, add a small amount of stock, and blend in an electric blender until puréed. Combine the strained stock, rabbit pieces, and puréed mushrooms. Simmer about 10 minutes and add remaining sliced mushrooms. Simmer another 5 minutes or so. Beat the egg yolks with heavy cream, stir in a little of the hot soup, and then stir the mixture into the soup. When heated again to simmering, serve at once. Do not boil. Pour into soup tureen or ladle into soup plates. Serve with French bread. Makes 6 to 8 servings.

NOTE: If you prefer to make a *potage* as in the original recipe, cook the rabbit another 30 to 60 minutes, until it is *very* tender. After removing meat from the bones, purée it in an electric blender and return it to soup.

Liver Dumplings in Beef Soup

Kansas pioneers who made this soup for supper used soup bones to make the stock. No doubt, it was most frequently made after a steer had been butchered.

Liver grinds more easily if partially frozen. And while grinding the liver, you might as well grind the onion, too, instead of chopping it.

1½ to 2 quarts beef stock	¼ teaspoon marjoram
½ pound beef liver	⅛ teaspoon mace
1 small onion	½ teaspoon salt
2 tablespoons melted butter	⅛ teaspoon ground black pepper
1 egg	¼ teaspoon lemon peel
½ cup dry bread crumbs	Chopped parsley

Heat the stock to simmering. Meanwhile, grind the liver and onion and mix with melted butter. Beat in the egg; mix in bread crumbs. Crush marjoram and add along with mace, salt, pepper, and lemon peel. Blend thoroughly. Drop the mixture by the tablespoonful into the simmering stock. Cover and simmer the dumplings 15 to 20 minutes. Ladle soup and dumplings into soup plates or bowls and sprinkle with parsley. Serve with crisp crackers, or, even better, fresh homemade bread or rolls. Makes 4 generous servings.

Mackinac Bean-Vegetable Soup

A friend who lives in the Upper Michigan Peninsula, where the woods are beautiful and filled with game and there are many fish in the streams, makes this hearty soup. Her family of hunters and fishermen like it particularly after a day in the outdoors.

2 or 3 pounds ham hocks or a ham
   shank
½ cup dry lima beans
½ cup dry black-eyed peas
½ cup dry navy beans
2 quarts water
1 can (1 pound 12 ounces) tomatoes
2 tablespoons barley

2 tablespoons rice
1 cup diced onions
½ cup sliced celery
½ cup diced carrots
½ cup diced white turnips
Salt to taste
4 ounces bologna

Combine ham hocks or shank with lima beans, black-eyed peas, navy beans and water in a large kettle. Bring to a boil. Add tomatoes. Turn heat down and simmer for several hours, or until beans are tender. Add barley, rice, onions, celery, carrots, and turnips. Continue simmering until barley, rice, and vegetables are done. Remove the ham and cut it into pieces or slices. Add salt to taste. Return ham to soup. Cut bologna into ¼-inch squares and sprinkle over soup. Serve with raisin bread sandwiches. Makes 8 generous servings.

Hamburger-Vegetable Chowder

This is a family standby that can be made "by guess and by gosh." If your pot is well seasoned, no extra fat is usually necessary. In fact, if the ground meat is at all fat, then it's best to brown it first and pour off any excess. Leave out the evaporated milk, if you prefer, or pour in some red wine instead. And add any leftover vegetables that happen to be around.

1 pound ground beef
1 cup chopped onions
1½ cups pared diced potatoes
½ cup thinly sliced celery
½ cup diced carrots

1 1-pound can tomatoes
1½ cups water
2 teaspoons seasoned salt
½ cup undiluted evaporated milk
Black pepper, fresh ground, to taste

Brown ground beef in a heavy kettle or Dutch oven. Use a small amount of oil or butter if meat is very lean; if it is fat, brown it and pour off excess fat. Add onions and cook until lightly brown. Add potatoes, celery, carrots, tomatoes, and water. Season with salt and simmer 30 to 40 minutes, or until vegetables are tender. Just before serving, stir in evaporated milk and add fresh ground black pepper to taste. Makes about 6 servings. Hot corn bread, bread sticks, or crisp toast are all good with this chowder.

Washington Chowder

This hearty delicious chowder originated during World War II when meat rationing made menu planning difficult. Salt pork, which gives it its distinctive meat flavor, wasn't so hard to come by. My friend who created this recipe named it *Washington Chowder* in recognition of all the directives about food which came from the various Washington, D.C. agencies.

4 to 6 ounces salt pork	*¼ teaspoon black pepper*
1 medium-size onion, chopped	*¼ teaspoon marjoram or sweet basil*
3 cups hot water	*1 12-ounce can whole kernel corn or*
1 1-pound can tomatoes	* 1 10-ounce package frozen corn*
2 or 3 potatoes, pared and diced	*1 tablespoon fat from salt pork*
2 teaspoons seasoned salt	*1 tablespoon flour*
2 teaspoons salt	*1 small can evaporated milk*

Cut the salt pork into small pieces. Fry it in a heavy kettle until pieces are crisp and brown. Lift out, drain on paper towels and set aside. Pour off all but about 1 or 2 tablespoons of remaining salt pork fat; reserve 1 tablespoon for thickening. Add chopped onion to fat in kettle and cook until onion is lightly browned. Add hot water, tomatoes, diced potatoes, seasoned salt, plain salt, and pepper. Crush marjoram or sweet basil and add to soup. Simmer about 30 minutes, or until potatoes are tender. Add corn and cook about 10 minutes. Rub together 1 tablespoon of reserved salt pork fat with 1 tablespoon flour and stir into soup. Stir until soup comes to a boil and is slightly thickened. Add undiluted evaporated milk. When soup is simmering, ladle out into soup plates and serve very hot. Makes 4 to 6 hearty servings.

Mainly Beans and Other Vegetables

~~~

Aunt Sarah's Lima Bean Goulash

Aunt Sarah was married to one of the early day Mormon Driggses who made the trek west to Utah. For awhile she and her husband lived in California, but then returned to Utah where he died when he was 38 years old. She lived to be a very old lady—known to all the family and friends, as were most Mormon women, as "Aunt." Early versions of this goulash were probably made with dry red or white beans; but as years have gone by, Utah and Idaho have become "bean" country, and all kinds grow there now.

2 cups dry lima beans
Water to cover, about 1 quart
1 pound pork sausage
1 large onion
1 can (1 pound 12 ounces) tomatoes
¼ teaspoon black pepper

1 small hot dry red chili
1 teaspoon ground cumin or chili powder
¼ teaspoon Tabasco
1 tablespoon Worcestershire sauce
2 teaspoons salt

Soak lima beans in water overnight. In a large kettle brown pork sausage and pour off excess fat. Peel and chop onion, add to sausage and cook until onion is golden. Add soaked beans and their water, tomatoes, and pepper. Crush dry chili and add with ground cumin, Tabasco, Worcestershire sauce, and salt. Simmer goulash slowly 1½ to 2 hours, or until beans are done. Serve in soup plates or bowls accompanied by *Mormon Johnnycake* or other corn bread. Makes 6 to 8 servings. Very good reheated, too.

Lima Bean and Mushroom Chowder

An easy-to-make luncheon or supper soup with a delicious herb flavor.

3 or 4 slices of bacon
½ cup chopped onion
1 quart chicken stock
¼ teaspoon sweet basil
¼ teaspoon oregano
1 cup diced carrots
1 cup diced potatoes
1 cup sliced fresh mushrooms
  or 1 4-ounce can sliced mushrooms

1 10-ounce package frozen lima beans
⅛ teaspoon garlic powder
  or ½ clove garlic
½ to 1 teaspoon salt
¼ teaspoon black pepper
2 cups half and half
½ teaspoon dill weed

Cut bacon into 1-inch pieces and fry it in a heavy kettle until crisp. Lift out bacon pieces, drain, and reserve until chowder is ready to serve. Drain off all but 1 tablespoon of bacon drippings. Add chopped onion and cook in drippings until lightly browned. Add chicken stock. Crush sweet basil and oregano and stir into soup. Add carrots, potatoes, mushrooms (if using canned mushrooms, add liquid too), lima beans, and garlic powder. Or crush fresh garlic and add to soup. Stir in ½ teaspoon salt and the pepper. Simmer until vegetables are tender, about 30 minutes. Just before serving, add half and half. If needed, add remaining salt. Heat to simmering, but do not boil. Sprinkle bacon pieces and dill weed over chowder. Ladle into soup bowls and serve with crisp crackers, hot French bread or muffins. Makes 6 servings.

Fava alla Paesana

Peasant Bean Soup

This hearty Italian-style bean pot goes well with a plate of antipasto and Italian or French bread.

1 pound large dry lima beans
4 cups water
2 cups beef or ham stock
1½ teaspoons salt
½ cup chopped onion
1 clove garlic, crushed

¼ cup chopped green pepper
¼ cup chopped celery
1 8-ounce can tomato sauce
2 teaspoons spaghetti sauce mix
Grated Parmesan or Romano cheese

Wash and pick over lima beans. Place them in a large kettle and add water. Soak overnight. Or bring to a boil and boil hard 5 minutes, turn off heat and let soak for 1 hour. Add beef or ham stock, salt, chopped onion, crushed garlic, chopped green pepper and celery, tomato sauce, and spaghetti sauce mix. Cook soup slowly for about 1½ hours, or until beans are tender. Ladle into soup bowls or plates and sprinkle with grated cheese. Makes 6 to 8 servings.

Julia's Autumn Vegetable Chowder

Many years ago Julia was head of the Home Economics Department of a large food chain. This hearty whole-meal soup was one of her favorites.

1 cup large dry lima beans	1 cup fine egg noodles
3 quarts water	¼ cup chopped green pepper
4 teaspoons salt	2 cups shredded cabbage
½ cup barley	4 or 5 slices bacon
1 clove garlic	¼ teaspoon black pepper
½ teaspoon oregano	Grated Cheddar or Parmesan cheese
½ pound fresh green beans	Chopped parsley

Combine lima beans and water in a large kettle. Bring to a boil and add salt and barley. Turn heat down to simmer. Crush or chop garlic and add to beans along with oregano. Simmer until beans and barley are done, 2 or 3 hours. Cut fresh green beans into ½-inch lengths and add to soup. Simmer about 20 minutes, then add egg noodles, chopped green pepper, and shredded cabbage. Fry bacon slices until crisp, crumble and stir into soup along with the drippings. Add the pepper. Ladle into soup plates or bowls and sprinkle with cheese and chopped parsley. Toasted French bread or crisp whole-wheat toast makes an excellent accompaniment. Makes 8 servings.

Lily's Bean Soup

Thirty-five years ago Lily was the cook at a sorority house at one of the border-state universities—so her cooking was partly northern and partly southern-style. Her bean soup, with tuna and egg-salad sandwiches, was Friday fare. She used celery salt and a good dash of Worcestershire instead of today's popular all-purpose seasoned salt and smoked salt.

1 *cup dry navy or pea beans*	¼ *cup diced carrots*
1 *quart warm water*	½ *cup chopped celery*
2 *teaspoons seasoned salt*	¼ *teaspoon summer savory*
1 *small clove garlic, chopped*	2 *cups cooked or canned tomatoes*
2 *tablespoons chopped onion*	2 *cups rich milk or undiluted evapo-*
1-*inch piece bay leaf*	*rated milk*
¼ *teaspoon black pepper*	*Smoked salt*

Wash and pick over beans. Combine with water in a large kettle and simmer gently for 1 hour. Add seasoned salt, garlic, onion, bay leaf, pepper, carrots, and celery. Crush savory and add to soup along with tomatoes. Cook soup until beans are tender. Mash with a potato masher or put beans through a food mill. Add milk and heat just to simmering. Season to taste with smoked salt or additional seasoned salt. Makes 6 to 8 servings.

Creole Red Bean Soup

Hearty enough for a main course for lunch or supper—another delicious soup from a collection of Creole recipes.

½ *pound dry red kidney beans*	1 *teaspoon Worcestershire sauce*
2 *quarts water*	1 *cup finely chopped baked or boiled*
2 *tablespoons butter*	*ham*
½ *cup chopped onion*	2 *teaspoons salt*
½ *cup chopped celery*	¼ *teaspoon black pepper*
2 *cloves garlic*	½ *cup claret wine*
1-*inch piece bay leaf*	2 *hard-cooked eggs, chopped*
¼ *teaspoon thyme*	*Lemon slices*

Wash beans and cover with water. Bring to a boil and let boil for 5 minutes. Turn off heat and let soak 1 hour. Meanwhile, melt butter in a frying pan. Add onion and celery and cook over low heat until soft but not brown. Crush garlic and add to onion and celery. Add to beans and simmer for about 2 hours, or until beans are done. Meanwhile, crush thyme and add to beans along with bay leaf and Worcestershire sauce. When beans are tender, mash or force a part of the beans through a food mill or wire sieve. Combine the puréed beans with the cooked beans and liquid. Add chopped ham and salt and pepper. When ready to serve, heat to boiling. Spoon a tablespoon of claret into each hot soup bowl. Pour in soup and garnish with chopped egg and a lemon slice. Makes 6 servings.

Grandmother Isola's Minestrone Soup

Every Italian family has its own recipe for *Minestrone*. And this one is the family recipe of my little granddaughter's Italian great-grandmother; *her* grandmother taught her to make it. Grandmother Isola sends home a jar with each member of the family and puts some away in the freezer. Quite a project to make, so it's good to end up with such a quantity.

The interesting sauce called *pesto* can now be purchased in cans, or you can make your own. Although most Italians insist that only fresh basil should be used, I make a very close facsimile with the dry herb.

I live where it's easy to buy Italian food products—Italian beans, curly green cabbage, *rigatoni* (a special shape of pasta), and Parmigiano by the piece that you grate yourself—and even, in some markets, fresh basil. But you can use red or white dry kidney beans or dry pink beans instead of the Italian beans; regular cabbage or Napa or Chinese cabbage; any large-size macaroni, and the usual packaged grated Parmesan cheese.

1 pound dry Italian beans	½ head curly green cabbage (about 1 pound)
3 quarts water	
½-pound piece salt pork	2 tablespoons pesto or to taste
4 tablespoons olive oil	2 cups rigatoni or other large macaroni
1 tablespoon salt	
¼ teaspoon pepper	Freshly grated Parmigiano cheese or grated Parmesan or Romano cheese
4 large potatoes (about 1½ pounds)	
4 carrots (about 1 pound)	
6 stalks celery	

Soak the beans in water to cover overnight. Next morning pour 3 quarts water into a very large kettle and bring to a boil. Chop the salt pork into small pieces and drop into the boiling water. Add olive oil, salt, and pepper. Drain the soaked beans and add to soup. Turn heat down so soup just simmers. While soup is simmering, pare potatoes and grate on a large or coarse grater. Scrape carrots and grate. Cut celery stalks in half lengthwise and then slice them very thin. Add the vegetables to soup and continue to simmer. Chop the cabbage into small pieces and add to soup. Continue to simmer, about 3 hours altogether. Half an hour before time to serve, stir in the *pesto*. Add the *rigatoni* or other macaroni and cook until it is just tender, not too soft. Ladle into soup plates. Pass the grated cheese to sprinkle over soup. Makes 16 to 20 servings.

TO MAKE PESTO:

Combine in an electric blender ½ cup olive oil, ¼ cup grated Parmigiano or Parmesan cheese, 1 tablespoon soft butter, 3 cloves garlic, crushed or chopped, ¼ cup coarsely chopped fresh basil (or ¼ cup coarsely chopped parsley and 1 tablespoon dry basil), ¼ teaspoon salt and a dash of pepper. Blend sauce until it is smooth. This is good, too, tossed with fresh-cooked spaghetti.

Saints' Soup

Because genealogy is an important part of the Mormon religion, we have become acquainted with and are very friendly with many of one branch of the Driggs' family and know about their early struggles in settling the West. These rugged pioneers—the men were all called "saints"—often had a hearty soup such as this as their entire meal. Admittedly, the celery is a slightly modern touch—although it didn't take long before these hardworking people were raising all kinds of fruits and vegetables.

1 pound green split peas	¼ teaspoon thyme
3 quarts water	1 pound pork sausage meat
2 teaspoons salt	1 large potato
½ teaspoon black pepper	1 large onion
¼ teaspoon sage	1 cup thinly sliced celery

Combine the split peas and water in a large kettle. Bring peas to a boil and turn down to simmer. Add salt, pepper, sage, and thyme, and simmer gently for 1 hour. Form the sausage meat into small balls and drop them into the soup. Simmer for another hour. Pare and dice potato; peel and dice onion. Add to the soup along with sliced celery. Simmer for 30 minutes. Ladle into soup bowls or plates and serve with warm fresh-baked bread. Makes about 12 servings.

Mountain Dew Chowder

A sophisticated friend who liked to cook got this recipe from his bootlegger. He always poured in a good slug of bootleg corn whiskey, and I agreed that it did give this very filling soup a lively flavor. These days when I make it, I use bourbon.

¼ *pound piece of bacon*
1 *large onion*
6 *ears fresh corn*
3 *or 4 new potatoes*
4 *cups water*

1 *teaspoon salt*
⅛ *teaspoon black pepper*
¼ *teaspoon sugar*
2 *cups half and half*
½ *cup bourbon whiskey*

Cut the bacon into ½-inch cubes, and fry them until brown in a large kettle. Peel and slice the onion; add to bacon and bacon fat and cook until lightly browned. Meanwhile, cut corn from ears, and scrape new potatoes and cut into 1-inch cubes. When the onion is brown, add corn and potatoes. Brown lightly. Add water, salt, pepper, and sugar. Simmer the soup for about 30 minutes, or until the corn and potatoes are tender. Just before serving, add the half and half and bring just to simmering. Stir in the whiskey and serve at once, accompanied by crisp saltines. Makes 6 generous servings.

Cream of Corn Soup—Hong Kong Style

Quite different from most Chinese or Oriental soups, this one is more of a whole-meal soup than the usual cream soup. It's good for a supper or luncheon along with bread sticks and a salad.

1 *quart well-seasoned chicken stock*
2 *thin slices fresh ginger, finely*
  chopped, or 2 thin slices dry ginger,
  soaked in cold water and chopped
1 *1-pound can cream-style corn*
¼ *cup milk*

1 *teaspoon MSG*
1 *cup cooked or canned crabmeat*
2 *egg whites*
¼ *teaspoon salt*
1 *tablespoon rice wine or sherry*

Combine the chicken stock and chopped ginger in a kettle. Simmer for 10 to 15 minutes. Add cream-style corn, milk, MSG and crabmeat, and continue to simmer the soup. Meanwhile, beat the egg whites and salt just until whites are in very soft peaks. Fold them into hot soup. Stir in the wine and ladle into soup bowls or plates. Makes about 4 servings.

Grandma White's Potato and Onion Soup

This recipe for a hearty potato soup is a hundred years old. With plenty of bacon it makes a whole-meal soup along with a salad.

¼ to ½ pound thick-sliced or chunk
  bacon
4 or 5 medium-size potatoes (about
  1½ pounds)
4 large onions (about 1½ pounds)
2 teaspoons salt

¼ teaspoon black pepper
1½ cups water
1 egg
1 cup flour
1½ cups rich milk

Cut slices of bacon into 2 or 3 pieces each or slice chunk bacon into thick slices. Brown the bacon in a Dutch oven or top-of-stove casserole, and drain on paper towels. Pare and slice potatoes and onions. Pour off part of the bacon fat, if desired, but leave at least 3 or 4 tablespoons in the Dutch oven. Arrange slices of potato and onion in the pot in alternate layers with one layer of bacon in the center. Reserve some bacon for top. Sprinkle the layers with salt and pepper, using 1 teaspoon of salt. Pour water carefully into the Dutch oven. Cover and simmer until potatoes and onion are tender, about 30 to 40 minutes. Meanwhile, beat the egg slightly and mix in flour and remaining 1 teaspoon salt. Blend until the mixture is crumbly. Add milk carefully to potatoes and onions and arrange remaining bacon slices on top. Sprinkle with the egg and flour mixture. Cover and simmer about 20 minutes more. Uncover and place in a moderately hot oven, 400°F., for 10 to 15 minutes, or until the top is lightly browned. Spoon into soup plates or bowls with some of the crusty topping and bacon slices in each serving. Makes 6 servings.

Pennsylvania Dutch Kale Soup

Depending on the amount of meat left on the bone or how many ham hocks you use, this can be a whole-meal or an opening-course soup. Home-made bread, white or whole wheat, makes a good accompaniment. This is a prize recipe of a friend who is a home economist.

1 ham bone from baked ham
  or 1- to 1½-pound end of ham
  or 2 or 3 ham hocks
2 quarts water
1 large onion, chopped

4 medium-size potatoes
2 to 3 cups coarsely chopped kale
2 tablespoons chopped parsley
Salt to taste
⅛ teaspoon pepper

Place ham bone in a large kettle and add water. Add chopped onion and simmer slowly until the meat falls from the bone, about 1½ to 2 hours. Lift out bigger pieces and cut into ½-inch cubes. Remove excess fat and ham bone. Pare potatoes, dice, and add to soup. Simmer about 20 minutes.

Cut the kale from heavy stalks and chop it coarsely. Pack tightly into cup to measure. Add kale and ham cubes and heat until soup simmers again. Sprinkle with parsley. Add salt to taste—the amount will depend on saltiness of ham—and pepper. Ladle into soup plates or bowls. Makes 6 servings.

Ash Anar
Pomegranate Soup

This soup originates in Iran, formerly Persia. The original used the unstrained seeds, but most Americans like better to make juice from the seeds and use only the juice. Or you can buy pomegranate juice at health food stores. An unusual flavor but unusually good—the amount of sugar will depend on the tartness of the pomegranate juice. Lamb is more typical for the meatballs.

1 pomegranate and 1½ cups water or
* 1½ cups pomegranate juice*
6 cups beef or chicken stock
1 teaspoon salt
Meatballs (recipe below)
½ cup rice
1 cup chopped fresh spinach

½ cup thinly sliced green onions
½ cup chopped parsley
1 to 2 tablespoons sugar
1 tablespoon lime juice
1 tablespoon dried mint
¼ teaspoon ground cinnamon
¼ teaspoon black pepper

Break open the pomegranate. Take out the seeds and juice and combine with the water. Simmer about 15 minutes, or until the seeds lose their color. Strain through a wire sieve, pressing seeds to extract all of the juice. Or use bottled juice. Combine the pomegranate juice with beef or chicken stock. Make the meatballs. Add salt, meatballs, and rice to the soup and simmer about 15 minutes. Add spinach, green onions, and parsley and simmer another 15 or 20 minutes. Add sugar to taste and lime juice. Ladle into soup bowls. Combine the dried mint, cinnamon, and pepper and sprinkle over soup. Toasted English muffins are good with this, or bread sticks. Makes 4 or 5 servings.

TO MAKE MEATBALLS:

½ pound ground lamb or beef (prefer-
* ably lamb)*
¼ cup finely chopped onion
¼ teaspoon cinnamon

¼ teaspoon black pepper
¼ teaspoon salt
Combine the ingredients well and
* shape into balls the size of walnuts.*

Eggs Poached in Soup

~~~

Eggs poached in soup are in the cuisine of countries the world over. There are innumerable versions of this simple, nourishing meal. In different regions of the same country the soup in which the eggs are poached will vary. Eggs are often poached first and then added to the soup. A book of French provincial cooking will have four or five variations of poached eggs and soup.

Whatever kind of soup strikes your fancy, try one with poached eggs for a simple supper or lunch. And for a real quickie, just poach eggs in a favorite canned soup—chicken noodle, onion, vegetable beef, or bouillon or consommé. The safest technique is to break the eggs onto a dish and slide them carefully into the simmering soup, one at a time.

Consommé Colbert
Poached Eggs in Consommé with Spring Vegetables

A classic French soup made by poaching eggs in *consommé printanier* or consommé with spring vegetables. It's a favorite luncheon dish for me—easy to make and not too high in calories.

2½ cups consommé or 1 10½-ounce
  can condensed consommé combined
  with 1 can water
¼ cup thinly sliced fresh green beans
¼ cup shredded carrot
2 tablespoons shredded turnip

2 tablespoons fresh or
  frozen green peas
Salt to taste
½ teaspoon chervil
4 eggs

Heat the consommé to boiling in a saucepan. Add sliced green beans, shredded carrot and turnip, and fresh or frozen peas. Simmer about 10 minutes; the vegetables should be just crisp-tender. Add salt to taste and chervil. Break the eggs carefully into the simmering soup and poach them until done as desired. Or poach the eggs in an egg poacher, slip one into each soup bowl, and pour consommé and vegetables over them. Serve with toasted French bread or crisp Melba toast. Makes 4 servings.

Soupe de la Grande Plaine
Poached Eggs in Tomato Soup

France has its great plain country, where wheat is raised. From the area of Beauce, *"le grenier de la France"* (the granary of France), comes this delicious soup enriched by the addition of poached eggs.

¼ cup butter, sweet or unsalted, if available	1-inch piece bay leaf
	3 or 4 cloves
3 large onions, thinly sliced (3 to 4 cups)	3 or 4 peppercorns
	1 1-pound can tomatoes
1 clove garlic	Salt to taste
1 quart beef stock	4 to 6 eggs
⅛ teaspoon thyme	Chopped chives
1 tablespoon chopped parsley	Shredded Gruyère cheese

Melt the butter in a kettle. Add thinly sliced onions to melted butter. Crush the garlic and add to onions; cook over low heat, stirring frequently, until onions are soft and slightly yellowed. Add beef stock. Crush thyme and add to soup along with parsley, bay leaf, cloves, and peppercorns. Let the soup simmer. Meanwhile, force tomatoes through a sieve or food mill and add the tomato purée to the soup. Continue to simmer for about 30 to 40 minutes. Add additional salt, if needed. Poach the eggs in the soup. Lift them out into soup plates or bowls; pour soup over the eggs and sprinkle with chopped chives and shredded cheese. Serve along with toasted French bread. Makes 4 to 6 servings.

Soupe Aigo, Provençale
Mediterranean Soup

One of the best of the French soups with poached eggs is from the Mediterranean, with the same seasonings as *bouillabaisse*. It is especially delicious if a piece of fish is poached in it before the eggs are added and

then served with them. Or if there is any soup left over, poach a piece of fish in it.

1 medium-size onion	2 quarts water
3 leeks	1 tablespoon salt
¼ cup olive oil	¼ teaspoon white pepper
2 tomatoes	Pinch of saffron
4 cloves garlic	4 medium-size potatoes
⅛ teaspoon fennel seeds	4 to 6 eggs
½ teaspoon grated orange peel	Chopped parsley
¼ teaspoon thyme	Toasted French bread
¼ teaspoon oregano	

Slice the onion. Clean and slice leeks, using some of the green part. Pour olive oil into a large kettle, add onions and leeks, and cook until yellow but not brown. Peel, seed, and chop the tomatoes; add to onions and leeks. Crush garlic, fennel seeds, thyme, and oregano and add along with the orange peel. Add water, salt, pepper, and saffron. Boil the soup hard for 15 minutes. Pare potatoes and cut into chunks. Cook in soup until tender. Poach the eggs in the soup. Lift the eggs and potatoes out onto a serving platter. Sprinkle with parsley. Pour the soup into cups or bowls. Serve the soup and eggs and potatoes with toasted bread. Makes 4 to 6 servings.

Zuppa alla Pavese
Eggs in Consommé Pavia

This simple Italian version of poached eggs in soup makes a wonderful quick luncheon or supper dish, nourishing and easy to digest. Use canned chicken or beef stock or make the stock from bouillon cubes. Pavia is a town in the Lombardy section of Italy.

4 cups chicken or beef stock	4 slices toasted or sautéed French or
¼ teaspoon Italian herbs or sweet basil	Italian bread
4 eggs (or more, if desired)	Grated Parmesan or Romano cheese

In a deep frying pan or saucepan heat the stock to boiling. Crush herbs and add to stock. Break the eggs and slide carefully, one at a time, into stock. Turn heat down to simmering. Cook until the eggs are just set. Sauté the bread on both sides in butter. Arrange bread in soup plates. Lift out eggs onto bread. Pour hot soup over eggs and sprinkle with cheese.

Or pour the soup over each egg in a soup bowl, sprinkle the sautéed bread with the Parmesan cheese, and float the slices in the soup. Serve at once. Makes 4 servings.

Sopa Hueva Escalfado
Eggs in Soup Escalfado

In Spain, eggs are poached in soup made with garlic-flavored chicken stock and finely chopped ham.

¼ cup olive oil	1 teaspoon paprika
1 cup fresh bread crumbs	4 cups chicken stock
½ cup finely chopped or ground ham	Salt and pepper to taste
2 cloves garlic	4 to 6 eggs
2 tablespoons finely chopped onion	

Heat olive oil in a saucepan and add bread crumbs and ham. Crush the garlic and stir it and the chopped onion into the crumb mixture. Cook until onion is soft. Add paprika and stock. Simmer the soup about 15 minutes, or until onions are tender. Add salt and pepper to taste. Break eggs into soup. Poach the eggs over low heat until they are set. Lift eggs out into individual casseroles or soup bowls. Pour soup over eggs. Serve with crisp bread sticks. Makes 4 to 6 servings.

Portuguese Egg Soup

The Portuguese who emigrated to Hawaii make this soup; no doubt in Portugal there is a similar version.

2 tablespoons olive oil	1 teaspoon celery salt
1 cup chopped onions	¼ teaspoon thyme
1 clove garlic	¼ teaspoon black pepper
1 quart beef stock	4 eggs
1 tablespoon seasoned salt	4 slices French bread

Heat olive oil in a kettle or saucepan; add onions and cook over low heat until onions are yellow but not brown. Crush the garlic and add to onions, then add beef stock. Bring the soup to simmering and add seasoned salt and celery salt. Crush the thyme and add to soup along with pepper. Simmer the soup for 20 to 30 minutes. Break the eggs, one at a time, and slip into soup. Poach eggs in soup. Meanwhile, cut French bread

into cubes and dry them in the oven. When ready to serve, divide dry bread cubes among soup bowls. Ladle soup over bread and add a poached egg to each bowl. Serve at once. Makes 4 servings.

Papa Lorenzo's Red Onion Soup

In Caracas, Venezuela, Papa Lorenzo liked to have this soup for a late supper. Mama and the children liked it, too.

⅓ cup olive oil

2 cups sliced red onions (2 or 3 large onions)

1 clove garlic, finely chopped or crushed

4 to 6 slices French bread

4 cups hot well-seasoned beef stock

4 to 6 eggs

Chopped parsley and mint

In a top-of-stove casserole heat the olive oil. Add onions and crushed garlic and cook until onions are soft. Push the onions to one side and fry the bread in the oil on both sides. Keep bread warm in oven. Add the stock to onions, and simmer soup until onions are tender. Break eggs into soup and simmer just until eggs are set. Ladle soup into individual bowls. Float a slice of fried bread on the soup, and place the eggs on top of the bread. Sprinkle with chopped mint and parsley. Makes 4 to 6 servings.

Spenatsoppa
Swedish Spinach Soup

The Swedish poach eggs in a cream of spinach soup. They are likely to poach the eggs and then add them, but it's equally good to poach the eggs right in the soup.

1 bunch fresh spinach (¾ to 1 pound) or 1 12-ounce package frozen chopped spinach

4 tablespoons butter

2 or 3 tablespoons flour

2 cups veal or chicken stock

2 cups milk

½ teaspoon salt or to taste

Dash of quatre épice or Spice Parisienne or ⅛ teaspoon nutmeg

4 to 6 poached eggs

Wash spinach thoroughly and cook it in only the water clinging to leaves. Chop the cooked spinach thoroughly. Or steam frozen chopped spinach until completely thawed and heated through. Do not overcook spinach. Melt butter in a saucepan and stir in the flour. (If you like a thicker soup, use the larger amount of flour.) Slowly stir in the veal or chicken stock and cook, stirring constantly, until soup has thickened and is smooth and bubbling hot. Mix in the milk and cooked spinach. Season with salt and spice. Pour into soup plates and add a poached egg to each serving. Or poach eggs in soup, if desired. Lift out eggs into soup plates and pour soup over eggs. Serve with Swedish rye bread or crisp rye wafers. Makes 4 to 6 servings.

Kørvelsuppe
Danish Chervil Soup

In Denmark poached eggs are served in *Chervil Soup*. It is usually made with veal stock but it can be made with chicken stock, using bouillon cubes.

2 carrots (about 1½ cups, sliced)	3 tablespoons flour
6 cups veal stock	2 tablespoons chervil
3 tablespoons butter or margarine	4 to 6 poached eggs

Scrape the carrots and slice thinly. Simmer them in veal stock until tender. Melt butter or margarine in a saucepan and stir in flour. Add stock and carrots, stirring constantly until well blended. Simmer about 15 minutes. Just before serving stir in chervil. Poach eggs and place one or two eggs in each soup plate. Ladle soup over eggs. Serve with sourdough or rye bread. Makes 4 to 6 servings.

Poached Egg Potato Soup

The western pioneers often had to make a meal out of meager supplies. Potatoes, milk, and eggs made a simple nourishing supper. The addition of vinegar makes this soup similar to the traditional sour milk soups with eggs from Czechoslovakia, the national background of many of the pioneers.

2 medium-size potatoes	1 teaspoon sugar
3 cups water	1 cup rich milk or half and half
1 teaspoon salt	1 tablespoon flour
2 to 4 eggs	⅛ teaspoon black pepper
2 tablespoons vinegar	

Pare potatoes and cut them into quarters. Place them in a saucepan; add water and salt. Simmer potatoes until tender. Lift out potatoes and keep them in a warm place. Poach the eggs in the simmering potato water; lift them out and keep warm with potatoes. Combine vinegar, sugar, milk, and flour and blend until smooth. Pour mixture into potato water and cook, stirring constantly, until soup comes just to simmering and is slightly thickened. Ladle into soup bowls and add eggs and potatoes. Sprinkle with pepper. Makes 2 servings. The pioneers accompanied this with fresh-baked bread. Toast is good, too.

Chinese Chicken Soup with Poached Eggs

Almost everyone is familiar with Chinese egg drop soup where eggs are beaten slightly, then stirred into hot soup. But Chinese cooks poach eggs in soup, too. Use spinach if Chinese greens are not available.

½ uncooked chicken breast
2 to 3 tablespoons soy sauce
1 tablespoon peanut oil
4 cups chicken stock
½ cup thinly sliced celery
4 water chestnuts, thinly sliced,
*   or 4 large mushrooms, thinly sliced,*
*   or both*

2 tablespoons thinly sliced green onion
½ cup shredded Chinese mustard
*   greens or Chinese cabbage*
1 teaspoon cornstarch
4 to 6 eggs

Cut chicken from breast into thin slices. There should be about ½ cup slices along with the bits and pieces. Marinate the chicken for a half hour or so in 1 tablespoon soy sauce. Heat the peanut oil in a kettle. Add the chicken and cook over medium-high heat about 15 to 20 minutes, or until almost done. Add chicken stock, any soy sauce left from marinating chicken and an additional 1 to 2 tablespoons, or to taste. Bring soup to a boil; add sliced celery, sliced water chestnuts or mushrooms or both, and green onions. Turn down heat and simmer 15 to 20 minutes, or until chicken is done and vegetables tender but still crisp. Add mustard greens or cabbage. Blend cornstarch with a little cold water and stir into soup. When soup begins to bubble, break the eggs into soup. Turn off heat and let stand about 5 minutes, or until eggs are cooked. Lift them out into soup bowls and ladle soup over them. Serve bowls of steamed rice along with soup. Makes 4 to 6 servings.

Chawanmushi
Japanese Egg Custard Soup

This Japanese egg custard soup is considered to be a favorite of women and children. My friend Pearl Kimura says she serves it as a luncheon dish accompanied by a salad. At our house we think it's good for supper, but I agree, it would make a delicious entrée for a bridge luncheon along with a fruit salad and rice crackers. In Japan you would make this in cups or bowls with lids and steam in a special steamer. I use individual casseroles with lids and then put the casseroles in my electric frying pan, add water, cover, and steam.

4 whole dried mushrooms or 4 large halves of mushrooms (shiitake)
¼ cup cold water
2 cups cold Dashi (*Japanese clear soup, see recipe*) *or chicken or fish stock*
4 eggs
1 tablespoon mirin or sake, or sherry
½ teaspoon MSG
1 teaspoon soy sauce

Salt to taste
½ uncooked chicken breast, about ¼ pound
4 small pieces white fish or 4 small slices fish cake (kamaboko)
4 small uncooked shrimp
12 small slices bamboo shoot (take-noko)
4 green beans or pieces of spinach, or snow peas

Soak dried mushrooms in cold water for about a half hour. Place a mushroom in each of 4 individual casseroles with lids. Combine the water in which mushrooms were soaked with cold *Dashi* or soup stock. Beat in the eggs with a wire whip. Add wine, MSG, soy sauce, and salt to taste. (The amount of salt will depend on the saltiness of the stock.) Cut chicken breast from bone and cut into 4 pieces. Place a piece of chicken in each casserole along with a piece of fish or slice of fish cake. Shell shrimp and place one in each casserole. Add 3 slices of bamboo shoot to each casserole. Strain the custard through a wire sieve into the casseroles and cover them. Place in a flat-bottom kettle or electric frying pan. Pour in hot water until about an inch deep. Cover the pan and steam over medium heat for about 25 minutes. Meanwhile, cut each string bean into 3 pieces and simmer briefly in lightly salted water. About 10 minutes before serving time, remove cover of pan and of casseroles and arrange beans on the custard. Or if using spinach or snow peas as garnish, dip in boiling water to soften slightly and arrange on custard. Cover casseroles and pan again and continue to steam until done. *Chawanmushi* should be eaten with a soup spoon; use chopsticks for the pieces of chicken, fish, and vegetables, if desired. Makes 4 servings.

Dashi with Egg
Japanese Clear Soup with Egg

Serve the very clear *Dashi* with a poached egg for a light luncheon or supper dish. Or it makes an attractive opening course for a salad meal. In Japan it might be served at breakfast.

3 *cups clear well-seasoned* Dashi (*see*   4 *poached eggs*
   recipe)   *Thinly sliced green onion*

Heat *Dashi* to simmering. Pour into 4 soup cups. To each cup add a poached egg. The eggs should be poached separately, either in an egg poacher or in hot water, so that the clear *Dashi* will not be clouded. Sprinkle soup with sliced green onion. Makes 4 servings.

Miso Shiru with Egg

For a late supper dish we like an egg poached in *Miso Shiru*, the very nourishing Japanese soup made with bean paste. Since *Miso* keeps a long time in the refrigerator and I have packaged ingredients for *Dashi*, it's no trouble to make. Instead of the usual *Tofu* or bean curd, which doesn't keep well, you can add mushrooms or a few frozen shrimp, or snow peas, or sliced water chestnuts.

3 *or 4 cups* Dashi (*see recipe*) *or*   ½ *cup* Miso *or bean paste* (*see recipe*)
  other fish stock   *Soy sauce to taste*
2 *or 3 large mushrooms, sliced,*   3 *or 4 eggs*
  or 6 or 8 small shrimp or 6 or 8 snow   *Thinly sliced green onion*
  peas or other desired vegetables

Heat the *Dashi* to simmering and stir in *Miso* or bean paste. Add mushrooms, cleaned shrimp, snow peas, or sliced water chestnuts or a combination of any of these. Simmer until these are done. Add soy sauce to taste. Break eggs carefully into soup and continue to simmer very gently until eggs are done. Lift eggs out into soup plates or bowls and pour soup over eggs. Sprinkle with sliced green onion. Serve at once. Makes 3 or 4 servings.

Part III

STEWS AND
BOILED DINNERS

Mainly Poultry—
Chicken, Turkey, Duck

WHAT MAKES THE DIFFERENCE between a whole-meal soup or chowder and a stew? Not much, we must admit, and sometimes it's hard to decide just which is which. Generally speaking, you eat a soup or chowder with a spoon and a stew with a fork, sometimes with the help of a spoon and sometimes with the help of a knife.

A perfect stew depends even more on skill, good taste, and luck than does the preparation of a first-class steak or roast. Each part of the world and each section of our own country has its favorite stews. Usually a particular stew comes about because certain kinds of meats, fish, or fowl and certain kinds of vegetables and grains flourish in that particular region. The seasonings and accompaniments are important, too, and vary from one part of the world to another.

The same can be said of boiled dinners. Of course, none should really be *boiled*. All are best when gently simmered so that most of the flavor is left in the various components. The accompanying broth is meant to be sipped or drunk more as an appetizer than eaten as a soup.

Poule-au-Pot
"Chicken-in-the-Pot": Boiled Chicken with Vegetables

Henry IV of France, who lived in the late 16th and early 17th centuries and was known as The Tolerant, hoped, as did Herbert Hoover much later, that every family could have a chicken in their cooking pot whenever they so desired. *Poule-au-Pot* was his favorite meal, as it is with many French families today. A good French friend has passed on *her* family's version of this classic favorite. She tells me she doesn't always stuff her chicken. If you choose to make the stuffing, you will have an even more complete meal.

1 5-pound stewing chicken	*2 sprigs parsley*
3 quarts water	*½ bay leaf*
1 veal knuckle, if desired	*1 clove garlic, peeled and sliced*
1 tablespoon salt	*2 large or 4 small leeks*
4 or 5 black peppercorns	*6 or 8 small boiling onions*
1 stalk celery with leaves	*2 large or 4 small carrots*

Cut off the wing tips and neck of the chicken and combine in a very large kettle with the gizzard and heart, and add water. Add the veal knuckle, salt, and peppercorns. Tie the celery stalk, parsley, bay leaf, and garlic clove in cheesecloth or thin muslin and add this *bouquet garni* to the pot. Bring to a boil, skim, and simmer for about an hour.

Meanwhile, make stuffing, if desired, and fill the chicken. Sew up the opening and tie chicken securely. (Even if unstuffed, the chicken needs to be well trussed.) Add the chicken to the stock and simmer slowly until almost tender, about 2 hours. Clean the leeks and cut off most of green tops. Scrape carrots; cut large carrots in two. Peel onions. If desired, tie leeks and carrots with small onions in cheesecloth. This makes it easy to lift them out together, but I don't usually bother. Cover the pot and simmer for another 30 to 40 minutes, or until vegetables are done. While vegetables are simmering make *Velouté Sauce* (below). When vegetables and chicken are done, lift out the *bouquet garni* and discard. Lift out chicken and remove strings. Place the chicken on a large platter, carve, and arrange slices of chicken and vegetables around the chicken. Spoon stuffing out onto a platter. Serve some of the hot bouillon in cups and then follow with chicken, stuffing, vegetables and hot *Velouté Sauce*.

Makes 4 to 6 servings, with some leftover chicken to serve cold or hot and about a quart of extra stock.

TO MAKE STUFFING:

Cut 6 or 8 ounces link sausage into ½-inch pieces. (Very good, if you can get it, is French or Alsatian sausage.) Chop chicken liver and brown the sausage and liver lightly in a small frying pan. Add this to 4 cups of coarse dry bread crumbs, preferably French bread. Mix in ½ teaspoon thyme, 2 tablespoons chopped parsley, ¼ cup finely chopped celery, 1 teaspoon salt, and ¼ teaspoon black pepper. Mix in about ½ cup chicken stock and 1 egg. Stuffing should be fairly dry. Stuff loosely into chicken, then sew and truss.

TO MAKE VELOUTÉ SAUCE:

Melt 4 tablespoons butter in a saucepan and stir in 4 tablespoons flour. When mixture is well blended and bubbling slightly, add 3 cups chicken stock. Cook, stirring constantly, until sauce thickens and comes to a boil. Season to taste with salt and pepper. Spoon sauce over chicken slices and stuffing. Makes 3 cups sauce.

Burgoo

Burgoo is the celebrated stew which helped to make Kentucky famous. It is served on Derby Day, at political rallies, horse sales, picnics, and other outdoor events. It is made in enormous quantities by a Burgoo Master, who is as sought after and respected as the executive chefs of our best hotels or the barbecue chefs who preside over big functions in the Southwest.

When available *Burgoo* includes squirrel, rabbit or other game meat. In the old days, as a good omen for the *Burgoo,* a black minister (whose salary must have been paid) would wave a rabbit's foot at the end of a yarn string over the steaming caldron. Often *Burgoo* was made in quantities of twelve hundred gallons. This included a ton of potatoes.

It's a good dish to have at a supper party for 20 to 25 people. Serve mint juleps first, and hard cider with the *Burgoo.* Old-fashioned wilted lettuce, cracklin' bread, watermelon pickle, and a dessert of Southern pecan pie will make your guests feel as if it really were Derby Day.

1 to 2 pounds each *of pork shank or*
  shoulder, veal, beef, and lamb stew
  meat
4-pound stewing chicken
6 quarts water
3 tablespoons salt
1 bay leaf
1 pound potatoes (3 or 4 medium-
  size)
1 pound onions (3 or 4 medium-size)
3 or 4 carrots
1 cup sliced celery
1 large green pepper, cut in slivers or
  chopped

1 1-pound can tomato purée
1 can tomatoes (1 pound 12 ounces)
2 small hot dry chili peppers
1 1-pound can whole kernel corn
2 cups sliced fresh okra or 1 10-ounce
  package frozen okra
2 cups fresh, frozen, or canned lima
  beans
1½ cups chopped cabbage
1 tablespoon Worcestershire sauce
1 tablespoon A.1. Sauce
¼ teaspoon cayenne pepper
Additional salt to taste
½ cup chopped parsley

Combine meat, chicken, and water in a very large kettle. Season with salt and bay leaf. Simmer until the meat is tender and falls from the bones. Lift it out, cool, and cut all meat from bones. Cut meat into bite-size pieces. Skim off the fat or chill the stock and remove all hardened fat. Return meat and chicken pieces to the stock. Peel potatoes and onions, scrape the carrots, and dice the vegetables. Add to stew along with sliced celery, green pepper slivers, tomato purée, tomatoes, hot peppers, corn, okra, lima beans, and cabbage. Simmer slowly until stew is thick and vegetables are done, 2 to 3 hours. (*Burgoo* should be thick but still soupy.) Season with Worcestershire, A.1. Sauce, cayenne, and additional salt, if needed. Just before serving, sprinkle stew with parsley. Serve in soup plates or bowls. Makes about 25 servings.

Brunswick Stew

Brunswick Stew, somewhat like *Burgoo,* dates from the days of Thomas Jefferson and is in one of his collections of favorites along with recipes for the French food he loved. In those days—and in parts of the South even now—it was traditionally made, at least in part, with squirrel. In many states it is now illegal to hunt these animals—and for non-hunters and for those where squirrel is unavailable, it's easier to make it with chicken or with chicken and domestic rabbit combined.

3-pound stewing chicken and 2- to
  3-pound rabbit or 5- to 6-pound
  stewing chicken or chicken parts

¼ cup bacon drippings
½ cup sliced fresh or frozen okra
1 cup thinly sliced onion

1 *teaspoon sugar*
½ *teaspoon Tabasco*
2 *teaspoons Worcestershire sauce*
1 *quart water*
1 *1-pound can tomatoes*
1 *tablespoon salt*

1½ *cups fresh or frozen lima beans*
  (10-ounce package)
1½ *cups fresh, frozen, or canned corn*
  (12-ounce can whole kernel or
  10-ounce package, frozen)
½ *cup toasted bread crumbs*
½ *cup sherry*

Have chicken and rabbit, if used, cut into convenient size pieces. Remove any excess fat. Heat bacon drippings in a large kettle. Brown the chicken and rabbit pieces until golden and remove. Add okra; cook until lightly brown and no longer sticky. Add sliced onion. When onion is lightly browned, return chicken to kettle and add water, tomatoes, salt, sugar, Tabasco, and Worcestershire sauce. Simmer until the chicken is very tender. Remove chicken and let cool. Remove meat from bones and cut into bite-size pieces. Skim off the excess fat from stew in kettle. (This much of the cooking can be done the day before, and the stew thoroughly chilled so the fat is easy to remove.) Return the chicken pieces to the stew; add lima beans and corn and simmer until vegetables are tender. Just before serving stir in toasted bread crumbs and sherry. Serve with spoon bread, rice, or hot biscuits. Makes 8 generous servings.

Old Kentucky Mulligan

Another of Kentucky's famous stews especially good to serve for a party of a dozen or so. A favorite salad—either fruit or cabbage slaw—and fresh baked bread or corn bread make this a complete meal.

2½- *to 3-pound stewing chicken*
2 *quarts water*
4 *teaspoons salt*
¼ *cup bacon drippings*
2 *pounds lean beef stew meat, cut in*
  1-inch cubes
1 *pound veal stew meat, cut in 1-inch*
  cubes
3 *or 4 medium-size onions (about 1*
  pound), peeled and sliced
½ *cup flour*
¼ *teaspoon black pepper*

1 *can (1 pound 12 ounces) tomatoes*
2 *cloves garlic*
1 *cup diced carrots*
2 *12-ounce cans whole kernel corn*
1 *10-ounce package frozen lima*
  beans
1 *10-ounce package frozen peas*
½ *teaspoon paprika*
Additional salt to taste
⅛ *teaspoon Angostura bitters*
½ *cup dry sherry*

Place the stewing chicken, whole or cut into pieces, in kettle with water and 1 teaspoon salt. Let simmer about 2 hours, or until chicken is tender. Lift it out and let cool. Reserve the broth.

In a very large kettle melt bacon drippings. Brown the beef and veal slowly; sprinkle with 2 teaspoons salt while browning. Or if easier, brown meat in a heavy frying pan and then transfer to large kettle. When meat is well browned add sliced onions; brown the onions and sprinkle with flour. When meat and onions are coated with flour, add the reserved chicken broth and cook, stirring constantly, until stew begins to simmer. Stir in pepper and add remaining salt and the tomatoes. Crush garlic and stir into stew. Add diced carrots. Remove the cooked chicken from the bones and cut into bite-size pieces. Add these to stew along with corn, lima beans, peas, and paprika. Simmer until vegetables are tender. Add additional salt to taste, if needed. Just before serving stir in Angostura bitters and sherry. Simmer another 5 minutes and serve in soup plates or bowls. Makes 12 to 16 servings.

Country Captain

Years ago this recipe came to my attention when it was included in a list of favorite foods of the Franklin D. Roosevelt family. Through the years I have made my own variations—now it's a favorite at my house.

2½ to 3 pounds chicken parts:	2 teaspoons curry powder
breast, thighs, or drumsticks	1 can whole tomatoes (1 pound 14
½ cup salad oil	ounces)
1 to 1½ teaspoons salt	2 tablespoons chopped parsley
¼ teaspoon white pepper	⅛ teaspoon mace
½ cup chopped onion	¼ cup currants
½ cup chopped green pepper	¼ cup slivered, toasted almonds
1 clove garlic	Steamed rice

Wash chicken parts; cut breasts into two pieces. Pat pieces dry with paper towels. Heat salad oil in a frying pan and brown the chicken. Sprinkle with about half of salt and white pepper. As pieces brown arrange in a casserole or baking dish.

To the hot oil in the frying pan add chopped onion and green pepper. Crush the garlic and stir in along with curry powder. Simmer until onions and pepper are tender but not brown. Add tomatoes, chopped parsley, mace, and currants. Add the rest of the salt and pepper. Pour the mixture over chicken in the casserole and cover. Cook in a moderate oven (350°F.) for about 40 to 45 minutes, or until chicken is tender. Just before serving, sprinkle with toasted almonds. Serve over steamed rice. Makes 4 or 5 servings.

Mac's Gizzard Stew

Mac, the mighty hunter, makes this from the gizzards of wild birds—ducks, geese, pheasant, and so on, but it is very good made from chicken or turkey gizzards. Serve for a buffet supper in a chafing dish along with steamed wild rice and you'll have a conversation piece.

2 to 3 pounds gizzards from wild birds, chickens, or turkeys
1 quart beer
2 bay leaves
2 cloves garlic, chopped or crushed
1 teaspoon sliced fresh ginger or 1 whole piece dried ginger, sliced

2 teaspoons seasoned salt
2 tablespoons butter
1 cup red table wine
1 tablespoon soy sauce
1 to 2 tablespoons cornstarch or arrowroot
Cold water

Cut off any excess gristle and fat from gizzards and cut large gizzards in half. Combine in a saucepan with the beer, bay leaves, chopped or crushed garlic, sliced ginger, and seasoned salt. (Dried ginger slices easier if you soak it for 20 to 30 minutes first.) Cover and simmer until gizzards are very tender, about 1½ hours, depending on birds. Cool the gizzards in the broth, preferably overnight.

When ready to serve, drain gizzards and slice thinly. In a chafing dish or an electric frying pan or saucepan, melt butter. Add sliced gizzards and brown lightly. Add 1½ cups of stock in which gizzards were cooked, red wine, and soy sauce. When gizzards are simmering, blend cornstarch with cold water and mix into gizzards. Stir and simmer until stew is slightly thickened. Keep warm. Serve with steamed wild or white rice. Makes 6 to 8 servings.

Pollo Habanero
Cuban Chicken Stew

From Havana comes *Pollo Habanero* with its unusual seasonings—mildly hot, spicy, sweet, and sour.

2 to 2½ pounds chicken parts
  or 1 broiler-fryer, cut in quarters,
  or 2 small broilers, split
2 tablespoons olive oil
1 teaspoon salt
½ pound ham, diced
3 or 4 fresh or canned green chilis
2 large onions, sliced
2 cloves garlic
1 tablespoon chopped parsley

⅛ teaspoon ground cloves
¼ teaspoon ground cinnamon
1 1-pound can tomatoes
1 cup water
¼ cup seedless raisins
¼ cup wine vinegar
1 firm ripe banana
2 tablespoons toasted, slivered almonds

Wash chicken and pat it dry. In a large heavy frying pan or Dutch oven, heat the olive oil. Brown chicken slowly in hot oil, sprinkling with ½ teaspoon salt. Remove chicken and set it aside while making sauce. Add diced ham to drippings and cook until lightly browned. Remove seeds and stems from green chilis and slice. Add to ham along with sliced onions. Crush garlic and stir into ham and onions along with chopped parsley. Add cloves, cinnamon, tomatoes, water, and remaining ½ teaspoon salt. Cover and simmer over very low heat for 30 to 40 minutes. Plump raisins in hot water; drain. Mix into sauce along with wine vinegar. Return browned chicken to the pan. Cover and continue to cook about 30 minutes, or until chicken is tender. Spoon sauce over chicken two or three times. At serving time, cut up banana and add to chicken. Spoon chicken and sauce onto large serving platter; sprinkle with toasted almonds. Serve with steamed rice. Making 4 servings.

Puchero
Philippine Stew

Puchero is a classic stew or boiled dinner of the Philippines. Other countries with a Spanish heritage have *pucheros*, too. Just what goes into the pot varies, as does the seasoning. In the Philippines, rice would be served with this, but crisp-fried tortillas are also good.

½ pound garbanzo or Spanish beans
2 quarts warm water
3½- to 4-pound stewing chicken
Ham bone or ham hock, if desired
1 tablespoon salt
1 small hot dry red chili pepper
¼ cup olive oil

1 cup chopped or ground onions
2 cloves garlic, crushed or finely
  chopped, or ¼ teaspoon garlic
  powder
1 8-ounce can tomato sauce
½ cup chopped cabbage
½ cup cooked green beans

Soak beans in cold water overnight; drain them and cover with 2 quarts warm water. Cut chicken into serving-size pieces and add to beans along with ham bone or ham hock, if used, salt and chili pepper. Simmer until beans and chicken are done, 1 to 1½ hours.

Meanwhile, pour oil into a heavy frying pan; add onions and garlic and fry until onions are golden and transparent. Add to chicken and beans. Remove ham, cut any meat into pieces, and return it to stew. Add tomato sauce. About 15 or 20 minutes before serving stew, add chopped cabbage and cooked green beans. Simmer until cabbage is crisp-tender. Serve in large bowls or soup plates with a piece of chicken and some of the ham in each serving. Makes 6 servings. If any stew is left over, remove the chicken from bones, discard bones and add chicken meat to stew. Bring to a boil and simmer until thoroughly heated.

Mole de Pollo
Chicken in Mexican Chili Sauce

One of the traditional Mexican dishes, chocolate and orange peel give *mole* it's distinctive flavor. Leftover roast turkey is good in a *mole* sauce also.

4- to 5-pound *stewing chicken*	½ *teaspoon ground cinnamon*
4 *cups water*	3 *tablespoons chili powder*
1 *tablespoon salt*	2 *teaspoons sugar*
¼ *cup bacon drippings or chicken fat*	1 *tablespoon peanut butter*
¼ *cup chopped onion*	1 *1-ounce cake unsweetened*
¼ *cup chopped green pepper*	*chocolate*
1 *clove garlic*	1 *teaspoon orange peel*
2 *cups tomato juice*	½ *cup dairy sour cream*
1 *8-ounce tomato purée*	

Place chicken in a kettle and add water and salt. Simmer until tender, about 2 to 3 hours. Lift out chicken, and reserve the stock. When cool enough to handle, remove chicken skin and bones. Separate or cut chicken into fairly good-size pieces. In a saucepan heat bacon drippings or chicken fat. Add chopped onion and green pepper, and cook until lightly browned. Add 3 cups of stock from chicken; simmer until vegetables are tender. Cool mixture slightly and blend in an electric blender until smooth or press through a wire sieve. Pour into saucepan or kettle. Crush garlic and add to sauce along with tomato juice, tomato purée, cinnamon, chili powder, and sugar. Simmer for about 1 hour and then blend in peanut butter. Add chocolate and orange peel. Simmer, stirring, until chocolate is melted. Add pieces of chicken and heat thoroughly. Just before serving blend in sour cream. Serve over steamed rice. Makes 6 to 8 servings.

Pollo con Chili
Chicken with Chili Sauce

The original of this, which comes from Bolivia and not Mexico, had even more chili powder. Increase it only if you like your chili hot, hot, hot!

3 to 3½ pounds chicken thighs, breasts, or drumsticks
¼ cup olive oil
3 tablespoons sesame seeds
2 medium-size onions, chopped
1 clove garlic, crushed or chopped
1 teaspoon salt

3 cups chicken stock
4 teaspoons chili powder
1 teaspoon caraway seeds
½ cup whole blanched almonds
½ cup pitted green olives
2 tablespoons cornmeal

Wash chicken and pat it dry; cut breasts into serving-size pieces. Heat olive oil in a heavy kettle or Dutch oven. Brown pieces of chicken in hot oil. Lift chicken out and add sesame seeds to oil; cook, stirring constantly, until seeds are brown. Add chopped onions and crushed or chopped garlic and cook until onions are soft. Return browned chicken to kettle; sprinkle with salt. Combine chicken stock and chili powder and pour over chicken. When stock begins to simmer, sprinkle caraway seeds over chicken. Cover and simmer for about 30 minutes. Add almonds and olives and continue cooking 20 to 30 minutes, or until chicken is tender. Sprinkle cornmeal into chicken and sauce, stirring carefully as sauce thickens almost at once. Celery, carrot, and green pepper sticks with a sour cream dip are good with *Pollo con Chili*. Makes 5 or 6 servings.

Peruvian Chupe

Perhaps *chupe* did originate in Peru but this one came from Venezuela. In Peru a *chupe* would be made with fish or seafood. The cheese used there is called Maracay; probably the closest to it in this country is Monterey Jack cheese. A more copious quantity of cheese is often used—but the number of people you are serving and the rest of the meal can help decide that.

3½- to 4-pound stewing chicken
2 quarts hot water
2 tablespoons salt
1 leek, sliced
1 large onion, cut in quarters
2 medium-size carrots, sliced
1 clove garlic, sliced
1-inch piece of bay leaf
1 chili tepin or other small hot dry red
chili pepper

4 medium-size potatoes, pared and
cut into cubes
2 cups fresh corn, cut from cob,
or 1 12-ounce can whole kernel
corn
1 tablespoon flour
½ pound Monterey Jack cheese, cut
into cubes
1 10½-ounce can evaporated milk

Cut up chicken and combine in a large kettle with hot water, salt, leek, onion, carrots, garlic, bay leaf, and red pepper. Simmer until chicken is tender, about 1½ hours. Strain the broth. Combine the strained broth and potatoes and simmer until potatoes are almost done. Meanwhile, bone and skin the chicken. Leave larger pieces serving-size and remaining bite-size. Add chicken to soup along with corn. When potatoes and corn are done, blend flour with a little cold water and stir into soup. Add the cubed cheese and undiluted evaporated milk. Heat just to simmering and when cheese is soft, ladle into soup plates or bowls. Serve with crisp fried tortillas or corn chips. Makes 6 to 8 servings.

Ffowlin Cymreig
Welsh Whole Chicken Stew

In Wales an old stewing hen was probably used to make a *Ffowlin Cymreig*, but we think a roasting chicken better. Serve with fried potato cakes, made either with shredded potatoes or leftover mashed potatoes, or the Irish *Boxty-on-the-Griddle*.

4- to 5-pound whole stewing or roasting chicken
1½ teaspoons salt
½-pound piece bacon
2 leeks
1 cup diced carrots

2 tablespoons flour
3 cups coarsely shredded cabbage
⅛ teaspoon black pepper
2 cups chicken stock
1 tablespoon chopped parsley
¼ teaspoon fines herbes

Wash chicken; twist wing tips and fasten so wings are akimbo and flat against back of chicken. Or if wing tips are cut off, skewer or tie chicken. Pat dry and rub about ½ teaspoon salt in body cavity. Dice the bacon and fry until crisp and brown in a Dutch oven or heavy, deep frying pan.

Brown the chicken in the hot drippings, turning to brown sides, breast, and back. Brown giblets, if desired, or save for another use. Sprinkle with another ½ teaspoon salt while browning. Remove chicken from pan.

Clean and slice leeks very thin, using just a small portion of the green tops. Add to bacon bits along with diced carrots. Cook until lightly browned; stir in flour and brown lightly. Add coarsely chopped cabbage, remaining ½ to 1 teaspoon salt, and pepper. (Amount of salt will depend on saltiness of stock.) Stir to mix thoroughly and when cabbage is slightly wilted, add chicken stock. Cook, stirring frequently, until simmering. Add chopped parsley; crush fines herbes and stir into vegetables. When stew is simmering gently, arrange chicken on top. Cover and simmer very slowly until chicken is tender, 1 to 2 hours depending on its tenderness. (A very old stewing chicken may take even longer.) Turn chicken several times and spoon sauce over it occasionally. To serve, cut slices from breast and cut legs, thighs, and wings into pieces. Arrange chicken pieces on beds of vegetables. Serve with potato cakes and spoon the broth over vegetables, chicken, and potato cakes. Makes 4 servings, perhaps with some leftovers.

Pilic Guveci
Turkish Chicken en Casserole

Also known as the Sultan's Pleasure, you'll find this Turkish version of chicken in a casserole with eggplant, okra and squash a delightful meal for guests. It takes a little time to put together, but with *Cracked Wheat Pilaff* and a salad it makes a festive dinner.

2 *broiler-fryer chickens, about 2 pounds each*	1 *small eggplant, about 1 pound, pared and cut into 1-inch cubes*
½ *cup butter*	2 *yellow or green summer squash, sliced*
2 *teaspoons salt, or more to taste (Cayenne pepper)*	½ *pound green beans, cut into 1-inch lengths*
2 *large onions, sliced*	
½ *pound fresh okra, sliced, or 1 10-ounce package frozen sliced okra*	2 *large ripe tomatoes, peeled*
	2 *cups chicken stock*

Have chickens cut into quarters. Wash chicken and pat dry. In a large heavy frying pan, melt 2 or 3 tablespoons of the butter. Brown chicken quarters in butter, sprinkling with salt, using about ½ teaspoon. Set aside browned chicken quarters. To the drippings, add the sliced onions. When onions are brown spoon them into a very large casserole. (Or use two medium-size casseroles.) Next add sliced okra to frying pan and brown. Then spoon it on top of onions in the casserole. Brown each vegetable separately, adding more butter as needed and sprinkling each vegetable with about ¼ teaspoon salt. Cut tomatoes in chunks, removing some of the seeds. Add to drippings and cook until just soft. Add to vegetables in casserole. Arrange browned chicken on top of layered vegetables. Then add stock to drippings in frying pan; bring it to a boil and stir and scrape so that stock will dissolve all browned bits in pan. Pour it over chicken and vegetables. Cover casserole and bake in a moderate oven, 350°F., for 40 to 45 minutes. Remove cover for the last 10 minutes. Serve with *Cracked Wheat Pilaff*. Makes 6 to 8 servings, depending on size of chickens and appetites.

Poulet à l'Arachide
African Groundnut Stew

The groundnut or peanut is a staple in the diet of the West African. And when this crop fails starvation threatens. From the poorest to the richest all have groundnut stew as often as their finances allow. An acquaintance who is a scientist went to Nigeria to help improve the groundnut crop. (It is often attacked by ground molds.) From his notes comes this recipe.

¼ cup peanut oil
1 cup chopped onions
1 cup chopped fresh tomatoes
¾ cup dry-roasted salted peanuts
1 cup Coconut Cream (see Hong
Kong Chicken-Okra stew)

1 cup water
1½ teaspoons salt
⅛ teaspoon crushed dry red pepper
¼ teaspoon black pepper
3 to 3½ pounds chicken parts
Steamed rice

CONDIMENTS such as fresh or canned pineapple chunks, sliced tomatoes, sliced bananas, French fried onions, shredded coconut, and chutney.

In a large top-of-the-stove casserole heat peanut oil. Add chopped onions and tomatoes and cook until onions are slightly yellow. Meanwhile, crush peanuts in an electric blender. They should be like coarse meal. Stir them into onion and tomato mixture. Add *Coconut Cream,* water, salt, crushed red pepper, and black pepper. Simmer for about 30 minutes.

Add chicken parts and continue to simmer over very low heat for 1½ to 2 hours, or until chicken is very tender. Or place stew in a slow oven, 275°F., and bake for about the same length of time or longer. If necessary, add a little more water during the simmering. Serve with steamed rice and an assortment of condiments served with a curry such as those listed. Makes about 6 servings.

Adobo Baboy
Philippine Pork and Chicken Stew

Almost a national dish of the Philippine Islands, this stew has its origin in the native Tagalog cookery.

2 to 2½ pounds chicken breasts,
wings, or other parts
2 to 2½ pounds lean pork shoulder
2 tablespoons olive oil
1 teaspoon salt
1 large onion, chopped
2 cloves garlic
1 teaspoon freshly ground black
pepper

½ teaspoon paprika
¼ teaspoon ground allspice
¼ teaspoon ground ginger
¼ cup wine vinegar
1 cup beef stock
1 cup Coconut Cream (*see Hong* Kong Chicken-Okra Stew)

Cut chicken into 2- to 3-inch pieces, breasts into 5 or 6 pieces, wings into 2 pieces; cut meat from thighs or legs. (Use any bones to make chicken stock.) Cut the pork into 2- to 2½-inch pieces. Heat olive oil in a heavy kettle or top-of-the-stove casserole. Add chicken and pork and brown slowly. Spoon off excess fat, leaving about 2 tablespoons. Sprinkle with salt. Add onion and mix with chicken and pork. When onion is lightly browned, crush garlic and stir into stew along with freshly ground black pepper, paprika, allspice, ginger, wine vinegar, and beef stock. Cover and simmer over low heat until chicken and pork are tender, about 40 to 50 minutes. Just before serving add *Coconut Cream* and simmer about 10 minutes. Serve with steamed rice. Makes about 6 servings.

Kai Swan
Siamese Chicken with Ginger Sauce

A slightly Americanized version of a recipe of a Princess of Siam, this is not too different from one named Heavenly Chicken. Siam is now known as Thailand, but those of us who have read *Anna and the King of Siam* or seen a production of "The King and I" still think of it as Siam. This is elegant to serve from a chafing dish or electric frying pan at a small dinner party.

4 large or 6 small chicken breasts
½ pound cleaned raw shrimp or prawns
1 fillet of sole (about 4 ounces) or other delicate white fish
1 teaspoon salt
½ cup water
½ teaspoon ground ginger
2 tablespoons oil
2 tablespoons thinly sliced green onion

2 tablespoons thinly sliced crystallized ginger

GINGER SAUCE
½ cup dried mushrooms
½ cup water
2 teaspoons cornstarch
1 cup chicken stock
¼ cup vinegar
3 tablespoons sugar
1 tablespoon soy sauce

With a very sharp, pointed knife—a boning knife, if you have one— cut bones from chicken breasts. (Don't worry if the job isn't too neat. Use bones to make the chicken stock for the *Ginger Sauce*.) Cut large breasts in two. In an electric blender combine raw shrimp and fish with salt, water, and ginger. It's easiest if you add a few shrimp at a time; cut fish into small pieces and add a few pieces at a time. Blend at high speed. When you have puréed about half of the shrimp and fish, add the salt, water, and ginger and blend until smooth. You will have a very smooth paste. Then add the rest of the shrimp and chicken.

With a wooden meat hammer or rolling pin, pound out the chicken breasts. Spread each with the fish paste; roll them up and fasten with wooden or bamboo skewers. Heat oil in a heavy frying pan and brown chicken rolls slowly.

Meanwhile, make *Ginger Sauce*. Soak the dried mushrooms in water for about half an hour. Blend cornstarch with mushrooms and water in a saucepan and add chicken stock. Bring to a boil, stirring constantly. Turn down to simmering and add vinegar, sugar, and soy sauce. Pour sauce over the browned chicken rolls. Cover and cook over low heat or in a low oven, 300°F., for 30 to 40 minutes, or until chicken rolls are tender. (You can do this some time ahead; even the day before.) About 20 minutes before serving time (30 to 40 minutes, if rolls made the day before are refrigerated) remove skewers from rolls and reheat carefully. Add a little hot water or chicken stock, if needed. When hot, add sliced green onion and crystallized ginger. Arrange on a heated platter or serve from chafing dish or electric frying pan. Serve with steamed white rice. Makes 6 to 8 servings.

Hong Kong Chicken-Okra Stew

American families who live for a while in Hong Kong come home with favorite dishes that are really a combination of cuisines the world over. This delicious stew seems to be a cross between Southern gumbo and an East Indian curry.

1 *broiler-fryer chicken, about 2 pounds, cut in half*	1 *or 2 tomatoes*
2 *slices bacon*	1½ *quarts water*
12 *small fresh or frozen okra, sliced*	1 *tablespoon salt*
1 *cup chopped onion*	¼ *teaspoon white pepper*
½ *cup chopped green pepper*	1 *small green apple, chopped*
2 *leeks, thinly sliced*	1 *cup diced eggplant*
1 *clove garlic*	1 *cup Coconut Cream*
1 *tablespoon curry powder*	½ *cup shredded or grated coconut*
	Steamed rice

Cut as much meat as possible from one of the chicken halves and cut it into bite-size pieces. Cut bacon slices into 5 or 6 pieces and fry them until crisp in a large heavy kettle. Add the chicken pieces and sliced okra and cook until chicken and okra are brown. Add onion, green pepper, and leeks and continue cooking until vegetables are soft and lightly brown. Crush garlic and stir into vegetables along with curry powder and cook about 5 minutes. Meanwhile, peel and chop tomatoes and mix into stew. Add water, salt, and pepper, the uncut half chicken, and the bones and skin of chicken half from which the meat was cut. Cover and simmer about 30 to 40 minutes, or until the half chicken is done. Lift it out of stew along with chicken bones and skin from other half. Simmer stew about 30 minutes more. About half hour before serving, add chopped apple, diced eggplant, and *Coconut Cream*. Remove cooked chicken from the bones and cut into fairly large pieces. Remove any remaining small pieces from bones of chicken half from which meat was cut. Add to stew. Serve stew with steamed rice. Makes 6 servings.

Stew, if desired, may be thickened by blending 1 tablespoon arrowroot or cornstarch in 2 tablespoons of cold water. Mix into stew and cook, stirring constantly, until stew comes to a boil and is thickened.

COCONUT CREAM

Drain milk from fresh coconut and add half and half or evaporated milk to make 1 cup. If coconut has no milk, then grate about ½ cup fresh coconut or grate in a blender. Pour 1 cup hot milk over coconut and let stand until cool. Strain it and add to stew. Or add 1 cup hot milk to 1 cup packaged flaked coconut and proceed as for fresh coconut.

Turkey Monterey

From a collection of early California recipes, *Turkey Monterey* was originally for wild turkey or other game birds such as pheasant, grouse, or quail. I like to make it with turkey wings with a leg or two for those who like dark meat. But you can also use a broiler-size turkey, a turkey quarter, or a turkey roll. An excellent inexpensive party recipe—particularly good for a buffet.

6 *pounds turkey wings and legs or a*	¼ *teaspoon rosemary*
6- to 8 pound turkey or turkey quar-	2 *tomatoes*
ter or a 4- or 5-pound turkey roll	2 *tablespoons wine vinegar*
½ *cup flour*	1 *teaspoon dry mustard*
1 *teaspoon salt*	1 *tablespoon sugar*
¼ *teaspoon black pepper*	1 *teaspoon paprika*
⅓ *cup bacon drippings or salad oil*	1 *teaspoon chili powder*
½ *cup chopped onion*	½ *cup catsup*
4 *cups hot water or turkey stock*	*Dash cayenne pepper*
1 *clove garlic*	*Additional salt to taste*

If using whole wings, cut off tips and cut into two pieces at joint. Have turkey legs cut into one or two pieces. Have small turkey or turkey quarter cut into serving-size pieces. If using a turkey roll, let it thaw, if frozen, and cut into serving-size pieces. The pieces don't have to be perfectly uniform.

Combine flour, salt, and pepper. Heat bacon drippings or salad oil in a frying pan. Dip turkey pieces in seasoned flour and brown well in drippings or oil. As pieces are browned, arrange in large casserole. To the drippings in the frying pan, add chopped onion and cook slowly until golden. Stir in any remaining flour. When well blended, add hot water or turkey stock and cook, stirring constantly, until slightly thickened and smooth. (Use wing tips, odds and ends of turkey bones to make stock.)

When sauce is bubbling, turn heat down; crush garlic and rosemary and stir into sauce. Peel tomatoes and cut into chunks. Stir into sauce along with wine vinegar, mustard, sugar, paprika, chili powder, catsup, and cayenne pepper. Let sauce simmer for 10 to 15 minutes. Taste and add salt to taste; amount will depend on the saltiness of the stock. Pour the sauce over the turkey pieces. Bake in a moderately slow oven, 300°F., for 1 to 1½ hours, or until turkey is tender. Serve with *Monterey Rice*. Makes about 8 servings.

Monterey Rice

3 cups cooked rice	¼ teaspoon pepper
½ cup chopped celery	¼ cup milk
½ cup chopped onion	2 eggs
¼ cup finely chopped parsley	¼ pound Monterey Jack cheese,
¼ cup finely chopped green chilis	shredded or cut into small cubes
½ teaspoon crumbled sage	(about 1 cup)
¼ teaspoon salt or to taste	1 cup sliced ripe olives

Combine the cooked rice with chopped celery, onion, parsley, and green chilis; stir in crumbled sage, salt, and pepper. (Amount of salt will depend on the saltiness of the cooked rice.) Beat together milk and eggs and add cheese and ripe olives. Mix into rice. Pour into a well-greased 2-quart casserole. Bake rice along with *Monterey Turkey* for 30 to 40 minutes. Makes 8 servings.

Galos Kastana Salonika
Turkey and Chestnuts Salonika

From Salonika, the Greek city of Anatolia College, *Turkey and Chestnuts* makes a wonderful party food when accompanied by *Cracked Wheat Pilaff* (see *Accompaniments*) and a plate of sliced tomatoes dressed with olive oil and vinegar, sprinkled with crushed oregano and topped with anchovy filets.

8-pound broiler turkey or 6 pounds turkey wings or parts	½ pound pitted prunes
½ cup butter	2½ cups water
Salt	6 to 8 black Greek olives or large green olives
4 tablespoons finely chopped onion	1 bay leaf
1 pound chestnuts	

Have turkey cut into serving-size pieces. Or use turkey breast, wings, thighs, or legs, and cut into serving-size pieces. Melt butter in a large frying pan; brown the turkey pieces slowly, sprinkling each piece with salt. Set pieces aside as browned. Add the onion to drippings and brown lightly.

Meanwhile, roast the chestnuts in moderate oven, 350°F., and soak prunes in the 2½ cups water. Remove a few of hot chestnuts at a time; when cool enough to handle, peel off outside shell and inner skin. Cut each chestnut into 2 or 3 pieces. In a large top-of-stove casserole arrange the browned turkey, onions, chestnuts, and prunes. (Save the water.) Cut olives from seeds, and add to dish along with water in which prunes were soaked and the bay leaf. Cover and simmer very slowly on top of the stove or place in a low oven, 300°F., and cook for about 2 hours, or until turkey is tender. Serve with wheat pilaff. Makes about 8 to 10 servings.

NOTE: If time permits, simmer any turkey bones, wing tips, pieces of skin, etc., in lightly salted water. Strain and substitute this stock for part of the water called for in the recipe. Soak prunes in only about 1 cup of water and combine water with turkey stock to make 2½ cups. And use turkey stock in cooking the pilaff.

Portuguese Duck

Perhaps not really a stew and maybe not a Portuguese recipe. This unusual and delicious way of preparing duck came from a Swedish friend.

4- to 4½-pound duck	½ cup white table wine
2 teaspoons salt	1-inch piece bay leaf
¼ teaspoon black pepper	¼ teaspoon thyme
2 medium-size onions	1 cup rice
1 medium-size carrot	1 cup water
1 can tomatoes (1 pound 12 ounces)	1 tablespoon chopped parsley

Wash duck and cut off excess skin at neck. Remove giblets and rub inside of body cavity with 1 teaspoon salt and pepper. Cut one onion into quarters and slice carrot. Stuff body cavity of duck with onion and carrot. Prick duck on breast and back with fork. Place it in a heavy kettle or casserole and roast in a moderately hot oven, 400°F., for about 1 hour, or until duck is well browned. Turn once or twice while browning.

Pour off fat; reserve 2 or 3 tablespoons for rice and discard rest of fat. To the duck add tomatoes, white wine, and bay leaf. Crush thyme and sprinkle over duck. Cover and cook in a moderate oven, 350°F., for about 1 hour longer, or until duck is tender. Or simmer or top of stove, if preferred. Turn duck two or three times.

About 40 minutes before serving, place 2 or 3 tablespoons duck fat in heavy saucepan. Chop duck liver and add to fat. Chop remaining onion and add to duck liver. Cook over low heat, until onion is soft. Add rice and cook, stirring frequently, until rice is golden. Measure about 1 cup of liquid from cooking duck and add 1 cup of water. Add these 2 cups of liquid to rice and bring to a boil; add 1 teaspoon salt. Cover and turn heat down to simmer. Cook rice about 25 to 30 minutes, or until done. Fluff rice with fork. Carve duck into thick slices and return it to sauce in casserole. Sprinkle with parsley. Spoon rice onto plates and top with sliced duck and sauce. Makes about 4 servings. (For a second meal, strip meat from duck and combine with any leftover sauce. Serve on rice.)

Madame Vernier's Cassoulet Toulousaine

Madame Vernier has lived in the United States for a number of years and teaches French. When she first came, she took courses in English. This recipe she wrote as an assignment for an English class.

AS MADAME VERNIER WROTE IT FOR HER ASSIGNMENT	1 bowl of diced bacon rind
	2 onions
1 pound soaked white beans	2 tomatoes
4 pieces of goose	4 cloves grated garlic
4 fresh pork sausages	

Brown goose, sausages, and bacon rind in casserole. Pour off all but 1 tablespoon fat. Take meat out. Add onion stuffed with cloves, and tomatoes, and ⅓ cup flour. When brown, add beans, 2 cups water, garlic, parsley, thyme, salt, pepper, saffron. Add meats except sausage; cook slowly for 2 hours, adding boiling water. Add the sausage and cook for another 30 minutes.

American Cassoulet Toulousaine

Here's an Americanized version of Madame Vernier's recipe. If there isn't a hunter in your family, use domestic goose.

1 pound small dry white beans	2 cups hot water
2 cups diced bacon rind	4 cloves crushed garlic
½ wild goose, cut into 4 pieces	1 tablespoon chopped parsley
4 fresh sausages, about 1 pound	¼ teaspoon thyme
2 or 3 tablespoons flour	1 tablespoon salt
2 whole medium-size onions, peeled	¼ teaspoon black pepper
3 or 4 cloves	Pinch of saffron
2 tomatoes	

Wash the beans and cover them with warm water. Bring to a boil and boil 5 minutes. Remove from heat and let beans soak 1 hour.

Meanwhile, in a heavy kettle or flame-proof casserole, brown the diced bacon rind, the pieces of goose, and the sausages. (Fresh Italian sausage is good, but use what is available.) When meat is brown, lift it out and set aside. Pour off all but 1 tablespoon fat. Sprinkle in the flour and brown, stirring. Stick the whole onions with the cloves and add them to the pan. Peel and dice the tomatoes and add them with the hot water, crushed garlic, chopped parsley, thyme, salt, pepper, and saffron. Add beans, the browned goose and bacon rind and simmer for 2 hours, adding more hot water from time to time. When beans are tender, cut each sausage in half and add to beans. Cook another 30 minutes. Serve in soup plates with toasted French bread. Makes 6 to 8 servings.

Mainly Meat and Beans

BEEF

＊

Pot-au-Feu
"Pot-on-the-Fire": Boiled Beef with Vegetables

Pot-au-Feu is to the French family what corned beef and cabbage is to the Irish and *Bollito Misto* to the Italian. Each French family has its own favorite combination of meats and vegetables. Some use two or three varieties of meat and sausage and a chicken. This *Pot-au-Feu* is the family recipe of Madame Genevieve Guerrard, a very good friend now living in this country. Madame's addition of tapioca makes a variation of the bouillon. Tapioca thickens the bouillon ever so slightly and gives it a certain shininess. This recipe makes quite a lot of good beef stock, too, to use later in other soups and sauces.

2½ to 3 pounds beef shank cut in thick slices, or 1 to 1½ pounds each beef shank and beef ribs
4 quarts water
2 large yellow onions
2 or 3 sprigs parsley
1 large stalk celery with leaves
1 teaspoon chervil
¼ teaspoon thyme
2-inch piece bay leaf

4 teaspoons salt
4 or 5 whole black peppercorns
2 pounds small young carrots or 1 pound each carrots and new potatoes
1 small green cabbage (about 1 pound) cut into 6 or 8 wedges
1 to 2 tablespoons quick-cooking tapioca or miniature pasta

Cut off a few pieces of fat from the beef and fry in a heavy frying pan until pieces are brown. Then add beef and brown slowly. Meanwhile, pour water into a very large kettle or *marmite*, as the French call this kind of utensil. Leave the onions whole; scrub but do not peel. Add to water along with parsley, celery, chervil, thyme, bay leaf, salt, and peppercorns. Bring to a boil. When meat is brown add it to boiling liquid. Turn down to simmer and simmer slowly for about 2 hours, or until meat is tender. Skim the soup from time to time.

Scrape carrots and potatoes. Add carrots to simmering stock and potatoes, if desired. (Much preferred is to dip out about 2 cups of stock and cook the potatoes separately, as starchy vegetables tend to make the broth cloudy.) Simmer about 15 minutes and then add cabbage and continue to simmer about 30 minutes. Lift out meat and vegetables onto a platter and keep warm.

Strain 1 to 2 quarts of the stock through a wire sieve. Bring to a boil and add tapioca (about 1 tablespoon for each quart of stock). Simmer 8 to 10 minutes or until tapioca is clear. If preferred, add tiny pasta, about 2 tablespoons for each quart of stock. Serve this hot bouillon in soup cups along with toasted French bread or sprinkled with crisp croutons. Slice the meat and serve hot with vegetables along with *Tomato Sauce*, French mustard, sour pickles, and horseradish. Makes 6 to 8 servings.

Any leftover meat and vegetables can be reheated for a second meal in some of the stock or bouillon. Strain any leftover stock through a wire sieve. Chill and skim off the hard fat. Use stock in making soups and sauces, or reheat and serve as bouillon.

TOMATO SAUCE:

While the vegetables are cooking, fry 2 tablespoons salt pork cut into small cubes, or diced bacon, until crisp and brown. Add ¼ cup finely chopped onion and cook until onion is soft. Crush a clove of garlic and stir into the onions along with 4 tablespoons tomato purée. Dip out a cup of stock from *Pot-au-Feu* and stir it into the sauce. Simmer while vegetables finish cooking, about 10 minutes. Add 1 tablespoon chopped parsley and salt and pepper to taste.

Suji-Nabe
Japanese Boiled Dinner

If *daikon* or the large white radishes aren't available in your market, use white turnips. Scrape or peel the turnips and cut into chunks or slices. Japanese families who use chopsticks would probably cut the meat into chunks. However, I think the beef has more flavor if cooked in one piece and then sliced just before serving.

2 to 2½ pounds lean beef brisket	*Salt to taste*
2 quarts water	*1 to 1½ pounds* daikon *or large white*
2 tablespoons thinly sliced fresh gin-	*radish*
ger root or soaked dry ginger root	*Orange Sauce*
¼ cup soy sauce	

Have the beef brisket well trimmed and securely tied. Place in a kettle and add water. Bring to a boil and skim. Turn the heat down to simmer and add thinly sliced fresh ginger root. (Or soak dry ginger root for an hour or so in warm water and slice.) Simmer for about 30 minutes and skim, if necessary. Add soy sauce and continue to simmer for about 1½ to 2 hours, or until the meat is tender. Taste the stock and add salt, if needed. (Saltiness of stock will depend on how salty your soy sauce is.) Scrape the radish and cut into 1-inch-thick slices. Add radish to stock and simmer for about 20 minutes, or until crisp-tender. Take out the beef and slice it. Return the slices to the kettle. Serve meat, cooked radish and hot bouillon from the kettle or transfer to a soup tureen or casserole. Ladle hot bouillon into soup cups or bowls. Serve the sliced beef with hot steamed rice and the cooked radish accompanied by *Orange Sauce*. Makes 4 or 5 servings.

ORANGE SAUCE:

Combine an 11-ounce can of mandarin orange segments and syrup with ½ cup soy sauce, ¼ cup sake or dry sherry and 1 teaspoon freshly grated horseradish. (Or soak ½ teaspoon dehydrated horseradish in 1 teaspoon water for a few minutes and add.) Serve *Orange Sauce* cold or lukewarm.

Old English Beef Stew

This beef stew is made with ale. *Yorkshire Pudding* seems to be the best go-along with it, but mashed potatoes, rice, or noodles are good, too. If you like your stew a little thicker, then add another tablespoon or so of flour.

2 *pounds beef stew meat, rump or chuck*
2 *or 3 beef bones, about 2 inches in length*
2 *tablespoons salad oil*
2 *teaspoons salt*
3 *cups water*
1 *12-ounce bottle ale*
1 *1-pound can tomatoes*
2 *medium-size onions, thinly sliced*
Dash Tabasco
1 *tablespoon Worcestershire sauce*

1 *teaspoon anchovy paste*
2 *tablespoons chopped parsley*
1-*inch piece bay leaf*
2 *whole cloves*
½ *cup thinly sliced celery*
1 *cup diced turnips*
1 *cup diced parsnips*
1 *cup diced carrots*
2 *cups coarsely shredded cabbage*
1 *to 2 tablespoons (or more) flour*
2 *tablespoons cold water*

Have beef stew meat cut into 1½-inch chunks. Wipe off beef bones with damp cloth. Brown meat and bones in hot oil in a heavy kettle. When well browned sprinkle with salt and add water, ale, and tomatoes. Bring to a boil; skim stew and turn down to simmering. Add sliced onions, Tabasco, Worcestershire sauce, anchovy paste, chopped parsley, bay leaf, and cloves. Simmer for about 2 hours, or until beef is very tender. About 30 or 40 minutes before serving time, add sliced celery, diced turnips, parsnips, carrots, and cabbage. Cover stew and simmer another 30 minutes. Mix flour and cold water into a smooth paste and stir into stew. Cook until stew has thickened. Serve with *Yorkshire Pudding*, mashed potatoes, rice or noodles. Makes about 6 to 8 servings.

Five-Hour Stew

A favorite in the Midwest, a variation or two of this stew is found in almost every church or club cookbook. You'll find it a wonderful simple meal to put in the oven if you intend to be gone most of the day. You can shorten the cooking time by raising the temperature slightly, or lengthen it by turning your oven even lower than 250°F.

2 pounds beef stew meat, cut into
  1½-inch cubes
1 cup sliced celery
1 cup sliced carrots
3 medium-size onions, peeled and cut
  into quarters
1 1-pound can tomatoes

2 teaspoons brown sugar
1 ⅜-ounce package brown or herb
  gravy mix
1 teaspoon salt
2 tablespoons quick-cooking tapioca
1-inch piece bay leaf
1 cup cooked, canned, or frozen peas

In a large casserole combine beef stew meat, celery, carrots, onions, and canned tomatoes. Mix in brown sugar, gravy mix, salt, and tapioca. Add bay leaf. Cover and place in oven. Turn oven to low, 250°F., and let stew bake for 5 hours. When time to serve, add peas. Bake another 5 to 10 minutes, or until peas are hot. Meanwhile, prepare quick-cooking rice or instant mashed potatoes. Serve with a tossed salad. Makes about 6 servings.

Cocido
Spanish Stew

Every part of Spain has a version of this typically Spanish stew—and every Spanish family has its variation of it. This one comes from a friend, now a grandmother, who had Spanish grandparents born in California. She says that as she was growing up this was her family's Saturday night supper.

½ pound garbanzo beans
2 or 3 slices of bacon or salt pork,
  or 2 tablespoons olive oil, preferably Spanish
1 to 1½ pounds beef stew meat, cut
  in 1-inch cubes
2 medium-size onions, chopped
2 leeks
2 medium-size carrots

1 clove garlic
1 1-pound can tomatoes
1½ quarts water
Beef or veal bones or ham shank
6 or 8 ounces chorizo sausage, or
  more, if desired, or other highly seasoned sausage
1 large sweet potato or 2 medium-size
  white potatoes

Cover garbanzos with warm water and let soak overnight. Cut bacon or salt pork into pieces. In a large kettle, fry until crisp and brown. Or, if using olive oil, heat oil in kettle. Add cubes of beef and brown slowly. Stir in chopped onions. Clean leeks and slice into thin slices. Add to meat and onions. Scrape carrots and cut into 1-inch pieces; add to stew. Crush garlic and add along with tomatoes and water.

Drain and rinse garbanzos and add to stew with any beef or veal bones or ham shank or bones. (Use either fresh or from leftover roast.) Bring stew to a boil and turn down to simmer. Skim stew, cover, and cook slowly for about 3 hours, or until beans and meat are very tender. About 40 to 50 minutes before serving, add sausage. Pare potato and cut into 1½-inch cubes. Add to stew. When potatoes are done lift out sausage and cut into slices 1 to 2 inches thick. Arrange on platter with beans, meat, and vegetables. Pour the broth into cups and serve as a first course. Or if preferred ladle *Cocido* into soup plates and eat with a spoon. Serve with French or Italian bread or crisp-fried tortillas. Makes about 8 servings.

Gulyás
Hungarian Beef Stew

Gulyás is the classic goulash or stew of Hungary. Seasonings vary, of course, according to family recipes. We like *Gulyás* served with egg noodles tossed in sour cream with a touch of caraway. Dill pickles or coleslaw seasoned with dill make good accompaniments.

1½ pounds lean beef stew meat cut in 1½-inch cubes	½ cup green pepper, cut in slivers
½ teaspoon ground coriander	1 clove garlic
¼ teaspoon ground allspice	1 cup red table wine
1 tablespoon paprika, Hungarian preferred	1 1-pound can tomatoes
1 teaspoon salt	2 cups beef stock
1 tablespoon flour	1 tablespoon chopped parsley
2 ounces salt pork	¼ teaspoon mixed herbs for beef or fines herbes
3 medium-size onions	2 or 3 medium-size potatoes

Combine ground coriander, allspice, and paprika. Mix salt and flour together. Cut salt pork into small pieces and fry until crisp in a heavy frying pan. Dip each piece of meat in the combined spices and then roll in flour. Brown meat in salt pork drippings. Peel and slice onions; stir into browned meat along with slivered green pepper. Crush garlic and add to meat along with red wine, tomatoes, beef stock, and chopped parsley. Crush herbs and add to stew. Simmer stew over low heat for about 1 hour, or until meat is almost tender. Pare potatoes and cut each into quarters. Add to stew and continue simmering 30 to 40 minutes, or until potatoes are done and meat is tender. Makes 6 servings.

Steak Diane

Most Americans wouldn't think of *Steak Diane* as a stew. But this Australian version (sent by a cousin now living Down Under, who got the recipe from one of her friends) is definitely in that classification. It's not what we know here as *Steak Diane*—but it's delicious. Note the large amount of garlic—for some reason it doesn't seem too much.

1½ *pounds lean round or chuck steak,* *cut about ½ inch thick*	1 *cup water*
3 *tablespoons butter*	½ *cup claret wine*
1 *tablespoon chopped garlic*	1 10-ounce can condensed tomato soup
1 *teaspoon salt*	1 *cup rich milk or half and half*
⅛ *teaspoon black pepper*	

Trim fat from meat and cut meat into thin strips. In a heavy frying pan melt butter and add chopped garlic. Cook for a few minutes and then lift out garlic pieces before they brown or burn. Pound meat strips with meat hammer until very thin. Season with salt and pepper, then brown strips in garlic butter. Combine water and wine and pour over meat. Return chopped garlic to pan. Cover and simmer for about 30 minutes. Combine condensed tomato soup and half and half. Stir into steak. Heat just to simmering, but do not boil. Serve at once with mashed potatoes or noodles. Makes 4 to 6 servings.

Five Flies Beef Stew

A friend who does a great deal of traveling brought back this unusually spiced stew, the specialty of the very, very old Five Flies Restaurant in Amsterdam.

1½ *pounds round steak,* *cut 1-inch thick*	¼ *cup salad oil*
⅓ *cup flour*	2 *beef bouillon cubes*
¼ *teaspoon ground cloves*	2 *cups hot water*
¼ *teaspoon ground ginger*	2 *tablespoons butter*
¼ *teaspoon curry powder*	¼ *cup slivered almonds*
¼ *teaspoon garlic salt*	1 *4-ounce can mushrooms*
¼ *teaspoon black pepper*	1 *cup drained sour red cherries*
½ *teaspoon salt*	1 *cup dairy sour cream*

Cut steak into 1-inch cubes. Combine flour with ground cloves, ginger, curry powder, garlic salt, pepper, and salt. Dip pieces of steak in the seasoned flour. In a heavy frying pan or Dutch oven heat salad oil. Brown the meat in hot oil. When meat is well browned, sprinkle with any remaining seasoned flour. Stir until flour is well browned. Dissolve bouillon cubes in hot water and pour over browned meat. Cover and simmer over low heat for about 2 hours, or until meat is tender. Meanwhile, melt butter in a small saucepan. Add nuts and cook until dark brown. At serving time stir nuts into stew along with mushrooms and their liquid and drained cherries. Simmer about 10 minutes or until bubbling hot. Blend in sour cream and serve at once, accompanied by buttered noodles or steamed rice. Makes 6 servings.

Grandma Greco's Pizzaiola

Why an Italian would call this wonderfully filling stew a "little pie" is as unexplainable as calling the elegant dessert *Zuppa Inglese* "English Soup." This came from a friend with an Italian grandmother. If any is left over, use it as a sauce for spaghetti.

1 pound top round steak	½ teaspoon black pepper
2 cans (1 pound each) tomatoes— Italian peeled tomatoes, if available	1 teaspoon oregano, or more if desired
	1 tablespoon chopped parsley
3 cloves garlic	1 teaspoon olive oil
2 teaspoons salt	1 tablespoon grated Romano cheese

Cut off fat from meat and cut meat into thin strips. Combine with tomatoes in casserole. Crush garlic and oregano and add along with salt and pepper. Stir in parsley, olive oil, and cheese. Bake uncovered in a moderate oven, 350°F., for 2 hours. Serve in soup bowls or plates with crusty Italian or French bread for dunking. Sprinkle with additional cheese, if desired. Makes 4 or 5 servings.

Swedish Short Ribs

Coffee and cream, along with allspice, in the sauce give *Swedish Short Ribs* their distinctive flavor. Potatoes would be the most usual accompaniment in Sweden, but noodles or rice are good, too.

3 or 4 pounds beef short ribs	½ teaspoon whole allspice
½ teaspoon salt	1-inch piece bay leaf
¼ cup chopped onion	½ cup undiluted evaporated milk or heavy cream
2 beef bouillon cubes	
2 teaspoons instant coffee	1 tablespoon cornstarch
2 cups hot water	

Cut off some of fat and fry out in a large heavy kettle. Add short ribs and brown on all sides. When meat is well browned, pour off all but a tablespoon of fat. Sprinkle with salt. Stir in chopped onion and cook until brown. Dissolve bouillon cubes and instant coffee in hot water. Pour over short ribs and add allspice and bay leaf. Cover and simmer slowly 2 to 2½ hours, or until meat is tender. Blend evaporated milk or cream with cornstarch. Skim excess fat from sauce of short ribs. Stir in cream mixture; cook until sauce is thickened, stirring constantly. Serve with noodles, mashed or boiled potatoes, or steamed rice. Makes 4 to 6 servings.

Mandarin Short Ribs

During World War II a group of Army officers was sent to Chinese Language School and later to China. The men in this group learned the Mandarin dialect—different from the Cantonese spoken by most Chinese here in the United States. All of the instructors were from North China and so their food was different, too, from the Chinese food served in most local Chinese restaurants. Instructors and students became good friends and invited each other to dinner. This way of preparing short ribs came from one of the teachers at the school. She used star anise; but anise seed is more readily available, so we have used it in this recipe. The flavor is practically the same.

2½ to 3 pounds beef short ribs, cut into serving-size pieces	4 or 5 dried mushrooms, whole or sliced (about ½ ounce)
⅟₁₆ teaspoon anise seed	½ cup water
3 tablespoons soy sauce	1½ cups beef stock
½ cup red table wine	2 teaspoons cornstarch
½ clove garlic	1 tablespoon cold water
⅛ teaspoon ground ginger	¼ cup thinly sliced green onions

Place short ribs in a deep bowl. Crush anise seed thoroughly and combine it with the soy sauce and red wine. Crush garlic and add it to soywine mixture along with ground ginger. Pour this over the short ribs. Marinate the ribs several hours at room temperature or overnight in the refrigerator.

Meanwhile, combine dried mushrooms and water and let soak. Lift short ribs out of marinade and brown in a heavy frying pan with cover. (There should be enough fat on the short ribs without adding any extra. But if needed, add a small amount of salad oil to frying pan.) After the short ribs are browned, pour off excess fat. Combine the marinade with the soaked mushrooms and their liquid and the beef stock and pour over short ribs. Cover and simmer slowly 2 to 2½ hours, or until ribs are very tender. Blend cornstarch with cold water and stir into short ribs. Simmer until sauce comes to a boil and thickens slightly. Just before serving sprinkle with sliced green onions. Serve with steamed rice. Makes 4 or 5 servings.

Rough-and-Ready Meatball Stew

Rough and Ready is a town in the Mother Lode country dating from the days of the Gold Rush, still very much in existence and by no means a ghost town. *Meatball Stew* was a part of the free lunch in the local saloon. This old recipe probably dates from around the turn of the century, since California olive trees were not productive as early as the '50's.

1 pound lean ground beef	2 tablespoons flour
½ pound country sausage	1 12-ounce bottle or can beer
1 egg	1 8-ounce can tomato sauce
¼ cup finely chopped onion	1 cup green ripe olives, pitted or cut
1 teaspoon salt	from pits
⅛ teaspoon black pepper	

Mix together well the ground beef, sausage, egg, finely chopped onion, salt, and pepper. Shape into 1-inch balls. In a hot frying pan, without additional fat, brown the balls slowly. As meatballs brown set them aside. Pour off all but 2 tablespoons fat; sprinkle in the flour and stir until flour is well browned. Stir in beer and tomato sauce and cook, stirring constantly, until sauce has thickened. Return the meatballs to the sauce. Add olives. Spoon the stew into a small casserole, bean pot, or chafing dish and keep warm over a small electric plate, candle warmer, or the like. Serve with sourdough or other homemade bread. Makes 4 or 5 servings.

Greek Meatballs in Lemon Sauce

After her retirement a professional friend of mine spent some time at Anatolia College in Salonika, Greece, organizing Home Economics courses. She passed on to me several of the recipes she collected. *Meatballs in Lemon Sauce* makes a wonderful simple family supper, particularly appealing to those who like the slightly tart flavor of the lemon sauce.

2 *pounds lean ground beef*
½ *cup rice*
1 *teaspoon salt*
¼ *teaspoon black pepper*
½ *cup finely chopped onion*
¼ *cup chopped parsley*
¼ *teaspoon oregano*

3 *egg whites*
½ *cup flour (approximately)*
2 *quarts beef stock*
3 *egg yolks*
¼ *cup cold water*
¼ *cup lemon juice*

In a mixing bowl combine ground beef, rice, salt, pepper, chopped onion, and parsley. Crush oregano and mix into meat mixture along with egg white. Combine thoroughly. Shape into balls about 1½ inches in diameter; the mixture should make about 24 meatballs. Roll them in flour. Heat beef stock in a large kettle and add meatballs. Simmer for about 1 hour or until meat and rice are done. Just before serving, beat egg yolks with cold water and lemon juice. Stir in about ½ cup of the hot broth from the meatballs. Then add the egg mixture slowly to meatballs. Heat just to simmering; do not boil. Ladle into soup plates and serve at once. Makes 6 to 8 servings.

Sauerklöpse
German Sausage and Meatballs

An old, old German recipe that has been in a friend's family for three generations. If you can't find German sausages in your market, then use small pork sausage links.

1 *quart water*
6 *whole allspice*
2-inch *piece bay leaf*
1 *teaspoon salt*
⅛ *teaspoon pepper*
1 *cup coarsely chopped onion*
1 *pound German sausages*

MEATBALLS:
3 *tablespoons flour*
3 *tablespoons cold water*
¼ *teaspoon sugar*
½ *cup cider vinegar*
2 *tablespoons bread crumbs*

In a large kettle combine water, allspice, bay leaf, salt, pepper, and chopped onion. Bring to a boil and simmer 5 minutes. Add sausage and simmer for about 20 minutes. Make meatballs (page 163). Add meatballs and continue to simmer for 15 minutes. Blend flour and cold water together and stir into the stew. Add sugar and vinegar. Bring back to simmering, stirring constantly. Add bread crumbs and simmer about 5 more minutes. Serve with boiled potatoes or noodles. Makes 6 to 8 servings.

MEATBALLS FOR SAUERKLÖPSE:

1 pound lean ground beef
½ teaspoon salt
⅛ teaspoon pepper
¼ teaspoon sage

2 tablespoons flour
1 tablespoon fine dry bread crumbs
1 egg

Mix together ground beef, salt, and pepper. Rub sage and mix into ground beef along with flour and bread crumbs. Beat eggs slightly and mix thoroughly into ground beef mixture. Shape into balls about 1 inch in diameter.

Gypsy Slumgullion

This is the kind of stew to make on a camping trip, in your mountain cabin, or on your boat. It's good, too, for a patio supper. You can use canned mixed vegetables instead of the mixed frozen vegetables. If so, you may want to add a small can of corn, since canned mixed vegetables usually omit the corn. The friend who passed this stew on to me is quite a hunter and he tells me he sometimes makes it with ground venison.

1½ pounds lean ground beef
1 large onion, coarsely chopped
1 10-ounce package frozen mixed vegetables, or 1 1-pound can mixed vegetables
1 4-ounce can mushroom stems and pieces

1 1-pound can red kidney beans
2 4-ounce cans tomato sauce or tomato sauce with cheese
Grated cheese, if desired ·

Combine ground beef and coarsely chopped onion in a heavy frying pan or kettle. Cook slowly, separating meat with a heavy spoon, until meat loses its red color. Add undrained mixed vegetables, mushrooms, and beans. Mix well and add tomato sauce. Cover and simmer 20 to 30 minutes or until meat and vegetables are done. Sprinkle with cheese, if desired. Serve with chunks of crusty bread. Makes 4 to 6 servings, depending on appetites and the rest of the menu.

Hot Dog Ragout

Another good stew to take on an outdoor jaunt, either camping or a hunting or fishing trip. Or take it to the backyard or on a picnic, especially if there's a barbecue or fireplace to reheat or keep it hot.

2 *tablespoons bacon drippings*   ½ *teaspoon ground cumin*
3 *cups chopped onions (3 or 4 me-* ½ *teaspoon salt or to taste*
  dium-size)   ⅛ *teaspoon black pepper*
½ *cup chopped green pepper*   1 *cup elbow macaroni*
2 *1-pound cans stewed tomatoes*   1 *pound frankfurters*
1 *8-ounce can tomato sauce*   *Dairy sour cream*
½ *teaspoon oregano*   *Chopped chives*
1 *teaspoon chili powder*

In a heavy kettle or Dutch oven melt bacon drippings. Add chopped onions and green pepper and cook until soft but not brown. Add stewed tomatoes and tomato sauce. When sauce is simmering, crush oregano and add along with chili powder, ground cumin, salt, and pepper. Simmer 20 to 30 minutes. Meanwhile, cook macaroni in boiling salted water to cover until tender and then drain. Cut each frankfurter into three pieces. Add drained macaroni and frankfurters to the ragout and simmer another 10 to 15 minutes. Add additional salt to taste, if needed. When ready to serve, spoon into bowls (plastic or foil are good outdoors) and top with a spoonful of sour cream. Sprinkle with chopped chives. Serve with toasted buns or bread sticks. Makes 4 to 6 servings.

Réchauffé Bonaparte
Bonaparte Stew

Probably named for Louis Bonaparte rather than the Emperor, this hash with its regal name comes from Louisiana. Use leftover cooked or canned or frozen potatoes and carrots. *Réchauffé* means "warmed over."

4 *tablespoons fat cut from roast beef,* 1½ *to 2 cups leftover roast beef, cut*
  or 3 tablespoons salad oil   *in cubes*
1½ *cups chopped onions*   1½ *cups diced cooked potatoes*
2 *tablespoons flour*   ½ *cup sliced cooked carrots*
2 *cups beef stock, or 1 cup stock*   ½ *cup prune juice*
  and 1 cup leftover gravy   ½ *cup cooked prunes, pitted*
¼ *teaspoon thyme*

In a heavy saucepan fry pieces of fat cut from roast until crisp or heat salad oil; add onions and cook until soft. Stir in flour and cook, stirring constantly, until flour is well browned. Stir in beef stock or stock and leftover gravy. Cook and stir until sauce comes to a boil and is thickened.

Crush the thyme and add with cubed beef, potatoes, and carrots. When stew is simmering, stir in prune juice; just before serving, add prunes. Serve with hot biscuits. Makes 4 servings.

VEAL

*

Bollito Misto
Italian Boiled Dinner

This traditional Italian boiled dinner will give the average family a whole meal or so and plenty of cold meats for sandwiches and snacks. Use any of the suggested meats that you like.

3 quarts water
1 cup red table wine
2 medium-size onions
2 carrots
2 large stalks celery
2 tablespoons chopped parsley
About 1½ pounds smoked beef tongue
   or cottage roll or 2 to 3 pounds of
   corned beef

About 2 pounds rolled veal or pork
   roast or 2½ to 3 pounds of beef
   brisket or chuck
2 to 2½ pounds whole broiler-fryer
   chicken
10 to 12 ounces Italian sausage
Salt to taste
½ pound spaghetti
Grated Parmesan or Romano cheese

Combine water and wine in a very large kettle and bring to a boil. Add whole onions, whole carrots, celery stalks, and chopped parsley. Add two of the suggested meats: 1) smoked tongue or cottage roll or the corned beef and 2) veal or pork roast or the beef brisket or chuck. Simmer 1½ to 2 hours, or until meats are almost done. Then add the whole chicken and Italian sausage. Simmer another 30 to 40 minutes. Add salt to taste. When time to serve lift out meats, slice them, and arrange on a platter. Carve up the chicken. Keep hot. Ladle some of the hot broth into soup cups and serve. (Or keep broth hot while cooking spaghetti.)

To remaining broth add spaghetti and cook until tender. Drain spaghetti or lift out onto platter and sprinkle with cheese. Serve the hot broth as a first course and the sliced meat and chicken and spaghetti next. A good mustard sauce goes well with this, and Italian or French bread. Makes 6 to 8 servings.

Danish Veal Stew

Veal stew is a favorite in Denmark at Easter time.

*2 to 2½ pounds veal stew meat, cut
    in 1½-inch cubes
4 cups water
2 teaspoons salt
1-inch piece bay leaf
5 or 6 whole black peppercorns
5 or 6 whole cloves
¼ teaspoon thyme
½ cup sliced celery
1 small boiling onion*

*4 medium-size carrots
¼ cup chopped parsley
¼ cup butter
1 cup chopped onion
½ pound small whole fresh mushrooms
3 tablespoons flour
2 egg yolks
2 tablespoons lemon juice
1 teaspoon dill weed*

Combine veal stew meat, water, and salt in a large kettle. Bring to a boil; turn down to simmer and skim well. Simmer for about 20 minutes, skimming from time to time. Add bay leaf, peppercorns and cloves; crush thyme and add it to stew. When veal has cooked for about an hour add sliced celery. Peel boiling onion. Scrape carrots and cut into thirds. Add the whole onion, carrots, and chopped parsley to stew. Simmer for about another hour, or until meat and vegetables are tender.

Meanwhile, melt 2 tablespoons butter in frying pan or saucepan. Add the chopped onion and cook until lightly browned. Add mushrooms and about ½ cup of stock from stew. Simmer until onion and mushrooms are tender, about 10 minutes. Melt remaining butter in a large heavy pan. Stir in flour. Drain stock from meat and vegetables and stir into this flour and butter *roux*. Cook, stirring constantly, until sauce is thickened. Beat the egg yolks with lemon juice; add a little of the hot sauce, then stir egg yolk mixture into sauce. Blend in the onion and mushroom mixture. Remove bay leaf, peppercorns, and cloves from meat. Then add veal and vegetables to the sauce. Heat just to simmering; add additional salt to taste, if needed. Sprinkle with dill weed and serve with boiled or mashed potatoes. Makes 6 servings.

Ragoût de Veau Normande
Veal Stew with Applejack

In Normandy the apple brandy would be Calvados, but it is sometimes hard to find, and it's expensive. Other apple brandy or applejack will give this veal stew the flavor of France.

2 to 2½ pounds veal stew meat	2 cups chicken stock
1 teaspoon garlic salt	1-inch piece bay leaf
½ teaspoon finely chopped parsley	¼ teaspoon thyme
⅛ teaspoon white pepper	½ cup applejack, apple brandy, or
¼ cup flour	cider
2 to 3 tablespoons butter	½ cup dairy sour cream
1½ cups sliced onions	

Have meat cut into 1½-inch cubes; pound cubes with meat hammer until slightly flattened. Combine garlic salt, chopped parsley, pepper, and flour. Dip pieces of veal in the seasoned flour. Heat butter in a heavy frying pan. Brown veal in butter. When well browned add the onions and cook until golden. Pour chicken stock over the meat; crush bay leaf and thyme and sprinkle over meat. Cover and cook over low heat about 1 hour, or until meat is tender. Or cook in a moderately low oven, 300°F., for about 1 hour. Just before serving stir in apple brandy and sour cream. Heat about 5 minutes. Serve with steamed rice, noodles, or small browned potatoes. Makes about 4 servings.

Vitello Cioppino
Italian Veal and Seafood Stew

The Italian flavor of San Francisco's North Beach and Fishermen's Wharf is in this combination of veal and seafood. Serve in bowls with toasted French or Italian bread or spoon the rolls and sauce over spaghetti and sprinkle with Romano or Parmesan cheese.

1 to 1½ pounds very thin veal steak
6 or 7 ounces fresh or frozen crab-
    meat, or 1 6- to 7-ounce can crab-
    meat
¼ cup olive oil
1½ teaspoons salt
1 cup chopped onions
1 cup sliced fresh mushrooms
2 cloves garlic
1 can (1 pound 12 ounces) Italian-
    style tomatoes

2 cups red table wine
3 tablespoons tomato paste
1 cup water
⅛ teaspoon black pepper
1-inch piece bay leaf
1 teaspoon mixed Italian herbs
1 cup cooked, cleaned shrimp, fresh,
    frozen, or canned

Pound veal steaks thin with a wooden mallet and cut into 6 or 8 pieces. Divide crabmeat and spoon onto veal pieces. Roll up veal and fasten with skewers. In a heavy frying pan or Dutch oven, heat 2 table-spoons of olive oil; brown veal rolls slowly, sprinkling with ½ teaspoon salt. Set aside while making the sauce.

Heat remaining 2 tablespoons olive oil in a heavy kettle. Add chopped onions and sliced mushrooms and cook slowly until onions are golden. Crush garlic and add to onions and mushrooms along with tomatoes, wine, tomato paste, and water. Add pepper and bay leaf. Crush herbs and stir into sauce along with remaining 1 teaspoon salt. Simmer for 30 to 40 minutes. Add browned veal rolls to sauce and continue to cook for another 30 minutes or until veal is tender. Add the shrimp and when thoroughly heated, serve in soup plates or bowls along with French or Italian bread. Or spoon stew over hot, cooked spaghetti and sprinkle with grated Par-mesan or Romano cheese. Makes about 6 servings.

Black Bean Pot Martinique

Quite a number of years ago my brother-in-law, who was then a teenager, ran across this recipe and asked me to make it. Through the years, when-ever I have served this it has caused lots of conversation because of the different liquids: beer, wine, coffee, brandy. One friend once, after tasting it, teasingly said, "I think it needs some vermouth!" It really is delicious, and a good dish for a buffet supper. If you can't find black beans—they aren't always in the supermarkets—then use Mexican or red kidney beans.

1 pound dry black beans
1 pig's foot, split
1 veal shank
1 fifth claret wine
1-inch piece bay leaf
¼ teaspoon each thyme and rosemary
2 green onions, cut in half
1 large white onion
6 whole cloves

1 tablespoon seasoned salt
1 tablespoon salt
2 cups hot coffee (2 cups hot water
  and 1 tablespoon instant coffee)
½ teaspoon dry mustard
1 12-ounce can beer
¼ cup olive oil
¼ cup brandy

Wash the beans; cover with warm water and let soak overnight. Next morning early, drain beans. In a bean pot or big casserole combine beans, pig's foot, veal shank, and claret wine. Add bay leaf; crush thyme and rosemary and add to beans along with halved green onions. Stick cloves into the white onion and bury in beans. Add seasoned salt and salt. Cover and bake in a slow oven, 250°F., 6 or 7 hours. In the afternoon mix in the coffee, dry mustard, and beer. Continue baking 2 or 3 more hours or longer. About half an hour before serving, stir in the olive oil and brandy. Makes 8 to 10 servings.

NOTE: This *Bean Pot* can bake as long as 12 hours or even more. The flavor actually improves.

LAMB

*

White Beans Indienne
Indian Beans and Lamb

From a collection of recipes from India, this has been adapted to American tastes. Pork or bacon or a piece of ham may be substituted for the lamb, or meat may be omitted. The stew is still very tasty—pleasantly pungent but not hot.

1 *pound dry white beans*
2 *quarts water*
½ *to 1 pound lamb stew meat, cut*
   into cubes
2 *tablespoons butter*
½ *cup chopped onions*
¼ *cup chopped green pepper*
2 *cloves garlic*
   or ¼ teaspoon garlic powder

¼ *teaspoon ground ginger*
1 *teaspoon ground turmeric*
1 *teaspoon ground coriander*
1 *teaspoon seasoned salt*
½ *teaspoon black pepper*
1 *large tomato, peeled*
1 *teaspoon salt, or to taste*
1 *tablespoon lemon juice*
2 *tablespoons chopped parsley*

Combine the beans and water; bring beans to a boil and let boil 5 minutes. Remove them from heat and soak for 1 hour. Add lamb and simmer for about 1 hour, or until beans are almost tender. About 1 hour before serving, melt butter in frying pan; add onions and green pepper and cook gently for 5 to 10 minutes. Crush garlic and add to onions and pepper along with ginger, turmeric, coriander, seasoned salt, and pepper. Cut tomato into quarters. Add cooked vegetables, seasonings and tomato to beans. Continue to simmer for another hour. Add salt, if needed. Just before serving, stir in lemon juice and sprinkle with parsley. Serve in bowls accompanied by a green salad and toasted French bread. Makes 6 to 8 servings.

Lancashire Hot Pot

From the north of England comes this traditional stew, very closely related to Irish stew. It should be cooked in an earthenware pot in the oven. The oysters can be added at first, but I like to add them the last half hour.

2 *pounds lamb neck slices*
   or shoulder stew meat
3 *or 4 large potatoes, sliced*
2 *large onions, sliced*
½ *pound mushrooms, sliced*
3 *lamb kidneys, split and sliced*

1 *to 2 teaspoons salt*
¼ *teaspoon pepper*
3 *cups hot water or beef stock*
1 *10-ounce jar oysters*
2 *tablespoons cornstarch*

Arrange half of the lamb stew meat in bottom of an earthenware pot. Top with a layer of sliced potatoes, then a layer of onions and mushrooms, and then kidneys. Repeat layers, reserving enough potato slices to form a top layer. Season each layer with salt and pepper, using less salt if stock is salty. Pour hot water or stock over meat and vegetables. Cover and bake in a moderately slow oven, 325°F., for about 3 hours, or until meat is tender. About ½ hour before serving, add the oysters, carefully placing them under layers of meat and vegetables. Moisten cornstarch with a little cold water and mix into stew without disturbing layers. Bake another half hour. Spoon into bowls and serve with oatmeal bread or toasted scones. Makes 6 to 8 servings.

Malaysian Denningvleis
Malaysian Spiced Stew

From Cape Town comes a Malaysian spiced stew similar to curry. It's served there with *atjar*, a condiment like chutney. Serve it with rice and the usual curry accompaniments—coconut, sliced bananas, chutney, chopped onions, and chopped salted peanuts.

2 tablespoons fat trimmed from lamb stew meat	1 quart water
	1 bay leaf
2 to 2½ pounds lamb stew meat, cut into cubes	6 to 8 whole allspice
	2 small hot dry red chili peppers
2 teaspoons salt	3 whole cloves
4 large onions, sliced	2 tablespoons vinegar
3 cloves garlic	2 tablespoons cornstarch
¼ teaspoon nutmeg	2 or 3 tablespoons cold water

Brown fat cut from lamb in a large kettle; add pieces of lamb and brown well. As meat is browned sprinkle with 1 teaspoon of salt; remove meat from pan and reserve.

Pour off extra fat, leaving about 2 or 3 tablespoons in the kettle. Add sliced onions and cook until well browned. Crush garlic and stir into onions; add nutmeg, water, bay leaf, and allspice. Crush chili peppers and add to pan along with cloves and remaining 1 teaspoon salt. When sauce begins to simmer return browned lamb to kettle. Cover stew and simmer slowly about 1 hour, or until meat is tender. Just before serving, stir in the vinegar. Blend cornstarch and cold water and mix into stew. Stir and simmer until sauce bubbles and is clear and thickened. Serve with steamed rice and curry condiments. Makes about 6 servings.

Vindaloo
Indian Lamb Stew

Vindaloo comes from North India where diets include more meat than in Southern India—partly because there is more meat there and partly because religious restrictions aren't as rigid. If you live in an area where you can buy imported foods you may be able to find *Garam-Masala* (it means mixed spices). You can often find this spice mixture in university areas where Indian students are enrolled. But you can mix your own. I have, and think it even better than that I purchased. If you like your food less hot, omit the black pepper in the *Garam-Masala*.

1½ pounds lean lamb stew meat	*2 or 3 slices fresh ginger, or dry ginger slices soaked in water*
2 tablespoons salad oil	
1 pound small new potatoes	*½ teaspoon ground cumin seed*
2 medium-size onions, thinly sliced	*½ teaspoon chili powder*
1 teaspoon salt	*1 teaspoon turmeric*
½ to 1 cup vinegar	*1 teaspoon Garam-Masala (see Accompaniments)*
3 cloves garlic, peeled	

Cut the meat into 1½-inch cubes. In a heavy kettle heat the salad oil. Add meat and brown over high heat. While meat is browning, scrape or peel new potatoes. Add potatoes to meat along with sliced onions and salt, and continue to cook over high heat until brown. In an electric blender combine ½ cup vinegar, garlic cloves, sliced ginger, ground cumin, chili powder, turmeric, and *Garam-Masala*. Turn the blender to high speed until garlic and ginger are well blended with the spices. Pour over meat and vegetables and simmer over very low heat until tender, adding more vinegar if stew becomes too dry. Serve with hot steamed rice. Makes about 6 servings.

Lamb Shank Stew with Dill

A family recipe of a good friend who grew up in San Francisco and whose parents were Irish, this stew makes use of lamb shanks—in the olden days inexpensive. Today they are not always a *bargain*, but they are always a *good* buy because they are meaty and flavorful.

4 to 6 lamb shanks (about 3 or 4 pounds)
1 quart hot water
1½ teaspoons salt
¼ teaspoon ground white pepper
¼ teaspoon garlic powder
    or 1 clove garlic

4 juniper berries
1 teaspoon dill weed
2 tablespoons flour
1 1-pound can small new potatoes
    or 8 to 10 small new potatoes, cooked and peeled
1 tablespoon lemon juice

Cut excess fat from the lamb shanks and place them in a large kettle. Add hot water, salt, pepper, and garlic powder. If using fresh garlic, crush clove of garlic and juniper berries and add to lamb shanks along with dill weed. Cover and simmer slowly until shanks are tender, about 1½ hours. Just before serving blend flour with a little cold water and stir into stew. Drain canned potatoes. Add potatoes and lemon juice to stew. Simmer until potatoes are thoroughly heated. Hot biscuits go well with this stew. Makes 4 or 5 servings.

Spring Lamb Stew

This version of an old New England stew was made in early spring after the killing of the first lambs. In the early days young sprouted onions were used, with plenty of the green sprouts. Dried winter onions added their flavor, too.

1 cup dry white beans
1 teaspoon salt
2 pounds boneless lamb, shoulder or leg
4 slices bacon
½ cup chopped onion
2 tablespoons flour
4 cups stock—lamb, beef, or chicken
½ clove garlic

½ teaspoon thyme
½ teaspoon oregano
½ teaspoon marjoram
¾ cup chopped green onions, including the green tops
8 small white boiling onions or 1 8-ounce can small whole onions

Soak the beans 6 to 8 hours or overnight; drain them and cover with warm water. Add salt and bring to a boil; turn heat down to simmer. Cut lamb into 1- or 1½-inch cubes. After beans have cooked about an hour, dice bacon and fry in heavy frying pan. Add chopped onion and cook until bacon is crisp and onion lightly brown. Lift these out and add to beans. Brown the lamb in bacon drippings. When lamb is brown lift it out and add to beans. Stir the flour into the fat in the pan to make a smooth *roux*. Add the stock, stirring constantly, and cook until sauce is slightly thickened and smooth. Crush garlic, thyme, oregano, and marjoram and add to sauce; then add sauce to beans. Simmer for about 1 to 1½ hours, or until beans are tender. About 30 minutes before serving, add green onions and small white onions. Add additional salt, if needed. Simmer about 30 minutes. Serve with toasted Italian or French bread sprinkled with Parmesan cheese. Makes 6 generous servings.

Idaho Ranch Lamb Stew

Many years ago my father-in-law owned a "spread" in Idaho. Although he never operated it himself, good friends raised potatoes and beans, and grazed lambs on the acreage. This lamb stew was a way of using ribs and breast of lamb after a butchering, for their own use. Potatoes and onions came from their ranch and usually the carrots and cabbage from their garden. The original didn't use herbs, but the herbs do much for the flavor.

3 pounds lamb ribs or breast of lamb
2 quarts water
1 tablespoon salt
¼ teaspoon pepper
½ teaspoon mixed herbs for lamb
6 new potatoes
4 to 6 small young carrots

4 to 6 small onions
4 to 6 wedges of young green cabbage
3 tablespoons flour
½ cup cold water
2 or 3 tablespoons chopped parsley

Cut lamb into serving-size pieces. Cut off excess fat. Heat a large kettle or Dutch oven, add the lamb and brown slowly. Pour off excess fat. Add water, salt, and pepper. Crush the herbs and add to stew. Simmer slowly until lamb is tender, about 1 hour. Scrub the potatoes, scrape them or not, as you prefer. Scrape carrots and peel onions. Add vegetables

to stew and simmer until almost tender. Add cabbage wedges. Simmer stew about 15 minutes more, or until cabbage is barely done. Blend together flour and cold water. Stir into stew. When stew comes to a boil and thickens slightly, spoon meat and vegetables onto large serving platter or soup tureen. Sprinkle with parsley. Serve along with fresh baked bread or rolls. Makes 4 to 6 servings.

Babootie
South African Lamb Stew

There are numerous versions of *Babootie*, a traditional South African dish, and there are several different ways to spell *Babootie*. One version is a timbale, another is baked in a crust as a pie. All seem to have much the same seasoning, curry powder, and fruits such as apricot, apple, and banana. *Babootie* is supposed to be of Malayan origin, brought by Malaysians who were slaves in South Africa. This recipe is a stew and comes from a former student at the University of California who has lived in South Africa.

2 *pounds lean ground lamb*	1½ *teaspoons salt*
2 *medium-size onions, chopped*	1 *green cooking apple*
2 *cloves garlic*	2 *tablespoons apricot preserves or jam*
1 *to* 2 *tablespoons curry powder*	2 *cups tomato juice*
1 *1-pound can tomatoes*	2 *firm bananas*
1½ *tablespoons sugar*	¼ *cup toasted slivered almonds*
2 *tablespoons vinegar*	*Steamed rice*

Break up the ground lamb into a large cold frying pan. Cook meat over low heat until it is separated and no longer red. Drain off excess fat. Add chopped onions and continue to cook until onions are transparent. Crush garlic and stir into lamb along with curry powder. Add tomatoes, sugar, vinegar, and salt. Simmer for about 15 minutes. Peel and chop apple and stir into *Babootie* along with apricot preserves and tomato juice. Simmer stew slowly about 1½ hours. Just before serving, peel bananas and cut them into 1-inch slices. Stir into stew. Pour *Babootie* into a large serving dish or casserole. Sprinkle with toasted almonds. Serve with steamed rice accompanied by chutney. Makes 6 to 8 servings.

Nargisi Koftas
Indian Meatballs

In India *koftas* or meatballs stuffed with hard-cooked eggs are made with almost any kind of ground meat available—probably more often kid than lamb. If you have a hunter in the family, then use ground venison or moose or other game meat.

FOR THE KOFTAS

1½ *pounds lean ground lamb or other ground meat*
½ *cup finely chopped onion*
2 *cloves garlic*
1 *teaspoon salt*
1 *teaspoon* garam-masala (*see recipe*)
½ *teaspoon turmeric*
1 *to 2 tablespoons yoghurt*
1 *egg*
6 *hard-cooked eggs*
2 *or 3 tablespoons salad oil or clear butter*

FOR THE SAUCE

1 *tablespoon salad oil or clear butter, if needed*
½ *cup chopped onion*
2 *large tomatoes or 1 cup canned tomatoes*
½ *cup yoghurt*
1 *cup hot water*
1½ *teaspoons salt*
1 *teaspoon turmeric*
1 *teaspoon* Garam-Masala (*see Accompaniments*)
1 *thin slice fresh ginger or dry ginger soaked in water*
2 *tablespoons chopped fresh coriander (Chinese parsley) or ½ cup chopped green pepper*

TO MAKE THE KOFTAS

Combine the ground meat and chopped onion in a mixing bowl. Crush garlic and mix into meat along with salt, *Garam-Masala*, turmeric, yoghurt, and egg. Mix very thoroughly. Peel the hard-cooked eggs and shape some of the ground meat around each egg. If any meat is left over, shape it into a ball. Heat the oil or butter in a heavy frying pan and carefully brown the meatballs. Lift out and make sauce.

TO MAKE THE SAUCE

Add 1 tablespoon oil, if needed, to the pan. Brown onion in oil, scraping bits of browned meat into onion. Add tomatoes, yoghurt, water, salt, turmeric, and *garam-masala*. Stir until the sauce is simmering. Chop ginger very fine and add to sauce. Return meatballs to sauce and simmer very slowly until done, about 45 to 50 minutes. At serving time cut meatballs in half. Arrange them in chafing dish or hot serving dish. Spoon sauce over and around meatballs. Sprinkle with chopped parsley or green pepper. Serve with hot steamed rice. Makes 6 servings.

Lentil Stew à la Andy Akamian

My friend, Andy Akamian, who has his own advertising business, comes from an Armenian family. He tells me that this recipe of his mother's was a family stand-by as he grew up. His mother, he said, "cooked with authority"—meaning that she used plenty of garlic. Preferably this stew should be made with red lentils—available in stores in Armenian or Greek or Turkish neighborhoods. But the lentils at the supermarket are good this way, too. At our house we like this stew made with lamb stock, but Andy said that as he was growing up they often didn't have meat for such as that, so their stew was made with water.

2 cups lentils (red lentils, if available)	1 pint yoghurt
	2 or 3 cloves garlic
1 quart warm water or lamb broth	2 large onions
2 to 3 teaspoons salt	¼ cup salad oil

Soak lentils several hours or overnight in water. Drain and cover with about 1 quart fresh warm water or lamb broth. Liquid should be about ½ inch over lentils. Add 1½ teaspoons salt. Simmer for about 1 to 1½ hours, or until lentils are cooked and stew is thick.

Add ½ teaspoon salt to yoghurt; crush or chop garlic and mix into yoghurt. Chop onions coarsely and fry in hot oil until brown. At serving time heat stew to simmering. Spread yoghurt over top of stew and top with fried onions. Spoon out onto plates or into bowls.

Serve with *Lavash* (*Armenian Cracker Bread:* see recipe) or with matzoth or matzoth crackers, spread with soft butter and toasted in the oven. Makes about 6 servings.

PORK AND HAM

✳

Gramps' Navy Beans and Fresh Pork

My father-in-law, who lived to his late eighties, earned his way through engineering school by "boarding" some of his classmates. I understand this combination was on the table almost every meal, sometimes even for breakfast. It had been a staple in his father's family, and through the years his children and grandchildren always expected to have *Navy Beans and Fresh Pork* when they came visiting. In those days they had no seasoned salt; that's a recent addition.

3 cups dry Great Northern or navy beans
Water
2 to 3 pounds fresh pork—country spareribs, neck bones, shoulder cut in cubes, or fresh pork hocks

1 tablespoon seasoned salt
½ teaspoon sage
¼ teaspoon black pepper
Salt to taste

Pick over and wash the beans. In a large kettle, cover beans with warm water; bring to a boil and boil 5 minutes. Turn off the heat and let beans soak for 1 hour. Drain them and cover with 6 to 8 cups warm water. (Gramps would have soaked them overnight.) Add fresh pork and seasoned salt and bring to a boil. Crush sage and add to beans and pork along with pepper. Cover and simmer 2 or 3 hours, or until beans and pork are tender. Add salt to taste. Spoon beans and pork over dry bread or crisp toast, or serve with hot corn bread. Some of the family is sure to want catsup. Makes 6 to 8 or 10 servings, depending on whether it's the whole meal or a side dish.

Pigs in the Corn

From the Midwest corn country comes this old-time pork and corn stew. We must admit that the original probably had no garlic in it, for Midwesterners in the olden days didn't go much for garlic. In the winter time it was made with home-canned or dried corn.

2½ to 3 pounds pork spareribs
1 quart water
1 tablespoon salt
¼ teaspoon black pepper
1½ teaspoons chili powder
1 clove garlic, crushed or chopped
1 tablespoon chopped onion

1 tablespoon cider vinegar
1 10-ounce package frozen whole kernel corn or 1 12-ounce can whole kernel corn
½ package, about 6 ounces, frozen shredded potatoes
Additional salt, if needed

Cut spareribs into serving-size pieces. Spread them out in a flat baking

pan and bake in a moderate oven, 350°F., for about 45 minutes. Drain off all fat. Transfer browned ribs to a large heavy kettle. Add water to browned drippings in baking pan and bring to a boil, scraping off brown pits. Pour over spareribs. Add salt, pepper, chili powder, garlic, chopped onion, and vinegar. Cover and simmer until spareribs are tender, about 1 hour. Just before time to serve, add corn and shredded potatoes. Simmer for 15 to 20 minutes, or until corn and potatoes are tender. Add additional salt, if needed. Serve from soup tureen or large casserole. Ladle into soup plates or bowls. Serve with hot corn sticks or corn bread. Makes 6 servings.

Soul Food Stew

My good Negro friend, Fannie Johnson, says that her nieces and nephews prefer hamburgers and hot dogs to *Soul Food*. But those of us past a certain age who have lived in the Middle West and South, both Black and White, have eaten and enjoyed stews similar to this one. If fresh black-eyed peas and fresh okra are available, then use fresh instead of frozen.

2½ to 3 pounds ham hocks
5 cups water, or water and ham stock
   combined
1 cup chopped onion
½ cup chopped green pepper
1 10-ounce package frozen fresh
   black-eyed peas or 1½ cups
   fresh shelled black eyed peas

1 tablespoon vinegar
1 10-ounce package frozen small
   whole okra or ½ pound fresh okra
Salt and pepper to taste

Combine ham hocks, water and stock in a large kettle. Bring to a boil, turn heat low and simmer for about 1 hour. Add chopped onion and green pepper and black-eyed peas. Simmer another hour or so. Stir in vinegar and add okra. (If using fresh okra, wash thoroughly and cut off stems and tips.) Simmer an additional 30 to 40 minutes, or until okra and peas are tender. About 15 minutes before serving, taste and season with salt and pepper. (The amount will depend on the saltiness of the ham hocks.) Serve in soup plates accompanied by hot corn bread. Or if preferred, serve over steamed rice. Makes about 6 servings.

Cuban Bean Stew

In the 1920's Grandmother Jackson lived in Cuba. Among her effects was an old, old "receipt" book. From it comes this whole-meal stew. One interesting ingredient is pumpkin used as a vegetable, as it is in many countries particularly those in the Tropics or in the Southern Hemisphere.

1 pound dry pink beans	*½ teaspoon ground coriander*
1½ quarts water	*¼ teaspoon black pepper*
1½ pounds lean pork shoulder or ribs	*2 teaspoons salt*
or 3 fresh pork hocks	*¼ teaspoon oregano*
Piece of bacon or ham rind, if desired	*1 medium-size tomato*
¼ cup chopped onion	*1 medium-size potato*
2 tablespoons chopped green pepper	*1 cup pared, diced pumpkin*
2 cloves garlic	*or yellow winter squash*

Wash the beans. Combine beans and water in a large kettle, bring to a boil and boil 5 minutes. Remove beans from heat and let soak for 1 hour. Cut meat into cubes or pieces. (If using pork hocks, have each hock cut into two pieces.) Add meat to beans with bacon or ham rind, onion, and green pepper. Crush garlic and add along with coriander, pepper, and 1 teaspoon salt. Crush oregano and add to beans. Simmer until beans are almost tender, about 1 hour. Add remaining salt. Peel tomato and potato, cut them into cubes and add to beans along with diced pumpkin. Simmer 30 to 40 minutes, or until vegetables and meat are tender. Serve in bowls, accompanied by hot French bread. Makes 6 to 8 servings.

Pozole
Pork and Hominy

Almost every Mexican family has its favorite version of this classic stew —some made with tomatoes and onion, some quite hot, some not so hot. All are made of pork and either hominy or corn. Interestingly, *Pozole* is supposed to be of Aztec origin and was introduced to other Indians and Spaniards by the Franciscan fathers at the Missions. This version of *Pozole* can be as hot as you like. The *Green Chili Sauce* can be added in desired amounts to the stew—or not at all, if preferred. Those who like can add additional sauce to make their bowls of *Pozole* hotter. The one tablespoon called for makes a rather mild stew.

2 *pounds pork shoulder roast*
   or other pork cut such as hocks, leg,
   butt, or country spareribs
2 *quarts water*
1 *teaspoon salt*
2 *cans (1 pound 13 ounces each)*
   hominy, preferably white
Green Chili Sauce (*recipe below*)

1 *teaspoon oregano*
Additional salt to taste
Shredded lettuce
Sliced radishes
Sliced green onion
Cubes of Monterey Jack cheese
Fresh lime or lemon wedges

In a large kettle combine pork, 1 quart water, and 1 teaspoon salt. Simmer until pork is tender. Lift meat out and chill it and the broth. Cut extra fat from meat and skim off fat from broth. Add hominy to broth and simmer for an hour or so, or until hominy is tender. Cut meat into bite-size pieces and add to hominy along with any pork bones, 1 tablespoon of *Green Chili Sauce*, ½ teaspoon oregano, and remaining 1 quart water. Simmer for another hour or so; add additional salt to taste. When time to serve, combine shredded lettuce, sliced radishes, and sliced green onions. Crush remaining ½ teaspoon oregano and toss with lettuce mixture. Ladle *Pozole* into bowls. Each person tops *Pozole* with a spoonful or two of the lettuce mixture, *Green Chili Sauce* to taste, cubes of cheese, and a squeeze of lemon or lime juice. Makes about 8 servings.

Green Chili Sauce

3 *or 4 long green chilis (about ¼*
   pound), or 1 4-ounce can green
   chilis

½ *clove garlic*
½ *teaspoon seasoned salt*
2 *teaspoons wine vinegar*

If using fresh chilis, place them under broiler until skin is charred. Peel and scoop out seeds; cut off stems. Chop peppers and garlic coarsely and combine with salt and vinegar in an electric blender. Blend until smooth. Makes about ⅓ cup *Green Chili Sauce*.

Feijoada Carioca
Brazilian Black Beans and Pork

Two different friends on trips to Brazil collected a recipe for the traditional complete black bean meal of that country. Though versions of *feijoada* vary slightly, all of them seem to have a variety of smoked and fresh meats. Smoked tongue, pig's feet, beef jerky, and fresh and Portuguese sausage seem to be the staples. Other meats, depending on what's on hand or how many people are to enjoy it, are added.

Brazilian-style rice, *farofa*, a hot *Pepper and Lemon Sauce*, steamed kale (if you like), sliced oranges, and rum to drink are the traditional accompaniments to the beans, and make a wonderful menu for an informal party. In Brazil *farofa* is made from manioc meal. In this country farina makes a good substitute.

2 pounds dry black or pinto beans	1½ cups chopped onion
Water	3 or 4 tomatoes (1 pound), peeled
1 tablespoon salt	and cut into chunks
2 or 3 pig's feet, cut into quarters	3 cloves garlic
½ pound smoked bacon or salt pork	2-inch piece bay leaf
2 or 3 ounces beef jerky strips	2 small hot dry red chili peppers
1 smoked beef tongue (about 2 pounds)	Strip of fresh orange peel
	1 pound fresh pork sausage
1½ pounds fresh or smoked pork shoulder, or both, if desired	1 pound hot Portuguese or Italian sausage
3 tablespoons bacon drippings	Additional salt to taste, if needed

Soak the beans overnight in water. Next morning drain and cover beans with about 8 cups fresh water in a very large kettle. Add salt, and heat to simmering. Wash pig's feet and smoked bacon or salt pork and add to beans. Bring beans to a boil and skim well. Add beef jerky and turn heat down very low.

Meanwhile, wash beef tongue and cover with water. Simmer tongue for about 1 hour; drain it and let it cool slightly. Remove the skin and trim off excess fat. Add tongue to beans along with fresh or smoked pork shoulder. Simmer for another hour.

Meanwhile, heat bacon drippings in a frying pan. Add chopped onion and tomatoes; crush garlic and stir into onions and tomatoes. Cook until vegetables are soft. Stir this mixture into beans and meat. Add bay leaf; crush red peppers and add to beans along with orange peel. Cut each sausage into 2 or 3 pieces and add to beans. Simmer for another hour, or until meats are tender. Add additional salt, if needed. (Saltiness of the various meats will determine if more salt is needed.) When time to serve, lift out tongue, smoked bacon or salt pork, and shoulder meat. Slice the meat and arrange on a platter. Pour beans and remaining meat into a large tureen or casserole. Each person then serves himself to meat and beans. Accompany with *Rice Brazilian Style*.

Farofa is sprinkled over the beans and the *Pepper and Lemon Sauce* is spooned over the meat—and the beans, if desired. Sliced oranges go on the same plate, along with steamed kale, if served. (The kale isn't really needed; there's a complete meal without it.) Makes 12 to 15 servings.

Rice Brazilian Style

3 tablespoons bacon drippings	2 cups long-grain rice
1 cup chopped onion	5 cups water
2 cloves garlic	1 teaspoon salt

In a heavy pot with lid, melt bacon drippings. Add onion and cook until lightly browned. Crush the garlic and stir into onion along with rice. Cook until rice is lightly browned. Add water and bring it to boiling; stir in salt. Cover rice and turn down the heat. Cook over very low heat until rice is tender, about 25 minutes. Just before serving fluff rice with fork.

Farofa
Brazilian Garnish

½ pound butter	1 pound farina
¼ cup chopped onion	Salt to taste

Melt the butter in a heavy frying pan; add onion and cook until it is brown. Stir in farina and cook over low heat, stirring constantly, until farina is lightly browned. Add salt to taste. Serve *farofa* from a bowl with a spoon so that it can be sprinkled over beans and rice.

Môlho de Pimenta e Limão
Pepper and Lemon Sauce

2 tomatoes	1 cup chopped onion
2 small hot dry red chili peppers	1 tablespoon chopped parsley
2 cloves garlic	1 cup liquid from cooked black beans
½ cup lemon juice	Salt to taste
½ cup vinegar	

Peel the tomatoes; cut in pieces and put into electric blender. Crush red pepper and garlic and add to tomatoes. Blend them until smooth. Mix in lemon juice and vinegar. Add chopped onion and parsley and stir in liquid from beans. Add salt to taste. Make sauce about an hour before serving. Be sure to keep any leftover sauce in refrigerator, or it will ferment. CAUTION: Be sure to warn your guests that this sauce is very hot.

Goulash

Sauerkraut makes this goulash just a little different—but it retains the flavor of Middle Europe. Serve it with cooked noodles tossed with butter and caraway seeds.

2 *pounds lean boneless pork or veal,*	2 *teaspoons paprika*
cut into 1½-inch cubes	2 *cups hot beef stock or hot water*
2 *tablespoons salad oil or butter*	1 *1-pound can sauerkraut*
1 *teaspoon salt*	2 *teaspoons cornstarch*
¼ *teaspoon black pepper*	1 *cup dairy sour cream*
3 *or 4 large onions*	

Brown pork or veal cubes in oil or butter in a heavy kettle or Dutch oven. Season with salt and pepper. Peel onions and cut into slices. When meat is brown, add onion slices and cook until onions are lightly browned, stirring often. Stir in paprika; mix thoroughly. Add beef stock or hot water and the undrained sauerkraut. Cover and simmer for about 1 hour, or until meat is tender. When time to serve blend cornstarch with a little cold water and stir into goulash. When goulash is simmering again and slightly thickened, stir in sour cream. Heat to simmering and serve with caraway noodles accompanied by dill pickles. Makes 6 servings.

Bohemian Pork Stew

For this stew, adapted from one served in a beer garden in Bohemian Czechoslovakia, beer makes the best accompaniment. In that part of the world the beer would be the famous Czech Pilsner beer.

2 *pounds lean pork shoulder*	1 *teaspoon caraway seeds*
1 *teaspoon salt*	*1-inch piece bay leaf*
⅛ *teaspoon pepper*	1 *can or bottle (11 or 12 ounces) beer*
1 *can (1 pound 14 ounces) sauerkraut*	1 *1-pound can red kidney beans*

Cut pork into 1½-inch cubes. Cut off a piece of fat and fry out in heavy kettle or a top-of-stove casserole. Brown pork slowly; sprinkle with salt and pepper. Drain sauerkraut and add to browned meat. Sprinkle caraway seeds over meat and kraut and add bay leaf. Pour beer into casserole. Simmer stew on top of the stove for about 1 hour, or until meat is tender. Drain beans and mix into stew. Continue simmering until beans are hot. Serve with black bread and boiled potatoes and plenty of beer. Makes 4 or 5 servings.

Japanese Curry with Noodles

Japanese curry is not as well known, of course, as that from India. For one thing, it is served with noodles instead of rice—preferably the *soba* or buckwheat noodle, but vermicelli or fine egg noodles if *soba* isn't available to you. Japanese curry powder is also a little different in flavor, but any one of your favorite curry powders will taste good, too.

1 to 1½ pounds lean, boneless pork	*1 teaspoon soy sauce*
shoulder or pork tenderloin	*¼ teaspoon MSG*
1 large onion, thinly sliced	*1 teaspoon salt or to taste*
2 cups dashi (see recipe)	*1 tablespoon cornstarch*
or chicken or other stock	*1 tablespoon cold water*
1 tablespoon mirin, sake, or sherry	*4 ounces noodles or vermicelli*
wine	*3 or 4 tablespoons thinly sliced green*
1 teaspoon curry powder	*onions*

Cut off any excess fat and cut meat into 1½-inch slices or cubes. Heat a heavy frying pan or Dutch oven; add meat and cook until brown, turning it to brown all sides. Pour off any excess fat. Add onion and cook, stirring frequently, until onion is brown. Add *dashi* or stock, and wine. Mix in curry powder, soy sauce, MSG, and salt to taste. Simmer until meat is tender, about 30 minutes, stirring occasionally. Blend together cornstarch and cold water and mix into stew. Cook until slightly thickened and bubbling hot, stirring constantly.

Meanwhile, cook noodles in boiling salted water until tender. Drain and rinse and pour out onto serving dish or platter. Pour pork and sauce over noodles and sprinkle with sliced green onions. Makes 4 servings.

TRIPE AND SUCH

✱

Marcie's Menudo
Marcie's Hominy and Tripe

Our beloved Marcie, a young man from a Mexican-American family, lived with us while a scholarship student at the College of Arts and Crafts. We used to have many discussions concerning the relative flavor and heat of the various chili peppers as compared to horseradish and mustard. Frankly, this *menudo* isn't as hot as he liked it, but you can add more red chilis if you want.

1 to 1½ pounds beef tripe	1 small hot dry red chili pepper
1 or 2 veal shanks or pork hocks	¼ teaspoon oregano
3 cups hot water	¼ teaspoon ground coriander
1 cup red table wine	1 tablespoon salt, or to taste
1 1-pound can tomatoes	1 can (1 pound 13 ounces) hominy
1 medium-size onion, chopped	Chopped green onions
2 cloves garlic	

Wash the tripe. Pour boiling water over it and bring to a boil. Drain tripe and rinse in cold water. Let it cool. When cool enough to handle, cut into strips or squares. Combine tripe with veal shanks or pork hocks in a large kettle or Dutch oven. Add 3 cups hot water, red wine, tomatoes, and chopped onion and bring to simmering. When simmering, crush garlic, red chili, and oregano and stir into stew. Add ground coriander and 2 teaspoons salt. Simmer about 3 hours, or until tripe is tender. Drain the canned hominy and add it to stew along with additional salt, if needed. Simmer about 1 hour longer. Ladle into soup plates or bowls and sprinkle with chopped green onions. Bread sticks, corn sticks, or corn chips are good with *menudo*. Makes 6 servings.

Carmen's Menudo
Carmen's Beans and Tripe

Most *menudos* are made with hominy, but Carmen, a co-worker of mine some years ago, made hers with garbanzo beans. Not only does she use tripe, but also oxtails and pigs' feet. This makes a large pot of stew, so it will last for some time (and improve with reheating). A good friend takes a pot of *menudo* with him when he goes out on his boat. He agrees with still another friend who says that *menudo* is the best cure of all for "morning-after" ailments.

½ pound garbanzo beans
1 to 1½ pounds beef tripe
2 oxtails (about 2 pounds), cut up
4 pigs' feet (about 2 pounds), split
1 cup white table wine
6 cups water
2 cloves garlic
1-inch piece bay leaf
½ teaspoon caraway seeds
2 beef bouillon cubes

¼ teaspoon whole black peppercorns
1 tablespoon salt or to taste
2 small hot dry red chili peppers
2 tablespoons olive oil
2 medium-size onions, chopped
1 chorizo or an Italian sausage (about
  1 pound)
2 1-pound cans stewed tomatoes
½ teaspoon oregano

Cover garbanzos with warm water and soak overnight. Next morning drain them, cover with fresh warm water and cook until done. Meanwhile, wash tripe and cover it with cold water. Bring it to a boil and simmer about 30 minutes. Drain tripe and let it cool. When cool enough to handle, cut it into strips.

Combine tripe in a very large kettle with oxtail and pigs' feet. Add the wine and water. Crush 1 clove of garlic and add it, along with bay leaf, caraway seeds, bouillon cubes, peppercorns, salt, and chilis. Simmer until tripe is tender and other meat falls from the bone. Cool the meat. Remove bones, if desired, and skim off excess fat.

Heat olive oil in a frying pan; add chopped onions. Crush remaining clove of garlic and add to onions. Skin and break up sausage and add it to onions. Cook about 5 minutes, or until onions are lightly browned. Add the mixture to *menudo* along with stewed tomatoes and the drained garbanzos. Crush oregano and add to stew; simmer for about 1 more hour. Add salt to taste, if more is needed. Serve in bowls with French bread, corn chips, or bread sticks. Cold Mexican beer goes well with *menudo*. Makes 10 to 12 servings.

Andalusian Callos
Andalusian Beans and Tripe

In the working man's *bistro* in southern Spain there is always a selection of *tapas*, hot and cold snacks to go with the wine. *Callos* is a popular

snack, though it could easily make a whole meal, with bread and a salad. This one came from a *bistro* in Málaga.

½ *pound garbanzo beans or chick peas*
2 *pounds beef tripe*
2 *or 3 pigs' feet, split*
½ *pound linguica or other hard, highly seasoned sausage, such as pepperoni*
4 *ounces salt pork*
2 *cups chopped onions*

1-*inch piece bay leaf*
4 *or 5 whole black peppercorns*
2 *or 3 small hot dry red chili peppers*
2 *cloves garlic*
1 *fifth or quart white table wine*
Salt to taste

Soak the garbanzo beans in water to cover overnight. Next morning, drain them and place in a large heavy casserole. Cover tripe with cold water, bring water to boiling and simmer for 20 minutes. Pour off water and rinse the tripe in cold water. Let it cool. When cool enough to handle, cut tripe into 2-inch strips. Add tripe and pigs' feet to the casserole. Cut sausage into ½-inch slices and salt pork into ¼-inch cubes. Add to casserole along with chopped onions, bay leaf, and peppercorns. Crush dry red peppers and garlic and add to beans and meat. Pour wine into casserole. Simmer *callos* over very low heat or cook in a low oven, 250° F., for 5 to 6 hours, or until beans are done and meat is very tender. Add additional water from time to time, if needed. Remove some of the larger pigs' feet bones, if desired. Serve in soup plates or bowls. Makes 6 to 8 servings. *Callos* reheats beautifully.

Javanese Tripe Stew

The crystallized ginger gives this stew its interesting flavor. Be sure to serve the fried onions (French fried or fried in oil) and the chopped salted peanuts as accompaniments.

1 *pound beef tripe*
3 *tablespoons peanut oil*
6 *cups water*
2 *teaspoons salt*
3 *or 4 leeks*
1 *tablespoon chopped crystallized ginger*

1 *teaspoon vinegar*
1 *cup rich milk or half and half*
(*Dash cayenne pepper*)
Steamed rice
Fried onions
Chopped salted peanuts

Cut the tripe into strips. Wash and cover with water. Bring to a boil, drain tripe and discard water. Dry tripe on paper towels. Heat peanut oil in a large kettle; add tripe and cook until lightly browned. (Don't worry if it sticks a little.) Add the 6 cups water and salt and simmer tripe until it is tender, about 1 to 1½ hours. Wash and clean leeks. Slice thinly, using some of the green part. Add to tripe with crystallized ginger and continue to simmer until leeks are tender. Stir in vinegar and milk, and heat just to simmering. Spoon steamed rice into soup bowls and ladle stew over it. Top with onions and chopped salted peanuts. Makes 4 or 5 servings.

TO FRY ONIONS:

Peel and slice thinly 2 or 3 large onions. Fry in 2 or 3 tablespoons peanut oil until golden brown. Salt lightly. Or use frozen or canned French fried onions.

Son-of-a-Bitch Stew

There are more refined names for this very old stew from the cattle country such as son-of-a-gun stew or S.O.B. stew, but the old cowhands preferred this down-to-earth name. In the old cow camps of the Southwest when an animal was slaughtered out on the range to feed the hands, the first night a stew was made of the innards. In those days the stew was put into a cast-iron pot and buried in coals. A Dutch oven or heavy kettle or large heavy frying pan with cover will do.

You need to know your guests' tastes before serving this. It's good, usually, for a stag party, either a crowd of sportsmen or card players. Use all of the various kinds of variety meats—or omit any you care to, or can't find in your market.

1 small beef tongue, about 1 pound	4 cups hot water
½ pound beef tripe	1 tablespoon salt
½ pound beef kidney	¼ teaspoon pepper
½ beef heart, about 1 pound	2 teaspoons Worcestershire sauce
½ pound beef liver	¼ teaspoon marjoram
½ pound beef or veal brains	¼ teaspoon thyme
½ pound beef or veal sweetbreads	2 or 3 tablespoons flour
¼ pound salt pork	Cold water
3 or 4 medium-size onions	

First, prepare all the meats for the stew. Combine beef tongue and tripe in a kettle; add water to cover. Simmer for about 30 minutes, then lift out tripe. Let it cool slightly and cut into strips. Continue to cook tongue for another 30 to 40 minutes. Drain tongue and let it cool slightly, then pull off skin. Cut off fat and gristly portions and cut tongue into 1½-inch cubes.

Meanwhile, soak kidney in salted water for about 1 hour, then cut into cubes, cutting out all white veins and fat. Cut beef heart and liver into 1-inch cubes. Parboil brains and sweetbreads in lightly salted water for about 15 minutes. Drain them and cut brains into 1-inch cubes. Remove membrane from sweetbreads and cut or break into pieces.

Dice the salt pork. In a large heavy Dutch oven or kettle fry it until crisp and brown. Peel and slice onions and add to salt pork. Cook until brown. Add all pieces of meat except brains and sweetbreads. Cook meat in browned onions, turning and stirring frequently, for about 10 to 15 minutes. Add hot water, salt, pepper, and Worcestershire sauce. Crush marjoram and thyme and stir into stew. Cover and simmer for about 2 to 2½ hours, or until meats are tender. Add brains and sweetbreads and continue simmering another 30 minutes or so. If desired for thickening, blend flour with cold water and stir into stew. When stew simmers again and is thickened, it is ready to serve. (You may not want to thicken the stew.) Serve with whatever you wish—steamed rice, mashed potatoes, buttered noodles—or we like lots of crusty homemade bread. Makes 8 to 10 servings.

NOTE: Some versions, notably from Texas, are thickened by sprinkling in a little cornmeal and served with corn bread.

Kidney and Mushroom Stew

My sister lived with a family of English background in her college days in Montana. This was their Sunday breakfast dish. Long a favorite at Sunday brunches at my house, you'll find *Kidney and Mushroom Stew* slightly different from the usual British kidney stew. It's particularly good with *Hominy Grits Soufflé*.

2 *pounds beef or veal kidney*
Cold water
2 *tablespoons vinegar*
1 *pound fresh mushrooms*
½ *cup chopped onions*
¼ *cup butter or margarine*

⅓ *cup flour*
1 *teaspoon seasoned salt*
¼ *teaspoon fines herbes*
3 *cups beef bouillon*
1 *cup sherry*

Slice kidney and cut out the white portions. Cover with cold water, add vinegar and let stand an hour or so. Wash the mushrooms and slice. Melt butter in a large frying pan. Add chopped onions and cook until they are light yellow. Drain the kidneys and rinse in cold water. Add sliced mushrooms and kidneys to onions and cook over low heat until kidneys have lost their red color. Sprinkle flour over kidneys and mushrooms and mix well. Add seasoned salt. Crush the herbs and sprinkle over mushrooms and kidneys. Add beef bouillon and sherry and cook, stirring constantly, until mixture simmers and is thickened very slightly. (If you like a thicker sauce, you will need to add more flour. This makes a very thin sauce.) Pour stew into a 2-quart casserole. Cook in a moderately low oven, 300°F., for about 2 hours, or until kidneys are very tender. If desired, bake *Hominy Grits Soufflé*, spoon bread or other hot bread during last 30 minutes or so. Turn up heat to accommodate hot bread. Makes about 8 servings.

Hangover Stew

An old, old favorite of Westerners—particularly outdoorsmen—this tasty stew is supposed to be good for the next-day doldrums following a gay evening.

2½ to 3 pounds oxtails, cut in 2-inch pieces
1 teaspoon salt
¼ teaspoon black pepper
2 cans beer (each 11 or 12 ounces)
1 teaspoon brown sugar
1 tablespoon Worcestershire sauce
Dash of Tabasco
1 clove garlic

½ teaspoon mixed beef herbs or ¼ teaspoon each marjoram and thyme
1 8-ounce can small whole onions
1 8-ounce can sliced or small whole carrots
1 8-ounce can small whole potatoes or 8 or 10 small frozen potatoes
1 tablespoon flour

Trim excess fat from oxtails. Fry a few pieces of fat in a heavy kettle or Dutch oven for drippings. Add oxtails and brown slowly. Pour off excess fat and season with salt and pepper. Add beer, brown sugar, Worcestershire sauce, and Tabasco. Crush garlic and herbs and stir them into stew. Cover stew and slowly simmer about 2 hours, or until meat is tender. About 30 minutes before serving add undrained onions and carrots. Drain canned potatoes, and add them or frozen potatoes to stew. Simmer until vegetables are thoroughly heated and potatoes cooked.

Blend flour with 2 or 3 tablespoons cold water and stir into stew. Cook until stew is simmering and thickened. Serve with hot biscuits or fresh bread, and plenty of paper napkins, for this stew tastes better if you pick up the pieces of oxtail with your fingers and eat the meat from the bones. Makes about 4 servings.

Cowboy Pinto Stew

A favorite in the great Southwest, this stew is the kind to take in a pot on a camping trip or on a picnic. Or serve it on the patio along with barbecued steaks or hamburgers.

½ pound dry pinto beans
1 quart water
1 teaspoon salt
2 tablespoons bacon drippings
1½ cups chopped onions
1 1-pound can tomatoes

1 tablespoon chili powder
2 cups diced cooked corned beef or smoked tongue or 1 12-ounce can corned beef, cut in cubes
¼ pound Monterey Jack or Cheddar cheese, cut in cubes

Wash the beans and combine with water in a large kettle. Boil beans 5 minutes, turn off heat, and soak for 1 hour. Bring again to a boil and add salt. Heat bacon drippings in a frying pan, add onion and cook until onions are soft and lightly browned. Add onions to beans along with tomatoes and chili powder. Simmer for about 1 hour, then add corned beef or tongue and cook until done, about 40 to 50 minutes. Just before serving, add cheese cubes. Spoon over crisp tortillas, or ladle into bowls and top with crisp corn chips. Makes 6 servings.

GAME

✳

Mac's Venison Stew

My very good friend, Mac McLean, is an expert hunter and an expert cook—so good that he is always the camp chef for his deer-hunting friends, a group that has gone hunting together for many years. He makes his famous venison stew in camp as well as at home. Of course, he sometimes has to make a few changes in camp; for example, he may not have the sour cream to stir in. Most often he makes double this amount, but because I depend on his—and other friends'—gifts of venison I'm not quite so generous with amounts.

2 to 3 pounds venison stew meat
½ cup flour
1 teaspoon salt
¼ teaspoon freshly ground black pepper
¼ cup bacon drippings or salad oil
2 large onions, chopped
1 clove garlic
2 to 3 cups red table wine

1 tablespoon Worcestershire sauce or soy sauce
1 bay leaf
¼ teaspoon each sweet basil, oregano, rosemary, and thyme
1 or 2 tablespoons flour or cornstarch for thickening, if desired
½ to 1 cup dairy sour cream, if available

Cut meat into chunks about 1½ to 2 inches square. Combine flour, salt, and pepper and roll meat in seasoned flour. Brown meat in bacon drippings or oil in a Dutch oven or very heavy deep frying pan. When meat is well browned, add chopped onions. Crush garlic and stir into meat and onions. When onions are brown, pour wine over meat. Add Worcestershire sauce and bay leaf. Crush herbs and stir into stew. Cover and simmer over very low heat for 1 to 1½ hours, or until meat is very tender. At serving time, if thicker stew is desired, blend flour or cornstarch with cold water and stir into stew. Stir until stew again is simmering and has thickened. Mix in sour cream, if used. (Our personal preference is for no more thickening and the sour cream.) Serve stew accompanied by steamed wild rice or *White and Wild Rice Pilaff*. Makes about 6 servings, depending on appetites.

Tavsan Güveci
Rabbit Ragout

Turkish cuisine uses eggplant in hundreds of ways. Here eggplant is combined with rabbit in a flavorful stew. Serve with rice or wheat pilaff. If you live where you can buy the flat Turkish or Armenian bread, it makes a wonderful accompaniment. Or make your own (see recipe). Matzoth is a good substitute, particularly if spread with butter or oil, sprinkled with garlic salt and then heated briefly.

2½- to 3-pound frying rabbit, cut into serving-size pieces	*2 cloves garlic*
	2 cups chicken or beef stock
3 tablespoons flour	*1 tablespoon tomato paste*
2 teaspoons salt	*¼ teaspoon oregano*
⅛ teaspoon pepper	*1 teaspoon parsley*
¼ cup olive oil	*½ cup red table wine*
1½ cups chopped onions	*¼ cup sliced ripe olives*
1 eggplant, about 1 to 1½ pounds	*or chunks of black Greek olives*

Wash the rabbit and pat dry with paper towel. Combine flour, 1 teaspoon salt, and pepper. Dip pieces of rabbit in seasoned flour. Heat olive oil in a heavy frying pan or top-of-stove casserole. Brown the rabbit in the hot olive oil and set brown pieces aside. Add chopped onions to drippings. Pare eggplant, cut into 1-inch cubes, and add to onions. Crush garlic and stir into onions and eggplant along with remaining 1 teaspoon salt. Brown lightly; sprinkle any remaining seasoned flour over vegetables. When flour is lightly browned arrange browned rabbit over vegetables. Combine chicken stock with tomato paste; crush oregano and stir into stock along with parsley. Pour over rabbit and vegetables. Cover ragout and simmer slowly until rabbit is tender, about 40 minutes. Just before serving stir in red wine and olives. Heat to simmering. Serve from casserole or serving bowl. Makes 4 servings.

Mainly Fish and Shellfish

~~~~~

Fish Mulligan Creole

The fame of Creole cookery lies in the blending of flavors. Contrary to popular belief Creole recipes are not all hot with red pepper nor are they complicated. Though *mulligan* is usually made with fish, shellfish can be added, and tomatoes are a frequent addition.

⅓ *cup diced bacon or salt pork*	¼ *teaspoon black pepper*
1 *pound firm lean fish*	½ *teaspoon thyme*
2 *large potatoes, sliced ½-inch thick*	½ *teaspoon lemon peel*
1 *large onion, sliced ½-inch thick*	2 *tablespoons chopped parsley*
1 *large green pepper, cut in slivers*	⅓ *cup rice*
4 *cups hot water*	1 *slice dry bread or 2 soda crackers*
1 *cup white table wine*	½ *cup cooked peas*
2 *teaspoons salt*	¼ *cup sherry*

Fry bacon or salt pork in a heavy kettle until crisp and brown. Lift out crisp bits and drain. Cut fish into chunks and arrange in drippings with potatoes, onion, and green pepper. Pour hot water and wine over fish and vegetables. Season with salt, pepper, thyme, lemon peel, and parsley and bring to a boil. Sprinkle in the rice. Simmer about 30 minutes, or until fish and vegetables are done. Break up bread or crackers and stir into the *mulligan*. Add peas and sherry. Sprinkle with bits of bacon or salt pork. Serve in soup plates accompanied by hot corn bread. Makes 4 servings.

195

Papaz Yahnisi
Bishop's Stew

The Sultans of Turkey were supposed to have feasted on this fish stew
from the Black Sea.

¼ cup olive oil

3 large onions, peeled and sliced

3 green peppers, seeded and cut in
slivers

2 large potatoes, pared and thinly
sliced

1 quart fish stock or water

3 cloves garlic

4 or 5 whole black peppercorns

1 whole bay leaf

Salt to taste

2 teaspoons paprika

3 tablespoons tomato paste

3 pounds white fish fillets, rock cod,
halibut, sole, or the like

Heat the olive oil in a large kettle or top-of-stove casserole. Add onions,
green peppers, and potatoes and cook over low heat until vegetables are
slightly softened. Add fish stock or water. When mixture is simmering,
crush garlic and add to stock along with peppercorns, bay leaf, and salt
to taste. (Amount of salt will depend on saltiness of fish stock.) Cover
stew and simmer until vegetables are almost tender, about 30 minutes.
Blend in paprika and tomato paste. Cut fish into serving-size pieces and
add to stew. Continue simmering until fish is just done. Do not overcook
fish. Serve in soup plates or bowls along with steamed rice or wheat
pilaff. Makes 4 to 6 servings.

Matelote à la Dieppe
Dieppe Seafood Stew

At a café in Dieppe between the two great wars a specialty of the house
was a fish stew made with sole from the English Channel. The cider and
the touch of apple brandy give it the flavor of nearby Normandy.

2½ pounds sole or flounder

1 large onion, sliced

1 teaspoon chopped parsley

1 teaspoon salt

¼ teaspoon white pepper

1½ cups hard cider or white table
wine

1 dozen oysters

1 dozen trimmed mussels
or 1 can mussels (4 or 5 ounces)

½ cup cleaned raw shrimp

2 tablespoons butter

1 tablespoon flour

1 egg yolk

2 tablespoons Calvados or apple
brandy

Arrange fish in a large casserole. Cover with onion slices; sprinkle with

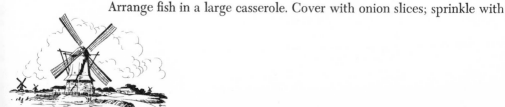

chopped parsley, salt, and pepper. Add cider or wine. Cover and cook in a moderately low oven, 300°F., for about 30 to 40 minutes. Add oysters, mussels and liquid, if using canned mussels, and shrimp. Continue to cook 30 minutes longer. Blend together butter and flour. Separate into small balls and drop into stew. Just before serving, beat egg yolk. Blend in some of liquid from stew and then stir into stew. This last can be done on top of stove, if desired. Add apple brandy and serve at once. Ladle soup into soup plates or bowls and top with crisp croutons or squares of fried bread. Makes 6 servings.

Scandinavian Fish Stew

The original of this recipe was translated from a Swedish cookbook. A white ocean fish seems to be just a little better in this stew than a fresh-water fish, but either is good, fresh or frozen.

2 pounds white fish—halibut, bass, flounder, cod, or the like	½ teaspoon salt
1 tablespoon butter	¼ teaspoon black pepper
1 tablespoon olive oil	½ teaspoon chopped parsley
4 tablespoons chopped onion	¼ teaspoon tarragon
1½ cups thinly sliced carrots	¼ teaspoon thyme
¼ cup thinly sliced celery	1 cup cream or half and half
2 cups fish or chicken stock	1 egg yolk
	½ teaspoon dill weed

If frozen, let fish thaw. Cut fish into chunks, cutting away skin and bone, if fish is fresh. Take any fish skin and bones and combine with 2½ cups water and simmer for about 20 minutes for fish stock. Meanwhile, heat butter and olive oil in a kettle; add onion and cook until golden. Add carrots and celery and fish or chicken stock. Add salt, pepper, and parsley. Simmer until vegetables are done, about 30 minutes. Crush tarragon and thyme and add to soup along with chunks of fish. Continue to simmer until fish is done, about 15 minutes. Beat cream and egg yolk together and stir into soup. Heat just to simmering. Sprinkle with dill weed. Serve at once accompanied by toasted and buttered split rye or whole-wheat buns or rolls. Makes 4 servings.

Bengal Fish Stew

From a collection of Indian recipes comes this stew with its rather unusual combination of spices. Pungent rather than hot, it shows that highly spiced foods don't have to burn.

1 *pound fresh or frozen white fish—*
halibut, haddock, sea bass or sole
1 *teaspoon ground turmeric*
1 *teaspoon ground cumin*
6 *or 8 anise seeds or a few drops of*
anise flavoring
¼ *teaspoon ground ginger*

¼ *teaspoon ground cardamom*
1 *teaspoon salt*
3 *tablespoons butter*
½ *cup chopped onions*
½ *cup white table wine*
½ *cup yoghurt*
1 *cup water*

Arrange the fish on a glass plate; sprinkle both sides with turmeric and rub it into the fish with fingers. Let stand about 1 hour. Combine cumin, anise seeds, ginger, cardamom, and salt. Crush seeds into spices and mix well. (If using anise flavoring, combine spices thoroughly, and add anise flavoring to wine and yoghurt.) Melt butter in a kettle; add onions and cook 4 or 5 minutes, or until they are slightly yellow. Stir in spice mixture. Add fish; combine wine, yoghurt, and water. Pour over fish and simmer about 30 minutes, or until fish is done. Spoon sauce over fish two or three times while fish is simmering. Serve with steamed or boiled rice. Makes 3 or 4 servings.

Cioppino North Beach
North Beach Fish Stew

San Francisco fishermen of Italian background all have their favorite recipes for this wonderful old-world fish stew. Bibs, aprons, paper napkins, are all in order, for *cioppino* isn't for the fastidious eater. Terrycloth finger-tip towels wrung out of hot water are welcome, too.

⅓ *cup olive oil*
2 *large onions, chopped*
1 *clove garlic, crushed*
1 *medium-size green pepper, chopped*
4 *stalks celery with tops, chopped*
1 *1-pound can tomatoes*
2 *8-ounce cans tomato sauce*
1 *teaspoon mixed Italian herbs, or*
½ *teaspoon sweet basil and*
¼ *teaspoon each rosemary and ore-*
gano

1 *teaspoon salt*
1 *teaspoon paprika*
½ *teaspoon black pepper*
1 *cup sherry*
¼ *cup chopped parsley*
1 *pound halibut, sea bass, cod, or*
other firm white fish
1 *pound raw or green shrimp*
1 *dozen clams in the shell*
1 *large crab, cleaned and cracked, in*
the shell

Heat oil in a large kettle. Add onions, garlic, green pepper, and celery. Sauté vegtables until tender but not brown. Add tomatoes, tomato sauce, herbs, salt, paprika, pepper, sherry, and parsley. Simmer at least 30 to 40 minutes, but longer if you have the time. Cut fish into 2-inch squares.

Wash shrimp and shell, if desired. Scrub clams. Make sure crab is well cracked. Add fish and other seafood to sauce and simmer for about 20 minutes. Serve *cioppino* in soup plates with hot French bread. A good red wine adds zest to the eating, too. Oyster or cocktail forks are good tools. Do provide bowls for the discarded shells. Makes 4 to 6 servings.

Cubillon
Cajun Fish Stew

Just where *Cubillon* originated is hard to say. It's thought to have been brought by the Acadians to Louisiana and other parts of the southern United States. The making of a dark brown *roux*—flour and butter mixture—is an essential for most Cajun recipes, and the very name *Cubillon* indicates a French origin. In one form or another *Cubillon* is a popular fish stew in the Gulf region and Southeastern United States where it's made with grouper fish or red snapper. In the Mississippi Bayou country it's made with fresh-water fish such as garfish or catfish. Sometimes *Cubillon* is made with crab, or crabmeat is added along with the fish.

2 pounds fish, either fresh-water or ocean fish	¼ cup butter or olive oil
2 cups water	2 tablespoons flour
2 stalks celery with leaves	1 large green pepper, chopped
1 medium-size onion, cut in quarters	1 large onion, chopped
½ bay leaf	1 clove garlic, finely chopped
2 teaspoons salt	2 1-pound cans tomatoes
6 whole black peppercorns	1 cup red table wine
	Salt and pepper to taste

Trim fish; cut out bones and cut fish into 2-inch chunks. Make a stock by combining the trimmings and bones with water, celery, quartered onion, bay leaf, salt, and peppercorns. Simmer about 1 hour. Strain stock and reserve it.

Melt butter or heat oil gently in deep soup pot; add flour. Turn up heat and cook the *roux*, stirring constantly, until it is a deep brown. Add chopped green pepper, chopped onion, and garlic. Cover and cook over low heat about 5 minutes. Add tomatoes and simmer 20 to 30 minutes. Stir in wine and the reserved fish stock. Place chunks of fish carefully on top; simmer gently 15 to 20 minutes or until fish is done. Season with salt and pepper, if needed. Serve in soup plates over steamed rice. Makes 6 servings.

Bacalao
Spanish Cod Stew

One of the classic fish stews of Spain, there are all kinds of variations of *Bacalao*. This particular version comes from San Francisco's Fisherman's Wharf—for a goodly number of these hardy fishermen are of Spanish background. They say that a taste for *Bacalao* is acquired, but those who like it are very enthusiastic about it. We like it with rice, for the blandness of the rice contrasts with the rather chewy quality of the cod and its marked saltiness.

1 *pound dry salt cod*	1 *4-ounce can pimentos*
2 *tablespoons flour*	1 *can (1 pound 12 ounces) tomatoes*
½ *cup olive oil*	2 *cups water*
3 *medium-size onions*	⅛ *teaspoon black pepper*
2 *cloves garlic*	2 *or 3 tablespoons fine dry bread*
1 *slice white bread, cut into cubes*	*crumbs*

Soak salt cod overnight or about 12 to 14 hours in cold water; change water once or twice, if possible. Drain fish. Place in a saucepan and cover again with cold water. Bring to a boil and simmer 5 to 10 minutes. Drain, separate into pieces, and remove any bones. Pat fish dry with paper towels and then dip fish pieces into flour. Heat olive oil in a heavy pan and cook fish until brown. Set aside. Peel and slice onions, crush garlic and add to hot olive oil. Cook until onions are yellow. Stir in bread cubes and cook until lightly browned. Cut pimentos into slivers and add along with tomatoes and water. Simmer for about 1 hour; stir in pepper. Spoon half of sauce into casserole or baking dish, add browned cod and then spoon rest of sauce over fish. Sprinkle with bread crumbs. Bake in a moderate oven, 350°F., for 30 to 40 minutes, or until *Bacalao* is bubbling hot. Serve with steamed rice or toasted French bread. Makes 4 to 6 servings.

Pinebark Stew

Pinebark Stew comes from the Deep South, made from river fish over a pinebark fire right by the stream and often eaten from a slab of pinebark. In Louisiana it's usually made with catfish; in the Carolinas from bass or bream. Almost any kind of flat fish will do.

½ pound bacon
6 medium-size potatoes (about 2 pounds)
6 medium-size onions (about 2 pounds)
2 to 3 pounds small catfish or fillets or steaks of catfish, bass, or bream

1½ teaspoons salt
¼ teaspoon pepper
3 to 4 cups boiling water
1 cup catsup
¼ cup Worcestershire sauce
1/16 teaspoon cayenne pepper
1 teaspoon curry powder, if desired

Cut slices of bacon into 2 or 3 pieces and fry until crisp in a heavy kettle. Remove bacon and set aside. Peel potatoes and slice two of them into bacon drippings. Peel and slice onions; top potatoes with two sliced onions. Top onions with half of the fish. Sprinkle with about half of the salt and pepper. Repeat layers of potatoes and onions; top with remaining fish. On top of fish arrange remaining slices of potatoes and onions. Sprinkle with the rest of the salt and pepper and pour boiling water over the stew, just to the top of the sliced onions and potatoes. Cover and simmer slowly until vegetables are tender, about 1 hour.

Meanwhile, mix together catsup, Worcestershire sauce, cayenne pepper, and curry powder. Spoon off 1 cup of liquid from stew and mix with this sauce, then pour it over the stew. Top with bacon. Simmer another 20 to 30 minutes. Ladle into soup plates and serve accompanied by corn bread or *Hush Puppies*. Makes about 8 servings.

Meurette Bourguignonne
Burgundy Fish Stew

A *Meurette* is a classic fish stew, similar to *Matelote*, from the province of Burgundy in France. Though usually made with red Burgundy wine and fresh-water fish, it can be made with other red wines or with white Burgundy (similar to the American Chablis) and with fish from the sea. In Burgundy, eel is often used along with fish. Serve with toasted French bread spread with garlic butter, preferably cut into heart shapes.

3 pounds fresh or frozen fish, such as bass, pike, or perch
2 cups chicken stock
2 cups Burgundy or other red table wine
¼ cup chopped onions
1 clove garlic, chopped or crushed
2 large carrots
2 leeks

¼ teaspoon thyme
1-inch piece bay leaf
Dash cayenne pepper
2 teaspoons seasoned salt
¼ cup brandy
1 cup small whole onions
1 cup small whole fresh mushrooms
1 tablespoon butter

Thaw frozen fish or wash fresh fish and cut into thick slices or chunks. Meanwhile, combine chicken stock, wine, chopped onion, and garlic in a large kettle. Scrape carrots and cut into thick slices; clean leeks and slice, using white portion only. Add these to soup. Crush thyme and mix into soup along with bay leaf, cayenne, and seasoned salt. Simmer for about 1 hour, or until vegetables are tender. Force mixture through a wire sieve or food mill, or purée in an electric blender. Add brandy to the puréed vegetables. Peel whole onions; clean mushrooms and remove stems. In a large casserole or Dutch oven arrange pieces of fish, onions, and mushrooms. Pour the puréed vegetables over fish, cover and cook in a moderate oven, 325°F., for about 1 hour, or until fish and vegetables are tender. Stir butter into stew. Ladle into bowls or soup plates over toasted pieces of garlic French bread. Makes 6 servings.

Sopa de Pescado y Almendras
Chilean Fish and Almond Stew

Serve this hearty seafood stew in bowls with lots of French bread. Or if you want to serve it from a casserole, add several slices of dry French bread to thicken the stew. The flavor of the saffron (the pure Spanish saffron takes only a pinch—too much and the flavor becomes almost medicinal) and the ground almonds along with the variety of fish and seafood make this unforgettable.

¼ cup butter	2 cups clam broth, fish stock, or water
½ cup chopped onions	1 pound cleaned raw shrimp
1 clove garlic	1 pound firm white fish
4 ounces ham or smoked sausage	½ pound fresh or frozen scallops
Pinch of saffron	1 pint or a 10-ounce jar fresh oysters
2 cups white table wine	3 or 4 ounces blanched almonds
1 small hot dry red chili pepper	2 slices white bread or French bread
1 dozen fresh clams	1 cup half and half
or 1 8-ounce can small whole clams	Chopped parsley

Melt butter in a large kettle; add chopped onions and cook until onions are yellow. Crush garlic and stir into onions. Cut ham into cubes, or skin sausage and cut into ½-inch slices. Add to onions and garlic along with saffron; brown lightly and add wine. Crush and add chili pepper. While mixture is simmering, scrub clams and steam until shells open. Take clams out of shells and add to soup. Strain off any clam broth and add enough water or fish stock to make 2 cups. Add to stew. (Or if using canned clams, drain and add water or fish stock to make 2 cups.) Add cleaned raw shrimp; cut fish into 1½-inch cubes and add along with scallops. Simmer stew for about 15 minutes, or until shrimp are red and fish firm. Add oysters and their liquor. Simmer until oysters' edges curl. Grind almonds or blend in an electric blender until like a coarse meal. Cut crusts from bread, cut it into cubes and stir into stew. Stir in almonds and half and half. Simmer another 10 minutes or so. Ladle into soup plates and sprinkle with chopped parsley. Makes 8 generous servings.

Creole Gumbo Filé

Gumbo Filé is my favorite way of using the bits and pieces and ham bone from a baked ham. My friend Fannie Johnson, who has a Creole heritage, makes hers almost like this but prefers to use the carcass from a turkey. The secret of flavor with this gumbo is, first, the browning of the okra, and then later, the brown *roux*, so characteristic of Creole dishes.

½ *pound fresh okra*	1 *small hot dry red chili pepper*
¼ *cup salad oil*	1-*inch piece bay leaf*
1½ *cups chopped onion*	½ *teaspoon thyme*
½ *cup chopped green pepper*	1 *can (1 pound 12 ounces) tomatoes*
1 *clove garlic, crushed or chopped*	2 *tablespoons flour*
½ *cup chopped celery*	1 *pound raw shrimp, shelled,*
1 *tablespoon chopped parsley*	*or ½ pound crabmeat*
1½ *quarts water*	1 *dozen oysters or 1 10-ounce*
1 *ham bone with meat*	*jar oysters*
or turkey carcass	1 *to 2 teaspoons gumbo filé powder*
2 *teaspoons salt*	

Wash okra, cut off stems and tips, and slice it into ¼-inch slices. Heat 2 tablespoons oil in a large kettle. Add okra and fry until it begins to brown and is no longer slippery. Add chopped onion, green pepper, garlic, celery, and parsley. Cook until lightly browned. Add water and ham bone or turkey carcass. Heat to simmering and add salt, small red pepper, bay leaf, thyme, and tomatoes. Simmer the gumbo for about an hour. In a frying pan, heat the remaining 2 tablespoons oil. Stir in the flour and brown it, stirring. Stir this *roux* into the gumbo. Add shelled shrimp or crabmeat; cook for about 15 minutes, or until shrimp are red. Add oysters and cook until edges curl. At serving time, bring gumbo to boiling and stir in the filé powder. Do not boil after adding powder. Serve over steamed rice in soup bowls. Makes 6 servings. Toasted French bread or hot corn bread or corn sticks are good accompaniments.

Portuguese Scallop Stew

For an interesting Sunday night supper for a guest or two, serve this spicy stew from a chafing dish. Rice or toasted bread go well with it. Make the sauce ahead, then it's a simple thing to finish at the last.

2 cups white table wine	6 black peppercorns
1 medium-size carrot, sliced (about ¾ cup)	1-inch piece bay leaf
1 medium-size onion, sliced	1 teaspoon seasoned salt
1 tablespoon chopped parsley	2 tablespoons olive oil
1 clove garlic, crushed	½ pound fresh mushrooms, sliced
1 can (1 pound 12 ounces) tomatoes	1 to 1½ pounds scallops
½ teaspoon ground cumin	Salt to taste
2 whole allspice	1 teaspoon lemon juice
	Chopped parsley

Combine the wine, carrot, onion, parsley, garlic, and tomatoes in a saucepan. Bring mixture to simmering; mix in bay, cumin, allspice, peppercorns, and seasoned salt. Simmer for about 45 minutes, or until carrot and onion are tender. Let the stew cool slightly and blend in an electric blender until smooth. In a chafing dish or saucepan heat the olive oil. Add mushrooms and sauté for 5 to 10 minutes. If scallops are large, slice into two or three pieces and add to mushrooms. Add sauce and simmer until mushrooms and scallops are tender. Add salt to taste. Just before serving mix in lemon juice and sprinkle with additional chopped parsley. Makes 6 servings.

Callaloo
Caribbean Seafood Stew

There are many varieties of this gumbo-like Caribbean dish and many ways of spelling it. This one originated in Trinidad. *Callaloo* is said to be a corruption of some long-lost word which slaves applied to the steaming kettles of soup. *Callaloos* have a wide choice of ingredients, but essentials are okra, onions, and some kind of seafood—crab, lobster, shrimp, and so on. Some *callaloos* call for chopped peanuts. Some have chicken

or beef added or even such a rare addition (to most of us anyway) as a slice of alligator tail.

¼ *pound piece salt pork or bacon*
½ *pound fresh okra or 1 10-ounce package frozen okra*
½ *pound spinach, finely chopped, or 1 10-ounce package frozen chopped spinach*
½ *cup finely chopped onion*
6 *cups water*

1 *whole hot green or red pepper, fresh, dry, or pickled*
¾ *pound fresh crabmeat or 2 cans (6½ to 7 ounces each) crabmeat*
2 *teaspoons salt*
½ *teaspoon black pepper*
2 *tablespoons flour*
¼ *cup light rum*

Cut salt pork or bacon into small pieces and fry in a heavy kettle or soup pot until crisp. Lift out bits of crisp pork and drain; reserve to garnish soup. Pour off all but 2 or 3 tablespoons drippings. Slice okra and add to hot drippings. Fry until okra begins to brown and loses some of its slipperiness. Add spinach, onion, 2 cups of water, and the hot pepper; simmer for 30 minutes. Add remaining water, salt, and pepper, and continue to simmer for another hour. Remove the hot pepper. Flake the crabmeat and add to soup. When thoroughly heated, mix flour with enough cold water to make a smooth paste. Stir into soup and continue to stir until soup is thickened. Add rum; sprinkle crisp pork or bacon bits over soup. Serve in soup bowls with hot garlic bread or toasted hard rolls, or serve over steamed rice. Makes 6 servings.

Eastern Shore Crab Stew

Some years ago I lived in Virginia and had a neighbor who came from Maryland's Eastern Shore. This rich crab stew of hers has gone through some changes (she used heavy cream), but it's still much the same.

2 *tablespoons butter*
2 *tablespoons finely chopped onion*
1 *to 1½ cups sliced fresh mushrooms*
2 *or 3 fresh tomatoes, or 2 whole canned tomatoes*
1 *pound crabmeat*

1 *teaspoon celery salt*
2 *cups half and half or rich milk*
Salt and pepper to taste
¼ *cup brandy*
2 *tablespoons chopped chives*

Melt the butter in a saucepan or in a chafing dish or electric frying pan. Add chopped onion and sliced mushrooms and cook until soft but not brown. Peel fresh tomatoes, scoop out most of the seeds, and chop. Or remove seeds and chop canned tomatoes. Add these to onion and mushrooms and cook for 2 or 3 minutes, stirring frequently. Add crabmeat, celery salt, and half and half. Heat the stew thoroughly. When stew is simmering, season to taste with salt and pepper. Stir in brandy. Spoon into soup plates and sprinkle with chopped chives. Serve with toasted large-size pilot crackers. Makes 4 servings.

Swedish Lobster Stew

It's the right combination of herbs and wine (a know-how of good Swedish cooks) and the flavor imparted by the flaming brandy that makes this stew superb. Two very hungry people can eat all of this, so you'll need more for a party.

2 10½-ounce packages frozen lobster tails, or a 1- to 1½-pound lobster, fresh or frozen	2 tablespoons brandy or Cognac
	½ cup canned tomatoes
	1 cup white table wine
3 cups boiling water	2 teaspoons seasoned salt
1 teaspoon salt	Dash cayenne pepper
½ teaspoon dill seeds	¼ teaspoon tarragon
1 tablespoon olive oil	2 teaspoons cornstarch or arrowroot
1 leek	1 teaspoon chervil or chopped parsley
1 small clove garlic	

Simmer the lobster tails or lobster in the boiling water seasoned with salt and dill seeds for 10 to 15 minutes. Strain out dill seeds and reserve the stock. Let lobsters cool slightly; remove the meat from the shells. Slice it into medallions. Pour the olive oil into a top-of-the-stove casserole or into an electric frying pan. Slice leek thinly—the white part and just a touch of the green; crush garlic. Add the sliced leek and garlic and the lobster medallions to the oil. Cook over low heat until the leek is slightly soft but not brown. Warm the brandy and pour it over lobster; set it aflame. Stir gently until flame dies down; then add tomatoes, white wine, reserved stock, seasoned salt, and cayenne. Crush tarragon and sprinkle over stew. Simmer over low heat 15 to 20 minutes. Moisten cornstarch or arrowroot in a little cold water and stir into stew. Stir until stew thickens slightly. Sprinkle with chervil or chopped parsley and serve in soup plates or bowls. Especially good to go along with *Swedish Lobster Stew* is hardtack or Melba toast made from pumpernickel or dark rye bread. Makes 2 or 3 generous servings.

West Indian Turtle Stew

As in Mexico the turtles in the West Indies are large sea turtles. Those in the inland areas of the United States are slightly different in size, but much the same in flavor. Use canned turtle if you can't get fresh or frozen turtle. Though the price of canned turtle may seem high, *Turtle Stew* makes an elegant and different meal.

¼ cup olive oil
½ cup finely chopped onion
½ cup thinly sliced celery
¼ cup chopped mushrooms
1 medium-size fresh tomato
1 clove garlic
1 tablespoon flour
1 cup Spanish-style tomato sauce
1 cup white table wine

1 teaspoon chopped parsley
1 teaspoon salt
¼ teaspoon each of sweet basil, marjoram, and thyme
2 cups cooked turtle meat and stock or 1 can (about 1 pound 4 ounces) turtle meat
¼ cup brandy

Heat the olive oil in a kettle; add chopped onion, celery, and mushrooms. Peel the tomato and cut into pieces, removing most of the seeds. Crush the garlic and add along with tomato to vegetables. Cook, over low heat, until vegetables are soft. Stir in the flour. Add tomato sauce, white wine, parsley, and salt. Stir until sauce comes to a boil and turn heat down to simmer. Crush herbs and add to sauce. Simmer sauce for 30 to 40 minutes. Cut turtle meat into ½-inch cubes and add meat to sauce along with about ½ cup stock and continue to simmer another 30 minutes. Just before serving pour brandy over stew and set ablaze. Stir into stew. Serve with steamed rice. Makes 6 servings.

Part IV

FINALE

Accompaniments

Seasoned Butters

One of the best go-alongs for any soup or stew is good bread spread with a seasoned butter, or crisp crackers, Melba toast, hot biscuits, or rolls. Here are several variations. Start out with butter and seasoned salt, then make whichever variation pleases you. Double amounts for more servings.

4 tablespoons soft butter or margarine   ½ teaspoon seasoned salt

Cream together butter and seasoned salt, then add any of the following:

PAPRIKA BUTTER
Blend in 1 teaspoon paprika and a dash of onion juice.

HERB BUTTER
Blend in ¼ to ½ teaspoon of your favorite herb (depending on what you plan to serve it with)—Italian herb mixture, fines herbes, tarragon, oregano, dill, chervil, or other herb. Add a few drops of lemon juice, if desired.

ONION OR CHIVE BUTTER
Blend in 1 to 2 tablespoons chopped green onion or chopped chives.

PARSLEY BUTTER
Blend in 2 tablespoons chopped fresh parsley and a few drops of lemon juice.

GARLIC BUTTER

Blend in 1 clove garlic, crushed, or ¼ teaspoon garlic powder. Or omit seasoned salt and add ½ to 1 teaspoon garlic salt.

NOTE: Amounts suggested are for dry herbs; if you use fresh herbs, increase amounts two to three times or to taste.

Dill-Flavored Sour Cream

Mix ½ cup dairy sour cream and ½ teaspoon each seasoned salt and dill weed. Use to garnish certain soups.

BREADS, SCONES AND THE LIKE

Garlic French Bread

What soup or stew isn't enhanced by garlic French bread! At least all my family and friends think so. Make it with butter or olive oil, fresh garlic or garlic powder, a loaf of French bread or hard French rolls, or even a reasonable facsimile with an unsliced loaf of regular bread, and with or without cheese.

1 loaf French bread, 4 to 6 French rolls, or 1 unsliced loaf of bread
¼ pound butter or ½ cup olive oil
2 cloves garlic or ½ teaspoon garlic powder

Shredded or grated Parmesan, Cheddar, or other cheese or 2 or 3 teaspoons finely chopped parsley
Paprika

Slice the loaf of French or regular bread in half, lengthwise. Then cut through, in 1½-inch slices, almost to the crust. Or split the French or hard rolls. Melt the butter; crush the garlic cloves. Stir the crushed garlic or garlic powder into melted butter or olive oil. Brush this over bread and down between the slices. Sprinkle bread with cheese or with parsley and paprika. Warm it in a moderately low oven, 300°F., for about 15 to 20 minutes. Serve hot. Makes 6 to 8 servings.

Croutons—Garlic and Otherwise

You can make these from almost any kind of bread that you have on hand or particularly like, and you can flavor them with garlic, your favorite herbs, or leave them plain. Good crisp croutons are the fitting garnish of hundreds of soups.

2 to 3 cups bread cubes
½ cup olive or salad oil, or butter
2 cloves garlic or ½ teaspoon garlic powder, if desired
1 teaspoon chopped parsley or ½ teaspoon seasoned salt

½ teaspoon of your favorite herb or herb combination such as sweet basil, oregano, summer savory, Italian mixed herbs, or chives

Use fresh or dry white or whole-wheat bread or any kind you like. Or use French bread for a distinctive flavor. Cut it into ¼-inch cubes. Pour oil into a large flat baking pan, or spoon butter into pan, and let it melt in the oven. Crush fresh garlic and stir it or the garlic powder into the oil or butter. If using oil, stir in seasoned salt. (You may not want the additional salt if you use butter.) Mix in the bread cubes, coating well with the oil or butter. Sprinkle with the herbs. Toast very slowly in a low oven, 250°F., for about 1 hour, turning cubes several times with a spatula, until croutons are crisp and lightly browned. (If bread is very fresh it may take even longer.) Makes 2 to 3 cups croutons, enough for 4 to 6 servings.

Cracklin' Bread

Originally cracklin' bread was made with the cracklings or crisp bits of pork left after lard was rendered.

¾ cup finely diced salt pork
2 cups cornmeal
1½ teaspoons baking powder
½ teaspoon baking soda

½ teaspoon salt
2 eggs
1 cup buttermilk
2 tablespoons salt pork drippings

Fry salt pork over low heat until it is brown and crisp. Drain the fat and reserve it. Mix together the cornmeal, baking powder, soda, and salt. Beat together the eggs, buttermilk, and salt pork drippings. Stir this into cornmeal along with the cracklings. Spread into a greased 7- × 11-inch baking pan. Bake in a moderately hot oven, 400°F., for 25 to 30 minutes. Serve with *Burgoo, Old Kentucky Mulligan, Brunswick Stew,* or other stews.

Old Virginia Spoon Bread

Years ago the George Washington Hotel in Winchester, Virginia, where I then lived, passed on their recipe for spoon bread to me. I cut it down, for it made more than I usually serve. It's a favorite in my family with fish and chicken stews—and excellent with kidney stew.

2½ cups milk	*1 teaspoon salt*
1 cup yellow cornmeal	*¼ cup melted butter*
3 eggs	*1 teaspoon baking powder*
2 tablespoons sugar	

Heat 2 cups milk to simmering and stir in the cornmeal. Remove from heat. Beat eggs and add remaining ½ cup milk, sugar, salt, and melted butter. Stir the egg mixture into the thick cornmeal and milk mixture. Add baking powder and blend thoroughly. Pour batter into a buttered 1½-quart casserole. Bake spoon bread in a moderately hot oven, 400°F., for about 45 minutes or until it is firm and brown. Serve at once. To serve, spoon out on plate and spread with butter or top with stew. Makes 6 to 8 servings.

Hush Puppies

Almost an American legend is the story of *Hush Puppies.* A part of the gastronomical history of the Deep South, these sizzling bits of fried corn pone were supposed to have been thrown to the barking, hungry puppies with the admonition "Hush, puppy!" A good lot of "puppies" were consumed, too, along with *Burgoo, Brunswick Stew,* or fried fish—whatever the crowd was feasting on that day. I think any bits and crumbs of the "puppies" that don't cling together are particularly delicious, well drained and sprinkled on top of a fish stew or chowder.

1 cup yellow cornmeal	*1 egg*
1 teaspoon salt	*½ cup finely chopped or grated onion*
¼ teaspoon black pepper	*2 tablespoons salad oil or melted*
2 teaspoons baking powder	*bacon drippings*
½ cup milk	

Combine the cornmeal, salt, pepper, and baking powder. Beat the milk and egg together and stir them into the cornmeal. Mix in onion and salad oil or bacon drippings. Drop the mixture by the teaspoonful into deep hot oil and fry until golden brown. Lift out and drain on paper towels. Keep warm in the oven until ready to serve. Makes about 2 dozen hush puppies.

Mormon Johnnycake

Probably the earliest johnnycake the Mormons made had no butter or eggs, and was made with molasses instead of honey. But before too many years had gone by Utah became a land of "milk and honey," and it still is.

1 egg
1 cup buttermilk
1 tablespoon honey
1 cup yellow cornmeal
¼ cup flour

½ teaspoon baking soda
½ teaspoon salt
1 tablespoon butter or bacon drippings

Beat together the egg, buttermilk, and honey. Combine cornmeal, flour, soda, and salt. Stir this into liquid mixture. Melt butter or drippings and stir them into batter. Pour it into a well-greased 9-inch-square cake pan. Bake in a moderately hot oven, 400°F., for 20 minutes, or until it is done and brown. Cut into 9 or 12 pieces.

Oatmeal-Pecan Bread

Good to serve with any number of stews and chowders is this *Oatmeal-Pecan Bread*. And it's especially good with an aspic or a fruit soup.

1 package active dry yeast
¼ cup warm water
1¼ cups cold water
½ cup quick-cooking oats
¼ cup molasses

1 tablespoon shortening
1 teaspoon salt
3½ cups flour, approximately
3 tablespoons non-fat dry milk
½ cup finely chopped pecans

Dissolve the dry yeast in warm water. In a saucepan bring 1 cup of the cold water to an active boil and stir in the oats. Cook for 1 minute, stirring constantly. Add molasses, shortening, and salt and stir until shortening is melted. Stir in ¼ cup cold water and let stand until lukewarm and then mix in dissolved yeast. Mix in about 3 cups of the flour, the non-fat dry milk, and the nuts. Add more flour if needed, to make a soft dough. Turn dough out on a lightly floured board and let it rest for about 10 minutes. Knead for about 5 minutes, using as little flour as possible. Shape kneaded dough into a ball and brush with oil. Place in a well-oiled bowl and let rise in a warm place until doubled in bulk. Punch dough down and knead once or twice. Divide dough into 2 loaves and place in 2 well-oiled 4- × 8-inch loaf pans. Brush oil over top of loaves and let rise again until doubled. Bake loaves in a hot oven, 425°F., for 10 minutes; turn heat down to moderate, 350°F., and continue to bake for 30 to 40 minutes, or until loaves are done and brown. Let cool in pans for about 10 minutes, then turn out and cool on a wire rack. Serve warm. Or chill and slice very thin. Freeze any bread that you don't use within a day or so.

Louise's Special Bread

Truly my own invention and I vary it from time to time. One time I will add some chopped onion sautéed briefly in oil or butter, another time a teaspoon of a favorite herb such as sage or dill weed, or another time a couple of teaspoons of caraway seeds. Freshly baked bread goes with almost any kind of stew, soup, chowder, *potage,* and the like.

2 *tablespoons sugar*	1 *cup milk*
2 *tablespoons butter, margarine, or shortening*	1 *egg*
	1 *package active dry yeast*
1 *teaspoon salt, or onion salt, or seasoned salt*	¼ *cup warm water*
	3 *cups flour*
1 *cup farina or cornmeal*	

In a mixing bowl combine sugar, butter, salt or seasoned salt, any preferred herbs, and farina or cornmeal. Heat milk to simmering and add it. Stir to mix thoroughly. Beat in the egg. Dissolve active dry yeast in warm water. When mixture in bowl has cooled to lukewarm mix in dissolved yeast. Beat in about 2 cups of flour. Add more flour until a soft dough is formed. Flour a board with remaining flour and turn dough out onto it. Knead until smooth and elastic, about 5 minutes. Shape dough into a ball and place in oiled bowl. Turn dough so it is completely coated with oil. Let it rise in a warm place, 80°F., until it has doubled in bulk, about 1 hour. Punch dough down and let dough rest for about 10 minutes. Turn out and knead again for 3 or 4 minutes. Shape dough into a loaf and place in an oiled loaf pan or an 8-inch round pan, if preferred. Let rise again until doubled, about 1 hour. Bake bread in a moderately hot oven, 400°F., for about 40 minutes or until done and brown. Turn out onto wire rack to cool and brush with oil or butter. Let cool, but serve while still fresh. Makes 1 loaf.

Herb Bread

Vary the herbs according to the kind of stew you are serving. Any leftover you can toast and serve with soup or make into croutons.

1 package active dry yeast
¼ cup warm water
¾ cup milk
2 tablespoons sugar
2 tablespoons shortening
½ teaspoon salt

1 egg
1 teaspoon celery salt
½ teaspoon chili powder
1 teaspoon oregano, summer savory, or fines herbes
3½ to 4 cups all-purpose flour

Crumble the yeast into lukewarm water in a mixing bowl. Let it stand 5 to 10 minutes and stir until dissolved. Meanwhile, heat milk just to simmering. Add sugar, shortening and salt; cool to lukewarm. Beat in the egg, celery salt, chili powder, and oregano. Add this mixture to yeast. Add 2 cups sifted flour and beat until smooth. Add enough of the remaining flour to make a moderately soft dough. Turn dough out onto a lightly floured board and knead until smooth and elastic, about 5 minutes. Shape dough into a ball and place in well-oiled bowl. Turn dough so it is oiled all over. Cover dough and let rise in a warm place, 80°F., until doubled, about 1 hour. Punch down; let rest about 10 minutes. Shape into round loaf and place in greased 8-inch round pan. Cover and let rise again until doubled, about 1 hour. Bake bread in a moderately hot oven, 400°F., 40 to 45 minutes, until done and brown. Brush it with melted shortening. Serve fresh baked. Makes 1 loaf.

Savory Biscuits

Good to serve with a variety of stews, these also make a wonderful accompaniment to a main-course salad. Very easy to make.

¼ cup butter
⅛ teaspoon garlic powder
1 tablespoon chopped chives, fresh, frozen, or dried

2 packages refrigerated ready-for-the-oven biscuits
1 tablespoon grated Parmesan cheese

Melt butter in a 7- × 11-inch baking pan. Stir in the garlic powder and chives. Open biscuit packages and arrange biscuits in melted butter and chive mixture. Let them stand in a warm place about 20 to 30 minutes, then turn biscuits over carefully with a spatula. Spoon butter and chives in bottom of pan over biscuits. Sprinkle them with grated Parmesan. Bake in a moderately hot oven, 400°F., for 15 to 20 minutes, or until biscuits are done and brown. Makes 6 to 8 servings.

Fifteen-Minute Miniature Pizzas

When I was in Naples, I saw a sign in English: "Pizzas, Just Like Mother Makes Back Home." These may not be just like mother makes, but they are good with minestrone soup and other vegetable soups. And they make a good snack lunch accompanied by a salad.

1 package of 10 to 12 refrigerated ready-for-the-oven biscuits
Marinara or spaghetti sauce—canned, made from a mix, or your own special recipe

Thin slices of Italian sausage, such as salami, mortadella, pepperoni, or whatever is available and you like
Mozzarella cheese

Roll out each biscuit on a lightly floured board to a 2½- to 3-inch circle. Top each with a tablespoon of sauce and then with a slice or two of sausage. Cut cheese into thin slices and place on top of sausage. Arrange pizzas on a well-greased baking pan. Bake them in a moderately hot oven, 400°F., for about 12 to 15 minutes, or until they are done and sauce and cheese is bubbling hot. Serve at once. Makes 10 or 12 pizzas.

Irish Soda Bread

Usually, Irish soda bread is made with white flour, but whole-wheat flour —especially if you can get stone-ground flour—is a delicious variation. It is good fresh or even several days old. In fact, Irish immigrants are supposed to have brought along a loaf or so to sustain them on the sea voyage to America.

2 cups whole-wheat flour, stone-
    ground preferably
1 cup sifted all-purpose flour
1 teaspoon baking soda

1 teaspoon sugar
½ teaspoon salt
1 tablespoon butter
1 cup buttermilk

In a mixing bowl combine whole-wheat flour, sifted all-purpose flour, soda, sugar, and salt. Stir with a fork to mix well. Work butter into the dry ingredients with fork or fingers. Stir in the buttermilk, then work with fingers to form a very stiff dough. Knead dough in bowl and shape it into a ball; then flatten it with the hands into a 1½-inch-thick circle. Place circle on a greased baking pan or a greased griddle. (I prefer the griddle.) Cut a deep cross across the top. Bake bread in a moderately hot oven, 400°F., for 20 minutes; turn heat down to moderate, 350°F., and continue to bake another 15 minutes or until it is done. Let bread "set," if possible, before cutting, about 2 or 3 hours. Cut bread into quarters, following the cross cut into bread before baking. Cut each quarter into wedges. Makes 1 loaf.

Boxty-on-the-Griddle

A modern version of an old Irish favorite, for the old time *Boxty* was made with mashed potatoes, shredded potatoes, flour, and soda or baking powder. In olden times it was eaten as a bread, but it's more like a potato pancake and goes with stews and creamed dishes and along with sausages and eggs.

Half of a 6-ounce package frozen
    shredded potatoes or about 1 cup
    shredded potatoes
½ cup biscuit mix

1 cup instant mashed potato flakes
1 teaspoon salt
2 cups milk
2 eggs

Let frozen shredded potatoes thaw in a mixing bowl. When potatoes can be broken apart, mix in biscuit mix, instant potatoes, and salt. Beat in milk and eggs. Drop this mixture by spoonfuls onto a greased griddle and fry until done and brown, turning once. Serve at once, or arrange on a hot platter and keep hot until served. Makes about 6 servings.

Fadge

Lots of butter is the flavor secret of this old, old Irish recipe—brought to this country by a friend's grandmother. Fine to serve with any good beef, lamb, or kidney stew.

3 or 4 medium- to large-size potatoes,	*¼ cup hot milk*
about 1½ pounds	*½ cup flour*
½ cup water	*⅓ to ½ cup melted butter*
1 teaspoon salt	*1 teaspoon caraway seeds*

Pare the potatoes and cut into quarters. Add water and salt and simmer until potatoes are tender. Pour off any water, for potatoes should be quite dry. Add hot milk and mash the potatoes. Mix in flour, most of the butter, and the caraway seeds. Spoon mixture into a buttered loaf pan, 4 × 8 inches, and pour the remaining butter over top. Bake in a moderate oven, 350°F., for 10 to 15 minutes or until fadge is lightly brown. (Or place in oven along with stew or bread at its temperature.) Turn the fadge out onto a platter along with stew, or onto a small platter or serving plate. Makes 4 to 6 servings.

Skirlie

In Scotland *Skirlie* is traditionally served with Scotch broth and other soups and stews. Oats have been for centuries the most important grain crop, and even in the days of Samuel Johnson were believed to be the source of strength in the Scottish people.

3 or 4 tablespoons bacon drippings	*½ teaspoon salt*
1 medium-size onion, chopped	*⅛ teaspoon pepper*
1½ cups quick-cooking oats	

Melt the bacon drippings in a frying pan. When they are hot, add chopped onion and cook, stirring frequently, until onion is lightly browned. Add oats, salt, and pepper and continue cooking, stirring frequently, until oats are brown, about 15 minutes. Spoon *Skirlie* into a bowl and pass to sprinkle over hot soup. Makes 4 to 6 servings.

Skirlie Fried Cakes

This is a slightly different version of *Skirlie.*

2 tablespoons bacon drippings	1½ cups quick-cooking oats
1 medium-size onion, chopped	½ teaspoon sage
1 cup boiling water	⅛ teaspoon pepper
½ teaspoon salt	

Melt the bacon drippings in a saucepan; add chopped onion and cook until onion is lightly browned, stirring frequently. Add boiling water and salt; mix in oats and cook about 15 minutes, stirring frequently, until oatmeal is thick. Crush the sage and mix into the porridge along with pepper. Spread mixture into a 6- or 7-inch-square pan or 8-inch pie pan and chill. When ready to serve cut into squares. Dip each square into flour and fry in hot bacon drippings. Serve as an accompaniment to stews or chowders.

Skirlie Bread

And still another version of this ancient Scottish food.

⅓ cup bacon drippings	¼ cup flour
2 cups chopped onions	2 teaspoons baking powder
1 egg	1 teaspoon salt
1 cup milk	½ teaspoon sage
2 cups quick-cooking oats	

Melt the bacon drippings in a frying pan; add onions and cook until lightly browned. Meanwhile, beat together milk and egg in a mixing bowl; stir in browned onions. Combine oats, flour, baking powder, and salt. Crush sage and mix into oats. Stir oats into onion mixture, mixing just until well moistened. Grease a 9-inch round cake pan with bacon drippings. Pour batter into the pan and bake in a moderately hot oven, 400°F., for 25 to 30 minutes, or until done and brown on top. Serve warm. Makes about 6 servings.

Oatmeal Scones

Here in this country we would call these biscuits, but in Scotland, Australia, and New Zealand they are scones. Their biscuits are sweet like our cookies. Serve them with the Scottish or English stews or those from Down Under.

1½ cups sifted flour
½ cup quick-cooking oats
½ teaspoon salt

3 teaspoons baking powder
3 tablespoons butter or margarine
½ cup milk

Mix sifted flour, oats, salt, and baking powder. Work in butter or margarine with a pastry blender or fork. Stir in the milk. Knead dough briefly and roll out about ½-inch thick. Cut into 1½-inch circles. Arrange circles on a cooky sheet. Bake in a moderately hot oven, 400°F., 10 to 12 minutes, or until done and brown. Makes about 16 to 18 scones.

Teisen Nionod
Welsh Onion Cake

Good either with hot or cold meat, *Welsh Onion Cake* goes well with stew, too.

3 medium-size onions, about 1 pound
4 medium-size potatoes, about 1½ pounds

⅓ cup butter
1 teaspoon salt
¼ teaspoon black pepper

Peel the onions and slice thin; pare potatoes and cut into thin slices. Butter an 8- or 9-inch round cake pan or casserole generously. Arrange a layer of potatoes and a layer of onions in pan. Using about a third of the remaining butter, place lumps of it on top of onions; sprinkle with part of the salt and pepper. Arrange another layer of potatoes and onions, butter, salt, and pepper. Top with a layer of potatoes, salt, pepper, and butter. Cover with a piece of heavy aluminum foil and bake in a moderate oven, 375°F., for about 50 minutes. Uncover the pan, turn heat up to 400°F., and bake another 10 or 15 minutes, or until top is brown. Cut into wedges to serve. Makes about 6 servings.

Yorkshire Pudding

Always good with roast beef, *Yorkshire Pudding* is delicious, too, with English beef stews and those from Scotland and Ireland—American ones, as well.

¼ *cup flour*	½ *teaspoon salt*
1 *cup milk*	1 *tablespoon water*
2 *eggs*	

Spoon the flour into a small mixing bowl. Add ½ cup milk and beat with a rotary beater or electric mixer until well blended. Break the eggs into the batter and continue beating for 3 or 4 minutes. Add salt and remaining ½ cup milk; mix to combine thoroughly. Set the batter in refrigerator for an hour to "rest." Meanwhile, in a casserole or baking pan (about 1-quart size) fry out some bits of beef fat cut from a roast or stew in a moderately hot oven, 400°F. Or spoon drippings from a roast into the casserole and place in oven until very hot. Blend water into the batter and pour it into the hot casserole. Return casserole to oven and continue baking about 15 to 20 minutes, or until pudding is puffy, crisp, and well browned on top. Serve at once or it will fall like a soufflé. Makes about 6 servings.

Swedish Flatbread

You can serve these thin, crisp wafers with almost any soup you choose —from the lightest bouillons to the heartiest chowders. They go particularly well with the various Scandinavian sweet soups.

1½ *cups all-purpose flour*	¼ *cup butter*
2 *tablespoons sugar*	½ *cup buttermilk, plus an additional*
¼ *teaspoon baking soda*	*tablespoon or two, if needed*
¼ *teaspoon salt*	

Mix together flour, sugar, soda, and salt. Add butter and with a pastry blender cut it into flour until mixture is crumbly. Stir in ½ cup buttermilk. If needed add a little more until you can shape dough into a firm ball. Pull off pieces of dough and shape them into 1-inch balls. Flour generously a pastry cloth and rolling pin covered with stockinette. Roll out each ball into a circle about 5 inches in diameter. Arrange on ungreased cooky sheet. Bake in a hot oven, 400°F., for 7 to 8 minutes, or until bread is done and lightly browned. Be sure to check once or twice; baking may not take as long, if you have rolled your flatbread very thin. Serve flatbread warm or cold. Makes about 30 wafers.

Reheat by arranging on a cooky sheet or baking pan and warming in a low oven, 300°F., for 4 or 5 minutes.

Finnish Rye Loaf

Truly a coarse peasant bread to go with a hearty fish or game stew. Or as Finnish people do, eat it with "clabber" on the side. Since making or buying "clabber" takes a bit of doing, we suggest yoghurt. You can find rye meal in markets that carry special kinds of flour or in health food stores.

2 cups buttermilk
1 package active dry yeast
1½ teaspoons caraway seeds
1½ teaspoons salt

½ cup golden syrup or treacle
2 cups rye meal
3 to 3½ cups flour

Heat the buttermilk until it is just warm; add yeast and stir until dissolved. Mix in caraway seeds, salt, and syrup. Pour mixture into a large mixing bowl and beat in rye meal. Add the flour about a cup at a time, until dough is stiff. After adding about 3 cups flour, turn dough out on a floured board and knead for about 5 minutes. Shape into a ball. Meanwhile, wash out the mixing bowl and oil well. Place dough in bowl and let rise in a warm place until doubled in bulk. Turn out on board and punch down; shape into 2 round loaves and place in greased 8-inch round cake pans. Let stand about 15 or 20 minutes and then bake in a moderately hot oven, 400°F., for about 40 minutes. Brush once or twice while baking with syrup diluted with a little water. Cool loaves on wire rack for a few minutes; then remove from pans. Makes 2 loaves.

Lavash
Armenian Cracker Bread

Available in areas where Armenians live (certain cities in California, for example) *lavash* isn't too hard to make. It reminds you of matzoth, but it has both salt and leavening. In Armenia *lavash* was baked in an oven in the ground or in the floor of the house. I find that a pizza pan makes a good baking pan.

1 cake fresh yeast	1 teaspoon salt
1 cup warm water	Additional lukewarm water
6 cups all-purpose flour	

Dissolve fresh yeast in 1 cup warm water. In a large bowl combine flour and salt. Make a depression in the center of the flour and add the dissolved yeast. Mix these and add enough lukewarm water to make a stiff dough. Knead it until it is smooth and elastic, about 5 minutes. (Turn dough out on a floured board, if it is easier for you, but I knead it in the bowl.) Cover dough with a damp cloth and let stand for 3 hours. Punch dough down and let rise again until doubled in bulk.

Pull off a piece of the dough (roughly about half a cup) and, on a well-floured bread board, roll it out until very thin—about ⅛-inch thick, if possible. Keep shape round to fit on a 14-inch pizza pan or use a cooky sheet. Bake in a moderately hot oven, 400°F., for 3 minutes. Turn on broiler and brown the top, about 3 more minutes. Remove from pan to a wire rack. Repeat until all dough has been baked. Stack and place all of the *lavash* in a warm oven for about 15 to 20 minutes, or until crisp and dry. A good way to do this is to turn the oven off after all the bread has been baked. It will stay warm enough to dry out the bread. Makes 8 to 10 14-inch circles of bread.

Lavash will keep indefinitely, if kept dry. It goes well with almost any kind of soup or chowder.

Mexican Spoon Bread

The traditional accompaniment to almost any of the Mexican or early California stews, you'll like *Mexican Spoon Bread,* too, with baked ham, sliced cold turkey, or broiled chicken.

2 eggs	½ teaspoon baking soda
¾ cup buttermilk	1 teaspoon salt
⅓ cup melted butter	1 4-ounce can green chilis
1 1-pound can cream-style corn	1½ cups shredded Monterey Jack or
1 cup yellow cornmeal	Cheddar cheese

Beat eggs slightly and mix in buttermilk, melted butter, and cream-style corn. Combine cornmeal, soda, and salt and stir into corn mixture. Pour half of batter into a well-greased 9-inch-square baking pan. Chop or cut green chilis into strips. Spread chilis and cheese over batter. Spoon remaining batter over chilis and cheese. Bake in a moderately hot oven, 400°F., for 45 minutes. Remove from oven and let stand for 4 or 5 minutes. Cut into squares. Lift out with pie server, spatula, or large serving spoon. Makes 8 or 9 servings.

Onion Bread

An easy-to-make onion bread that goes well with all kinds of soups and stews.

1 1-pound loaf frozen ready-to-rise bread dough	½ cup chopped onions
	½ teaspoon celery salt
¼ pound butter, or more, if needed	¼ teaspoon thyme

Let frozen bread dough rise in a well-buttered 5- × 9-inch loaf pan until about 1 inch above pan. (This takes about 4 hours at room temperature.) Turn it out onto a floured board and knead for 4 or 5 minutes. Roll it out or stretch into a 5- × 10-inch rectangle. Melt about 4 tablespoons of the butter in heavy frying pan. Cook the chopped onions in the butter until tender but not brown. Season with celery salt and thyme. Spread onions out over rectangle of dough. Roll up dough as for a jelly roll and return it to buttered loaf pan with the "seam" on the bottom. Tuck in the ends of loaf to hold in the onions. Spread any remaining butter over top. Let rise again until about 1 inch above pan, about 1 hour. Bake bread in a moderate oven, 350°F., for 35 to 40 minutes, or until done. Turn out onto a wire rack and cool slightly. Serve warm with hot stew. Makes 1 loaf.

Onion Squares

Onion Squares are very good with fish or seafood chowders and with many whole-meal soups.

1 13¾-ounce package hot roll mix	1 egg
1 cup warm water	1 cup dairy sour cream
3 cups thinly sliced onions	½ teaspoon celery salt
¼ cup butter	½ cup grated Parmesan or Romano cheese
½ teaspoon chervil, fines herbes, or finely chopped parsley	

Dissolve the envelope of yeast in the package of hot roll mix in warm water in a large bowl. Mix thoroughly and knead a few times. Turn the dough out onto floured board and roll or stretch it to fit a greased 10- × 15-inch shallow baking pan. Cook the sliced onions in butter until they are tender but not brown. Stir in the herbs and spread onions out over dough. Beat egg slightly; mix in sour cream and celery salt. Spoon this over onions. Sprinkle with grated cheese. Bake dough in a 450°F. oven for 15 to 20 minutes, or until done and cheese is brown. Cut into 12 to 16 squares.

Mushroom Pirozhki
Mushroom-Filled Miniature Turnovers

Serve these Russian tidbits with borsch or soups of Polish or Hungarian origin. They are good, too, as a cocktail snack or to go with a salad.

1½ cups sifted flour	*½ to ¾ cup dairy sour cream*
½ teaspoon baking powder	*1 egg yolk*
½ teaspoon salt	*2 tablespoons water*
¼ cup butter	*Mushroom Filling (below)*

Combine the flour, baking powder, and salt. Cut in the butter with a pastry blender. Blend in just enough of the sour cream to make a pastry that holds together. Chill it thoroughly. Roll out ¼-inch thick and cut circles with a biscuit cutter. Beat egg yolk and water together. Brush the circles with egg yolk. Spoon about ½ teaspoon mushroom filling on half of each circle. Fold over the circle and press edges together with the tines of a fork. Arrange turnovers on an oiled baking pan. Bake them in a hot oven, 425°F., for about 20 minutes, or until golden brown. Serve hot with borsch or other soups, cold or hot. Makes about 24 *pirozhki*.

MUSHROOM FILLING:

½ pound fresh mushrooms	*¼ teaspoon pepper*
1 small onion	*2 tablespoons finely chopped parsley*
½ teaspoon salt	*2 tablespoons butter*

Wash mushrooms well and trim the stem ends. Peel the onion and grind mushrooms and onion, using the fine blade of the meat grinder. Stir in salt, pepper, and chopped parsley. Melt butter in a frying pan. Add ground mushroom mixture and cook for about 10 minutes over low heat, stirring frequently. Cool slightly before using as filling.

NOTE: If you don't use all of the filling, freeze it and save to use later. Or the ground mushrooms can be added to soups, gravies, or sauces.

Quick Cheese Sticks

Be sure to get the baked sticks off your baking pan immediately, with a good strong spatula, for they tend to stick a little. But they are extra good, served warm, with almost any kind of soup or as a tidbit to go along with cocktails or as an accompaniment to a salad luncheon.

2 *cups biscuit mix*
2 *tablespoons chopped chives, fresh, frozen, or dried*
¼ *cup melted butter, bacon drippings, or salad oil*

¾ *cup milk*
1 *to 2 tablespoons shredded Parmesan or Romano cheese*

Mix together in a bowl the biscuit mix and chopped chives. Combine melted butter, drippings, or oil with ¾ cup milk and stir into the biscuit mix. Stir with a fork until well combined. Turn dough out onto a floured board and knead 2 or 3 minutes. Roll it into a 10-inch square. Cut into 1- × 5-inch strips. Dip each strip in the remaining milk and then roll it in shredded cheese. Arrange on a very well-greased baking pan and bake in a moderately hot oven, 400°F., about 15 minutes, or until sticks are done and brown. Makes about 20 cheese sticks.

Kraut Krispies

Good to go along with opening-course soups—both hot and cold. You'll find these an interesting accompaniment, too, to a main-course salad, or served hot with cocktails.

1 *1-pound can sauerkraut*
2 *tablespoons finely chopped onion*
½ *teaspoon seasoned salt*
¼ *teaspoon coarsely ground black pepper*

½ *cup soft butter or margarine*
2 *cups flour*
2 *tablespoons liquid from sauerkraut, or as much as needed*
Grated Parmesan cheese

Drain the sauerkraut well. (A good way is to dump it into a wire sieve and then press down until as much liquid as possible is drained off. Save some liquid.) Chop drained kraut coarsely. In a mixing bowl combine kraut with finely chopped onion, seasoned salt, and pepper. Blend in soft butter or margarine with a fork. Add flour (no need to sift it) a little at a time, blending into the sauerkraut mixture. If necessary add kraut liquid so that all of the flour is moistened. Shape mixture into two balls. Roll each ball of dough out into a large square about ⅛-inch thick. (Easiest to do if you use a well-floured pastry cloth and a covered floured rolling pin.) Sprinkle dough with grated Parmesan cheese. With a sharp knife cut into 2-inch squares. Arrange on an ungreased cooky sheet and bake in a hot oven, 425°F., about 15 minutes, or until done and brown. Makes about 4 dozen krispies.

RICE, PASTA AND DUMPLINGS

Steamed Rice

Plain or seasoned steamed rice goes well with many different soups and stews.

2 to 2½ cups water or chicken stock	1½ cups water or chicken stock
1 cup rice	1½ cups quick-cooking rice
Salt to taste	Salt to taste
or	

   Bring water or stock to a rapid boil. Add ½ teaspoon salt or less if using chicken stock. Amount depends on the saltiness of the stock. Add rice and stir with a fork. Turn heat down very low, cover pan tightly, and let rice steam—about 20 minutes for regular rice and 5 minutes for quick-cooking rice. Do not remove cover while rice is steaming. Uncover and fluff with a fork just before serving. Makes 4 to 6 servings.

GREEN RICE—Fluff steamed rice with a fork and mix in ¼ cup finely chopped parsley and 1 tablespoon butter.

CURRIED RICE—Add 1 teaspoon curry powder to chicken stock or water. Use onion salt instead of table salt.

SAFFRON RICE—Dissolve pinch of saffron in water or chicken stock. Use onion salt instead of table salt.

ROSY RICE—Substitute tomato juice for water or chicken stock. Use seasoned salt instead of table salt.

White and Wild Rice Pilaff

When wild rice is too expensive to serve, then combine half wild and half white rice. Or use one of the packaged mixtures of the two.

¼ *cup butter*	2 *cups hot water*
¼ *cup chopped onion*	2 *teaspoons chicken stock base*
¼ *cup chopped green pepper*	*or 2 chicken bouillon cubes*
½ *cup thinly sliced celery*	1 *cup mixed wild and white rice*

Melt the butter in a saucepan with a cover. Add chopped onion, green pepper, and celery. Cook vegetables until just yellow but still crisp. Add the hot water and the chicken stock base or bouillon cubes. Stir to dissolve them. Bring water to boil. When boiling stir in rice. Turn down to low heat. Cover pan and steam rice for about 30 minutes, or until it is tender and has absorbed all of the stock. Makes about 6 servings.

Cracked Wheat Pilaff

This is good to serve with almost any stew, but particularly with those of Middle East origin.

1 *cup cracked, or* **bulgur**, *wheat*	1 *teaspoon onion salt*
2 *tablespoons butter*	⅛ *teaspoon black pepper*
2 *cups chicken stock*	

In a heavy saucepan combine the cracked wheat with butter. Stir over medium heat until the wheat is coated with butter. Add the chicken stock and bring to a boil. Stir in onion salt and pepper and cover the pan. Turn heat down very low and cook until the wheat has absorbed all of the stock and is soft, about 25 minutes. Toss pilaff with a fork. Makes about 6 servings.

NOTE: *Cracked Wheat Pilaff* may also be cooked in a casserole in the oven. Bake it in a moderate oven, 350°F., for about 30 minutes.

Barley Pilaff

Serve with almost any good stew—beef, lamb, pork, or venison. Good, too, as an accompaniment to broiled meats—steaks, chops, or broiled wild ducks.

½ to 1 ounce dried mushrooms	1 cup barley
½ cup water	1½ cups beef stock or bouillon
¼ cup chopped onion	1 teaspoon seasoned salt
2 tablespoons butter	1 teaspoon chopped parsley

Soak the dried mushrooms in water for about ½ hour. In a heavy saucepan, cook the chopped onion in butter until it is a pale gold. Wash barley and stir it into onions. Add soaked mushrooms and their water and the beef bouillon. Heat to boiling; stir in seasoned salt and parsley. Cover the pan and turn heat down very low. Cook pilaff over a very low heat 30 to 35 minutes, or until barley is tender. Just before serving stir with a fork. Makes 6 to 8 servings.

Arabian Rice Pilaff

Saffron is a very potent seasoning, so take care not to use too much. Of course, different brands vary in their strength: if you are using a mild one, increase the amount a bit. *Arabian Rice Pilaff* is good with fish and lamb stews, especially those from the Mediterranean.

2 cups long-grain rice	1 large onion, thinly sliced
4 cups chicken stock	½ to 1 teaspoon salt
¼ to ½ cup olive oil	Pinch of powdered saffron
½ cup pine nuts	

Soak the rice in the chicken stock about 30 minutes. Drain it and reserve the stock. Heat ¼ cup olive oil in a heavy pan with a cover. Brown the pine nuts lightly, and lift them out and drain. Brown the onion; lift out and combine with nuts. Add the well-drained rice to the hot oil and brown it lightly, adding more olive oil if needed. Add 2 cups of reserved chicken stock, salt, and the saffron. (Amount of salt will depend on saltiness of chicken stock.) Cover the pan and cook over low heat 20

to 25 minutes, or until the rice is done. Turn pilaff out onto a platter and top with fried onions and pine nuts. Makes 6 to 8 servings.

Lentil Pilaff

A pleasant change from rice or wheat or noodles to go with your favorite stew is *Lentil Pilaff*. It's especially good with those from the Middle East or the Orient.

1½ cups lentils	*3 cups ham, chicken, or veal stock*
3 tablespoons butter or margarine	*½ teaspoon Worcestershire sauce*
⅓ cup finely chopped onions	*⅛ teaspoon pepper*
2 tablespoons chopped pimento	*Salt to taste*

Wash the lentils and let them drain. Melt butter or margarine in a saucepan; add the onions and cook over low heat until they are yellow. Stir in lentils and pimentos and cook until very lightly browned. Add stock, Worcestershire sauce, and pepper. Taste and add salt as needed; the amount will depend on saltiness of the stock. Pour mixture into a 2-quart casserole. Cover casserole and bake pilaff in a moderate oven, 350°F., for about 30 to 40 minutes, or until lentils are tender. Just before serving, toss carefully with a fork. Makes 6 to 8 servings.

Imjadara
Arabian Rice and Lentil Pilaff

Traditionally this pilaff would be served with lamb or chicken stews or with fish rather than with beef. But it's an interesting and unusual accompaniment to beef stews, too. If you live where you can purchase the red lentils, you'll find them more interesting, but the usual brown lentils from the supermarket are good, too.

1 cup lentils (red lentils, if available)	*2 teaspoons salt*
2 cups cold water	*½ teaspoon ground cumin*
2 whole cloves garlic	*⅛ teaspoon black pepper*
1 cup long-grain rice	*2 medium-size onions*
Boiling water	*⅓ cup olive oil*

Wash the lentils; add cold water. Peel the garlic and cut it into very thin lengthwise slivers. Add these to lentils and water. Bring lentils to a boil, turn down heat and simmer 20 minutes. Meanwhile, pour boiling water over rice and let stand off the heat while lentils cook. Then drain rice and add to lentils along with 1 more cup of boiling water. Add salt, ground cumin, and pepper. Cover pilaff and continue to simmer until liquid is absorbed and rice and lentils are tender, about 15 minutes.

Meanwhile, peel onions and slice into lengthwise slices. Fry onions in hot olive oil until crisp-tender and golden brown. Just before serving spoon fried onions and any oil in pan over the pilaff. Makes 6 to 8 servings.

Kasha
Baked Buckwheat Groats

An interesting pilaff kind of cereal dish to go along with all kinds of Russian and Middle-Eastern stews. We like it with almost all beef and lamb stews, regardless of their origin.

2 or 3 tablespoons butter or chicken fat	*1 cup coarse buckwheat groats*
½ cup chopped onion	*1 egg*
	2 cups hot chicken stock

Melt the butter or chicken fat in a frying pan. Add onion and cook slowly until it is lightly brown and tender. Spoon onion into a 2-quart casserole and set aside. Turn up the heat under the frying pan, add groats, and mix in egg. Stir constantly to keep groats from burning. When each grain is well coated with egg, mix into onions in the casserole. Pour hot chicken stock over the groats and onions and stir with a fork. Cover casserole and bake in a moderate oven, 350°F., for 50 minutes to 1 hour, or until *kasha* is tender. Makes 4 to 6 servings.

Buttered Noodles

There are many variations to buttered noodles, each very good. Just take your pick according to what you plan to serve along with them.

1 12-ounce package egg noodles	*4 tablespoons butter*
2 quarts boiling water	*1 teaspoon seasoned salt*
1 tablespoon salt	

Cook the noodles in boiling salted water until they are tender. Drain them and rinse in hot water. Meanwhile, melt butter in a large saucepan. Add seasoned salt and noodles. Toss noodles to thoroughly coat them with butter. Serve at once. Makes 8 servings.

VARIATIONS:

PAPRIKA NOODLES—Add 1 tablespoon paprika to melted butter.

PARSLEY NOODLES—Add ¼ cup chopped parsley to melted butter.

TOASTED ALMOND NOODLES—Add 3 or 4 tablespoons slivered almonds to butter. Toast almonds in butter until they are brown. Add noodles and toss to mix thoroughly.

SESAME SEED NOODLES—Add ¼ cup sesame seeds to butter. Cook, stirring constantly, until seeds are brown. Add noodles and toss to mix thoroughly.

NOODLES IN SOUR CREAM—Instead of butter, add ½ cup dairy sour cream and seasoned salt to hot drained noodles. Toss to mix thoroughly.

CHEESE NOODLES—Add ¼ to ½ cup grated shredded Parmesan or other cheese to the butter. Add noodles and toss to mix thoroughly.

Viennese Noodles

There are so many stews that *Viennese Noodles* go well with, and not all Middle-European. Don't hesitate to serve them with stews made from beef, wild game, chicken, or lamb—especially good for a buffet supper.

8 ounces egg noodles	1 teaspoon onion salt
2 quarts boiling salted water	⅛ teaspoon ground black pepper
2 10½-ounce cans condensed cream of	½ teaspoon paprika
celery soup	3 eggs
½ cup dairy sour cream	1 cup shredded Swiss cheese

Cook the noodles in boiling salted water until just tender. Drain them and rinse in hot water. Combine noodles with undiluted cream of celery soup, sour cream, onion salt, pepper, and paprika. Beat the eggs slightly and mix into noodles along with about ½ cup of the shredded cheese. Spoon mixture into a 3-quart casserole and sprinkle with remaining cheese. Bake noodles in a moderate oven, 375°F., until they are bubbling hot and cheese is melted. Makes about 8 to 10 servings.

Ricetti
Rice and Pasta

Good to serve with a number of stews, especially chicken. All kinds of variations are possible by using different herbs.

¼ cup olive oil or butter
1 cup rice
½ cup pastina (miniature pasta)
2½ cups chicken stock

½ teaspoon seasoned salt
¼ teaspoon herbs, such as an Italian herb mixture, or chervil, rosemary, basil, thyme, or a pinch of saffron

Heat oil or melt butter in a heavy saucepan. Add rice and cook over low heat, stirring frequently, until rice is golden. Stir in the pastina and the chicken stock. When stock comes to a boil, add seasoned salt. Crush the herbs and add to rice and pasta. Turn heat down very low. Cover pan and steam for about 25 minutes, or until rice and pasta are done and liquid is absorbed. Just before serving, fluff with a fork. Makes about 6 servings.

Cavatelli
Italian Potato Dumplings

Many Italian families call these delicious additions to a good stew *gnocchi*. But a very dear friend, whose Neapolitan family name is Constantini, calls them *cavatelli*. She tells me that as she was growing up they were often, with the addition of a good sprinkling of cheese, the complete meal on a Friday night. Other days a good hearty meat or chicken stew went along with them. Be sure to use "old" or baking potatoes; the potatoes must be dry. The moist new potatoes just do not make the same kind of dumpling.

1 pound potatoes (about 3 medium-size)
1 cup flour
1 cup ricotta cheese
½ teaspoon salt

1 teaspoon sweet basil
2 eggs
¼ cup butter
1 clove garlic or ¼ teaspoon garlic powder

Pare the potatoes and cook in a small amount of slightly salted water. Drain well and dry completely over very low heat. Cool potatoes slightly

and mash or press them through a food mill. Combine with flour, ricotta cheese, and salt and toss with a fork. Crush ½ teaspoon sweet basil and add to the potatoes and flour. Break the eggs and stir in, one at a time. Mix well and then shape mixture into sausage shapes about 1 inch in diameter and 2 inches long. Drop dumplings into boiling salted water and cook for about 8 to 10 minutes, turning them several times after they come to the surface. Lift out with a slotted spoon, draining well, and place on a platter.

Meanwhile, let butter soften. Crush the garlic and stir crushed garlic or garlic powder into butter. Crush remaining ½ teaspoon sweet basil and blend into garlic butter. Spoon this over the hot *cavatelli*. Makes about 24 dumplings, enough for 6 servings of 4 each.

Hominy Grits Soufflé

We like this especially with *Kidney and Mushroom Stew* or as an accompaniment to *Brunswick Stew, Burgoo,* or any stew with a Southern origin. Since it is quite adaptable to a wide range of oven temperatures, you can bake it along with other oven-prepared dishes.

1 quart water	3 eggs
1 teaspoon salt	1 teaspoon seasoned salt
1 cup hominy grits	Dash Tabasco or hot pepper sauce
½ cup butter	

Bring the water and salt to a rapid boil in a 2-quart saucepan. Add the hominy grits slowly, turn down the heat, and cook for about 5 minutes, stirring frequently. Remove grits from heat and stir in the butter. Separate the eggs. Beat in egg yolks, one at a time. Add seasoned salt and Tabasco to the egg whites and beat them until stiff. Fold beaten whites into cooked hominy grits. Spoon mixture into an ungreased 1½-quart casserole or soufflé dish. Bake it in a moderate oven, 350°F., for 30 to 40 minutes or until it is puffed and brown. If baking at a lower temperature, bake for 45 to 50 minutes; at a higher temperature, cut baking time to 25 to 30 minutes. Makes about 6 servings.

Herbs, Spices and Such

~~~

You will discover, I am sure, that most of the recipes in this book call for some kind of spice, herb, or other seasoning. Of course, a reasonably well-stocked spice and herb shelf will help you create these different soups and stews as they were originally prepared, for each part of the world and each section of this country has its favorite seasonings.

But it isn't always necessary to have the exact seasonings called for in the recipe. I have tried to suggest substitutes and alternatives in most recipes. Many of the herbs belong to the same botanical family and have similar flavors. The same is true of spices and other seasonings. There are also a number of herb mixtures on the market and these will vary slightly as to brand. I have used a wide variety of brands and find that, in almost every instance, each can be used interchangeably. Use the brand or mixture you prefer or the one that is available where you shop.

~~~

ON USING HERBS

*

Unless indicated we have used dried herbs in the recipes in this book. This is partly because I spent a number of years testing and writing recipes for a spice and herb company and partly because so many city dwellers haven't the facilities to raise their own herbs. You will find a wide selection of dried herbs in many different grocery stores, supermarkets, and gift and gourmet shops. If you do raise your own or have a friend who does or, as in some areas, you can purchase fresh herbs, then it's very simple to substitute the fresh for the dried herbs.

How Much and How to Use Herbs

Generally, you would use ¼ to ½ teaspoon dried herbs for each 4 to 6 servings. I like to give exact measurements, for what is a "pinch" to one cook is two or three times as much to another. When using some of the milder herbs such as dill weed, parsley, or chervil you may want to increase the amount to ½ to 1 teaspoon or more. It takes only a little practice to learn just how much you and your family prefer.

If you are using fresh herbs instead of dried, use from three to four times as much of the fresh as the dried.

The flavor of dried herbs is usually enhanced by crushing them before adding to liquid. (Dill weed, chervil, and dried parsley usually do not need to be crushed.) Crush by placing the herbs in the palm of one hand and rubbing with two fingers of your other hand. Or use a mortar and pestle.

If you are just starting an herb shelf, then we would suggest these as a beginning: sweet basil, bay leaf, marjoram, oregano, rosemary, sage, summer savory, tarragon, and thyme. After that add dill weed, chervil, chives, and parsley. You are more apt to be able to obtain these latter herbs in the fresh form, but it's nice to have some of the dried on your shelf in case of emergency.

A Few Different Herb Combinations

There are numerous combinations of herbs; almost every company and every grower of herbs has its specialties. One company may call its combination a *"bouquet garni";* another may call it "pot pourri" or "mixed herbs."

What to use if you don't happen to have one of the mixtures called for in some of the recipes? Here are some suggestions:

MIXED HERBS FOR BEEF—If you have Fines Herbes, then substitute this combination for Mixed Herbs for Beef. There are a number of different Fines Herbes on the market. Or use a combination of sweet basil, rosemary, sage, and thyme.

MIXED HERBS FOR LAMB—Again use Fines Herbes or a combination of rosemary, oregano, and tarragon.

MIXED ITALIAN HERBS—Combine sweet basil, crushed bay leaf, marjoram, and thyme or oregano. Or use chopped parsley.

BOUQUET GARNI—The most usual combination is parsley, thyme, and bay leaf. One simple bouquet is to tie a sprig of parsley around a celery stalk. Other combinations may contain sweet basil, chervil, tarragon, rosemary, or savory.

FINES HERBES—This traditional French combination of herbs is usually a mixture of parsley, chervil, chives, and tarragon.

SALAD HERBS—Most often a combination of chervil or parsley (chervil is considered to be the perfect salad herb), tarragon, chives, and thyme, so try any combination or use only one of these. Or substitute dill weed or use dill weed in combination with any of the other herbs mentioned.

CONCERNING SOME OF THE MORE
UNUSUAL HERBS AND SPICES

✳

You can purchase fresh coriander, fennel, and ginger as well as the dried in some areas. Fresh coriander and fennel are fresh green herbs; their seeds are sold in the dried form. Ginger is a spice.

CORIANDER or CHINESE PARSLEY—In its fresh green form it is called Chinese parsley in the Oriental markets and *cilantro* in Mexican and Central American markets. Coriander is also available as dried whole seeds or the seeds are dried and ground. To substitute for fresh coriander, use crushed seeds or ground coriander with fresh parsley.

FENNEL—Sold fresh in Italian markets as *finocchio,* both the roots and leaves, cooked or raw, are delicious. The seeds are dried. This plant, too, is related to parsley and both fresh fennel and the dried seeds have a slight licorice flavor.

GINGER—Fresh ginger root may be purchased in areas where there is a large Oriental colony or people from other Far Eastern countries such as India and Malaysia. It keeps, refrigerated, for some time, but will eventually start to mold. I like to cut it into thin slices and then freeze it to avoid this spoilage.

Ginger root can also be purchased in dried form. You can replace fresh ginger root with the dried root if you soak the dried for about an hour in cold water. Slice or chop and then use as you would the fresh.

Or you can wash the sugar from candied ginger and then slice or chop it and use instead of fresh ginger. Or for ginger flavor, use about ½ teaspoon ground ginger for each 6 servings.

From Faraway Places

SAFFRON—Considered by some to be an herb and by others a spice, saffron is one of the more exotic and expensive seasonings. It comes from the dried stigma of a crocuslike plant and it takes almost 100,000 of these flowers, all hand-picked, to make one pound of saffron.

Pure Spanish saffron, which I have used in these recipes, is extremely potent and should be used in the smallest amounts. Otherwise the flavor will be medicinal and bitter. With less potent saffron amounts can be increased to ⅛ to ½ teaspoon for 6 or so servings. Do taste carefully.

Most of the time I have suggested a "pinch of saffron." To be sure of a "pinch" we suggest measuring. Use a ¼ teaspoon measuring spoon. Fill the spoon, smooth it off, then cut off half of that amount. This ⅛ teaspoon portion should also be cut in half—and the remaining ⅟₁₆ teaspoon cut in half again. Thus you will have a ⅟₃₂ teaspoon measurement.

Another way to measure a "pinch" is to use a very sharp-pointed paring knife. The amount of saffron that you can lift with the very pointed end and that will stay on the point of the knife will be enough.

PARISIAN SPICE—This mixture of spices, used very much in French cooking, can be a mixture of different spices. (Spice Parisienne is the name given by one spice company to its particular mixture.) Parisian Spice may also be purchased in gourmet departments and gift shops as Quatre Épices, or Épices Fines. Or use your own combination of nutmeg, cayenne or white pepper, and allspice. Use only a small amount for this spice tends to be hot and pungent.

SOME OTHER SEASONINGS AND HOW TO USE THEM

✳

Other seasonings in the recipes are sometimes blends of spices, herbs, seeds, vegetables—sometimes combined with salt, or with oils, vinegar, fish, meat or poultry, fruit, or chemical products. Other seasonings are really vegetables, such as garlic, onion, horseradish, mushrooms, or the various kinds of peppers. You'll find several in fresh, dry or liquid form.

SEASONED SALT—There are quite a number of different seasoned salts on the market and under a variety of names. Many have a special brand name and, in addition, will be designated as seasoning salt, savory salt, flavored salt, herb salt, gourmet salt or seasoning, as well as a host of other names.

In preparing these soups and stews I have used at least a dozen different seasoned salts. I have found that, almost without exception, they can be used interchangeably. True, each will give a slightly different flavor, but not enough to concern you. I do suggest, though, that you try out several and find the one that *you* like the best. Some have more pepper, others more onion or garlic, others are sweeter, others have a more herby flavor.

If you wish to substitute plain table salt for seasoned salt, we suggest using half the amount and then adding any additional to taste. Or combine celery, onion, and garlic salts to make an equal amount of seasoned salt.

Or try making your own seasoned salt by combining ½ teaspoon table salt with ¼ teaspoon onion powder or ⅛ teaspoon garlic powder and ¼ teaspoon of your favorite herb. Be sure to crush the herb well and combine thoroughly.

GARLIC—Most of the recipes call for fresh garlic, either crushed or finely chopped. Occasionally whole cloves of garlic or thin slices are indicated. These are usually removed before serving the dish.

Garlic powder may be used in place of fresh garlic. Use ⅛ teaspoon garlic powder for a small to medium-size clove of fresh garlic or ¼ teaspoon for a large clove of garlic.

Liquid garlic and garlic juice are also on the market. Use the liquid garlic sparingly, for it is very strong. One-half teaspoon garlic juice will give about the same flavor as a small clove of fresh garlic.

ONION—Many varieties of onions, both green and dried, are available. You can also purchase many forms of dehydrated onions, both green and white, and onion powder and onion juice. One tablespoon of onion powder is about the same as ½ cup chopped onion and 1 tablespoon of instant minced dehydrated onion can be used in place of 2 tablespoons chopped onion.

Use about 1 teaspoon onion juice to give the same flavor as 2 table-spoons finely chopped onion.

CHIVES—Use fresh, frozen, or freeze-dried chives in the same amount.

MSG—This chemical flavor enhancer may have several brand names and is also marketed as monosodium glutamate, *aji no moto* seasoning, or gourmet seasoning powder. It is also an ingredient in most of the seasoned salts and seasoning mixtures.

However, many of the seasoning mixtures are now eliminating this chemical, and it has been taken out of many food products. I have used MSG in its pure form only in Oriental recipes, since it is considered an important ingredient by Oriental cooks. (*Aji no moto* is its Japanese name.) However, it may be omitted, even in these recipes, and additional table salt, seasoned salt, or soy sauce used instead.

SOY SAUCE—Different brands of soy sauce vary considerably as to strength. The Japanese sauces, sometimes called *shoyu* sauce, tend to be a little stronger than other soy sauces. Again it is well to taste to get the exact amount you like.

Curry Powder

Curry powders may consist of as few as five spices or as many as fifty. Different brands vary as to hotness and flavor. The flavor and the heat varies according to the country and the part of the country it comes from. And each family usually has its own particular mixture. Want to make one of your own? If you want it with less "heat" cut down on the red or black pepper or omit them. And make substitutions of spices—and of ground spices for whole or seeds—whatever pleases your fancy.

2 tablespoons coriander seeds	¼ teaspoon ground cumin
1 teaspoon mustard seeds	½ teaspoon ground cinnamon
1 teaspoon caraway seeds	½ teaspoon ground cloves
½ teaspoon fenugreek, fennel, or poppy seeds	½ teaspoon whole black peppercorns
	4 or 5 small hot dry red chili peppers

Combine all of these spices in an electric blender. Blend them thoroughly. You will have to turn the blender on and off a number of times and it will take several minutes. All spices should be well crushed. Sift mixture through a fine wire sieve, then use as any commercial curry powder. Makes about 4 tablespoons curry powder.

NOTE: Omit any spice you do not have or use ground instead of seeds or whole spices, using about half the amount. Or substitute ground ginger, ground mace, ground nutmeg, or paprika for any of the spices. Or add some garlic powder or any well-liked herb. Make it your own family recipe!

Garam-Masala
Indian Mixed Spices

This combination of spices is not too different from curry powder and is an important spice ingredient in many East Indian dishes. If you live in an area where there are students from India you may find a shop that sells this mixture. But it's easy enough to make.

1 teaspoon coarsely ground black pepper
1 teaspoon ground coriander
1 teaspoon ground caraway or caraway seeds

¼ teaspoon ground cloves
¼ teaspoon ground cardamom
½ teaspoon ground cinnamon

Combine all the spices and mix well. If you use caraway seeds, crush them with a mortar and pestle, or use the handle of a wooden spoon. Or if you start with whole spices, or part ground and part whole, combine all in an electric blender and blend until ground. Makes about 1 tablespoon *Garam-Masala*.

Coconut Cream

A little richer than coconut milk. Any left makes a wonderful flavoring for homemade ice cream.

Pour off any milk from a coconut. Grate 2 cups of the fresh coconut; either use a coarse grater or cut the coconut into chunks and then crush in an electric blender. Combine any milk from the fresh coconut and enough half and half or undiluted evaporated milk to make 1 cup. Heat milk to simmering and pour it over the grated coconut. Strain mixture through a fine wire sieve or a double thickness of cheesecloth. Press or squeeze it to extract all of the cream. Or pour 1 cup of hot half and half or undiluted evaporated milk over 1 cup of flaked or grated packaged coconut and proceed as for fresh coconut. Makes about 1 cup of *Coconut Cream*.

Coconut Milk

Not quite so rich. Drain the milk from a fresh coconut and add enough half and half or undiluted evaporated milk to make 1 cup. If coconut is dry and has no milk, then grate ½ cup fresh coconut, pour 1 cup hot milk over the grated coconut and let it stand until cool. Strain mixture through a fine wire sieve. Or pour 1 cup hot milk over ½ cup flaked or grated packaged coconut. Strain through a fine wire sieve. Makes about 1 cup *Coconut Milk*.

Index